CULTURAL POLITICS

Teaching women

CULTURAL POLITICS
general editors Jonathan Dollimore and Alan Sinfield

published with this volume

Teaching women
Feminism and English studies
edited by Ann Thompson and Helen Wilcox

MANCHESTER UNIVERSITY PRESS
MANCHESTER and NEW YORK

distributed exclusively in the USA and Canada by ST. MARTIN'S PRESS

Published by Manchester University Press,
Oxford Road, Manchester M13 9PL, UK
and Room 400, 175 Fifth Avenue,
New York, NY 10010, USA
Distributed exclusively in the USA and Canada
by St. Martin's Press, Inc.,
175 Fifth Avenue, New York, NY 10010, USA

British Library cataloguing in publication data
Teaching women: feminism and English studies. — (Cultural politics).
    1. Great Britain. Educational institutions. Curriculum subjects: English literature.
    Teaching.
    I. Thompson, Ann, 1947–   II. Wilcox, Helen   III. Series
    820'.7'1041

Library of Congress cataloging in publication data
Teaching women: feminism and English studies / edited by Ann Thompson
    and Helen Wilcox.
p.cm. — (Cultural politics) bibliography: p. 204. Includes index.
ISBN 0–7190–2603–2 : $35.00 (est.). ISBN 0–7190–2604–0 (pbk.) : $12.00 (est.)
1. English philology—Study and teaching (Higher)—Great Britain. 2. English literature—
    Women authors—Study and teaching (Higher)—Great Britain. 3. Feminism and litera-
    ture—Study and teaching (Higher)—Great Britain. 4. Feminist literary criticism—Study
    and teaching (Higher)—Great Britain. 5. Women college teachers—Great Britain—
    Attitudes. 6. English teachers—Great Britain—Attitudes. 7. Women and literature—Great
    Britain. I. Thompson, Ann, 1947– . II. Wilcox, Helen. III. Series.
    PE68.G5T4 1989
    820'.7'1141—dc19   88–12946

ISBN 0–7190–2603–2 hardback
    0–7190–2604–0 paperback

Photoset in Linotron Joanna
by Northern Phototypesetting Co, Bolton

Printed in Great Britain
by Hartnolls Limited, Bodmin, Cornwall

Contents

PART FIVE Beyond the boundaries of 'English'

Foreword: **Cultural politics**

The break-up of consensus in British political life during the 1970s was accompanied by the break-up of traditional assumptions about the values and goals of literary culture. Initially at specialised conferences and in committed journals, but increasingly in the mainstream of intellectual life, literary texts have been related to the new and challenging discourses of Marxism, feminism, structuralism, psychoanalysis and post-structuralism, and juxtaposed with work not customarily accorded literary or artistic standing.

Some recent developments offer a significant alternative to traditional practice; others are little more than realignments of familiar positions. But our belief is that a combination of historical and cultural context, theoretical method, political commitment and textual analysis offers the strongest challenge and has already contributed substantial work. We call this *cultural materialism*.

There are (at least) two ways of using the word 'culture'. The evaluative use has been more common when we are thinking about 'the arts' and 'literature': to be 'cultured' is to be the possessor of superior values and a refined sensibility, both of which are manifested through a positive and fulfilling engagement with 'good' literature, art, music and so on. The analytic one is used in the social sciences and especially anthropology: it seeks to describe the whole system of significations by which a society or a section of it understands itself and its relations with the world. Cultural materialism draws upon the latter, analytic sense, and therefore studies 'high' culture alongside work in popular culture, in other media and from subordinated groups.

'Materialism' is opposed to 'idealism': it insists that culture does not (cannot) transcend the material forces and relations of production. Culture is not simply a reflection of the economic and political system, but nor can it be independent of it. Cultural materialism therefore sees texts as inseparable from the conditions of their production and reception in history; and as involved, necessarily in the making of cultural meanings which are always, finally, political meanings. Hence the series title: Cultural Politics.

Finally, cultural materialism does not pretend to political neutrality. It does not, like much established literary criticism, attempt to mystify its perspective as the natural or obvious interpretation of an allegedly given textual fact. On the contrary, it registers its commitment to the transformation of a social order that exploits people on grounds of race, gender, sexuality and class.

The Cultural Politics Series seeks to develop this kind of understanding in a sequence of volumes that has intellectual coherence, but no restrictive format. The books will be both introductory and innovatory: introductory in that they will be clear and accessible; innovatory in their application of distinctive perspectives both to established topics and to new ones. In the tradition of Shelley, Arnold, Eliot, the Leavises and Williams, though often in terms very different from theirs, culture and politics are again at the centre of important intellectual debates.

Jonathan Dollimore
Alan Sinfield
University of Sussex

Preface

The emphasis of this book is on feminist teaching practice rather than on feminist theory or criticism. All the contributors are working (or have recently worked) in institutions of higher or further education in Britain. Most of them belong to Network, an organisation of women teaching literature in such institutions; the need for a book of this kind became evident in discussions amongst Network members. Contributors were invited to write specifically about their teaching experiences, concentrating, if they chose, on the teaching of a specific text or course, but also attending to the institutional context of the teaching and the individual positions and requirements of both teacher and students. The introductions to each Part are by Ann Thompson.

The resulting essays cover a wide range of texts, courses, institutions, teachers and students. It is clear that feminist pedagogy is exciting, diverse, demanding, sometimes difficult, and not always successful. Nevertheless we celebrate its existence and hope that this book will be of practical use as well as intellectual interest to everyone involved in this field.

Ann Thompson
Helen Wilcox

This book is dedicated
to women teaching women,
and especially to Mary Billing
and Margaret Boulton
A.T. and H.W.

PART ONE

Access for women

Introduction to Part One

All contributors to this book would agree that the first and fundamental issue is for women to have equal access to higher and further education. The extent to which female students are in fact still generally disadvantaged in the British education system has been analysed in such books as *Learning to lose: sexism and education* (Spender and Sarah, eds., 1980) and *Is higher education fair to women?* (Acker and Piper, eds., 1984), which discuss secondary and tertiary education respectively. It is apparent that girls and women are regularly undervalued by teachers and consequently allowed to underachieve. Their interests are not properly represented on the curriculum, they do not take up their fair share of class time, and they are discouraged from taking 'important' and 'difficult' subjects like science.

Even in what is perceived as a 'feminine' subject like English, female students still find themselves in a curiously subordinate position: while they are in a majority as 'consumers' of tertiary education courses, most of their teachers are men and they spend most of their time studying texts by male authors and male critics. The potential power of their numbers is undercut by the lowliness of their status and by the limitations on their input into course planning and administrative control.

While we take it for granted that women should in practice as well as in theory have equal rights to enter higher and further education, and that they should receive equal treatment once they have entered, we are also aware that the institutional structures of our education system, its assumptions about classroom practice and assessment procedures as well as about the curriculum, are often problematic for women. As feminists we find ourselves on the one hand championing the right of women to be educated in precisely the same ways that have been

deemed appropriate for men, but on the other hand we frequently want
to challenge existing procedures and find more appropriate alternatives.
This makes for some stimulating debates, but it can also lead to
bafflement and frustration. It is difficult simultaneously to empower our
female students by giving them proper access to the traditional privileges
of tertiary education and to question the very structures of authority on
which those privileges rest. Not least when we begin by questioning our
own positions of authority in relation to admissions procedures,
classroom behaviour and examinations.

The essays throughout this book are alert to these problems in
different ways. The three in this section focus specifically but not
exclusively on questions of access. Other essays in later sections (notably
those by Maggie Humm and Moira Monteith in Part II and those by Su
Reid and Ann Hancock in Part IV) are also highly relevant to this theme,
though they are not dominated by it to the same extent.

For Deborah Cameron, as indeed for everyone, access to language
comes before access to education. Language is the necessary medium of
education and the potential means whereby we can change both our
personal reality and our social reality, but subordinate groups, such as
blacks and women, have limited access to language. In discussing her
attempts to 'release people into language' in two very different contexts –
a community project with young black women in inner London and a
compulsory course for undergraduate students – Cameron confronts the
complexities of these situations: the initial resentment of black people
that she has knowledge of 'their' language which they themselves lack,
the very different resentment of antifeminist students who are obliged to
work on topics they see as peripheral or even unacademic. She develops
a critique not only of her own teaching practice but also of the standard
methods of undertaking linguistic research.

Elaine Hobby and Susan Sellers are both concerned in different ways
with questions of access for women who are 'returning to study', entering tertiary education as mature adults whose earlier experiences in this
area have left them with a sense of frustration and failure. Whether they
find themselves at the Cambridgeshire College of Arts and Technology,
at Hélène Cixous' Centre d'Etudes Féminines in Paris or at the Institute of
Andragology in Amsterdam, these women need to develop confidence
as much as they need to improve their study skills. The positive revaluing
of women's experience (the major theme of the essays in Part II of this
book) takes place alongside the exploration of small-group teaching
techniques and the dismantling of hierarchical authority. The issue of

1

'Released into language': the study of language outside and inside academic institutions
Deborah Cameron

Language is power, and . . . the silent majority, if released into language, would not be content with a perpetuation of the conditions that have betrayed them. But this notion hangs on a special conception of what it means to be released into language: not simply learning the jargon of an elite, fitting unexceptionably into the status quo, but learning that language can be used as a means of changing reality.

(Adrienne Rich, 1979)

At the heart of education should be questions about language – it sounds like hyperbole, or mere trendy rhetoric, but I believe that it is simply and quite literally true. Language, after all, is the stuff of education: not only the medium in which most knowledge is represented, but also the means whereby people learn and teach, through linguistic interaction with each other and with texts. To be educated in our society, and perhaps in any, is to have access to the culture's linguistic resources; to feel at home with them, to be aware of their potential, in some sense to control them for your own chosen purposes.

Representation and interaction, however, are not transparent and neutral processes. They come to us marked by history and the structures of power. For less privileged people, full access to language is impossible without an understanding of that fact and its implications. Education which does not make space to point this out, to reflect on language and our relation to it, is hardly worthy of the title *education* – especially if it purports to address those groups in society whose position is subordinate and whose relation to language is correspondingly less simple.

Exactly this point is made by Adrienne Rich in her essay 'Teaching language in open admissions' (1979). In the late 1960s, Rich taught English in New York City to students for whom education was no birthright: mostly women and men of colour from the Inner City ghettos. The experience led her to the following conclusion:

Language is . . . a weapon, and what goes with language: reflection, criticism, renaming, creation. The fact that our language itself is tainted by the quality of our society means that in teaching we need to be acutely conscious of the kind of tool we want our students to have available, to understand how it has been used against them, and to do all we can to insure that language will not someday be used by them to keep others silent and powerless. (p. 68)

This essay is about my attempts to help women understand and transcend 'the way language has been used against them'.

How has language been used against women? Any answer to that question must begin by acknowledging that neither 'language' nor 'women' is a homogeneous category. There are differences between languages and differences between women – as I hope the pages that follow will make clear. Yet speaking very generally, two things are apparent. First, that the norms of linguistic representation have constructed 'Woman' as man's Other, his negative: she is objectified, sexualised, stereotyped or excluded in the conventional discourse of a hundred different registers. (For a fuller account of how this is done, cf. Cameron, 1985, chapters 4 and 5.) Second, women have been restricted as interactors – participants in or active producers of language. Even in ordinary mixed conversation we are usually unsupported and frequently silenced; negative value judgements are made on our speech; we have less access than our brothers to the most prestigious registers, the ones which give us influence, status and control – to rhetoric, to literacy, to the production of literature.

Although they are not exact in every detail, there are striking parallels between this linguistic sexism and linguistic racism or class oppression. Black and working-class people too have been objects, not subjects of representation; their speech and writing has also been disparaged; they too have been silenced and stereotyped. For members of any of these three subordinate groups, their relation to formal, institutional language, and indeed to many aspects of most language they encounter, is likely to be ambivalent and problematic. No teacher can afford to pretend this is not so. It has to be acknowledged, made explicit and worked with. I want now to give a brief account of two contexts in which I have tried to do just that, and to explain how my experience has affected my notions of my role as a teacher and linguistic researcher.

The two contexts represent two different facets of my work as a teacher. One is 'institutional' – teaching linguistics to undergraduates, the vast majority of them young white women, in an Institute of Higher Education. The other is 'community involvement' – since publishing my book, *Feminism and linguistic theory* (Cameron, 1985), I am often asked to speak to women's groups and to organisations concerned with anti-sexist work in education and the youth service. The example to be discussed below is an extended project working with mainly Afro-Caribbean young women: like most work outside the institution where I am employed, it provided an opportunity for research as well as teaching, and this dual function should be borne in mind.

'Respect, please!': linguistics outside the institution

In 1985 I was asked to give a talk about sexism in language to a youth club discussion group. The club was in Southwark, an inner London borough with a large minority ethnic group population, and although its clientele is racially mixed, on this occasion the group consisted exclusively of Black (Afro-Caribbean) young people. I therefore chose to make explicit analogies between (for instance) the use of language to insult women (*slag*, *slut*) and the proliferation in English of racist insult terms. I also raised the topic of attitudes to 'patois' (i.e. the Caribbean creoles which are the heritage languages of most Black British people, and which are frequently dismissed as mere 'broken English', 'bad talk' and the like). The theme of racism in language was taken up enthusiastically, and it was decided that the group and I would work together to produce discussion material on the subject for use in educational and youth club contexts. What we eventually produced, after several weeks' discussion, was a twenty-minute video entitled 'Respect, please!'

'Respect, please!' is a mixture of taped discussions and role-play, scripted and performed by the group. The two central discussions concern, respectively, the experience of being insulted and having words like *foreigner*, *immigrant*, *native* and *black* used against you, and the complex, ambivalent feelings of the group and their parents about their creole linguistic heritage. Around these sections are woven a number of sketches. Some were taken from group-members' experiences (e.g. an episode where a Black British woman is asked by a well-meaning white fellow office worker where she 'comes from'; and another in which a woman's Cockney accent enables her to secure a job interview on the phone, but when she gets there in person, the job has gone). Others came from newspaper articles (e.g. an item about the police taking lessons in Jamaican creole, the better to converse with muggers and drug dealers). The title, 'Respect, please!' is intended to make the point whose profound significance we had all been led to see: that in order to affirm someone's dignity and status, it is necessary both to respect their language and to show that respect in your own use of language.

Although the video was important in itself, and gave a clear focus to our overall activity, in this particular enterprise, I would claim, the process was just as important as the product. That is, had the video not in the end been made, or had it proved useless, both I and the group would still have been changed by the discussions we had in the course of the project. This orientation to process rather than product is, in my view, a defining characteristic of teaching which 'changes reality' rather than 'fitting unexceptionably into the status quo'. I shall consider later on just how far it is possible in the exam-centred setting of the average institution.

Meanwhile, let me point out that process orientation is extremely untypical of most research as well, even where the researchers are politically well-intentioned (as they normally have been on the subject of Black language). A great deal of what academics know about Black speakers has been taken from Black communities without any direct benefit to them: in order not to 'bias' the findings, informants in sociolinguistic research are usually recorded by a researcher who deliberately conceals her true purpose, and who therefore avoids explicit discussion of language issues. The researcher then writes up her findings about the linguistic and social validity of patois for an audience of professionals – linguists and teachers, typically – in a way which immediately makes it inaccessible to those who not only provided the material, but who most need to know, for their own self-esteem, that their language is just as good as anyone else's and is under-valued for political, not linguistic reasons. Conventional research both silences Black speakers – the linguist speaks for them or on their behalf – and denies them the kind of theoretical understanding with which the more privileged researcher is equipped. This, needless to say, releases no one into language. It makes people into objects, with no chance to be subjects of either language or knowledge.

At this juncture, readers may be starting to feel uneasy about the patronising implication here that Black speakers are 'empty vessels' to be filled up with knowledge and theory by white researchers. So let me make it clear that my point is not about who is capable of producing knowledge – all creolists would have to acknowledge their debt to Black linguists, and take seriously their criticisms of the field – but about the *social distribution of knowledge* in the community. For it was clear to me in Southwark (and naively, I was surprised) that the knowledge which gives a history and validity to the languages of Black people had not passed into the common knowledge of the community, and that this deprivation is a form of oppression, one which the researcher/teacher has a responsibility to address.

Linguists have long rejected the popular stereotype of creole languages as 'broken' and 'primitive' because of their knowledge of how creoles are formed. Those of the Caribbean, for instance, developed in conditions of plantation slavery, where Africans with a common language were carefully separated. They had learned a 'pidgin' – that is, a simplified and restricted language based on the tongue of the European master – while awaiting shipment from the ports of West Africa, and as this language became their *lingua franca*, they drew on their African mother tongues and on universal linguistic strategies to enrich it, a process which their children continued and deepened. The consequence was a creole which was, and is, much more than 'debased European'; it might more fairly be regarded as a triumph of human communication over inhuman conditions.

The Southwark group were at first very ambivalent about their various ancestral patois; both they and their parents had internalised the 'broken language' view, with the result that some families had tried to prevent their British-born children acquiring patois at all. On investigation it turned out that no one in the group had ever been told about the history of creole languages in slavery; no one had ever heard of the African elements in creoles, or encountered the idea of their structural autonomy (i.e. the fact that creoles differ grammatically from both African substrate and European superstrate). The knowledge that would have allowed these speakers to value patois whole-heartedly as a cultural achievement had been denied them. And not surprisingly, their first reaction to my attempts to share my 'expert' knowledge about creoles was anger and resentment that I should possess it when they did not.

In the course of the project we were able to discuss both the history of patois and the reasons why it had been hidden from them. The discussion we eventually taped is testament to the fact that their reality was

changed by having access to new knowledge: not only did they express
pride in patois as *languages*, and especially in their connexion with African
languages, they spoke of their plans to help their own children acquire
patois from relatives who retained an active command. This dramatic
'renaming' of an aspect of the group's lives could not have come about
without the researcher's commitment to an active, process-oriented
teaching role.

At the end of the project, I formulated for myself four maxims of what
I called 'democratic research'. These were:

(1) *Make research relevant to those involved.* Let their interests and experience dominate, not yours. Listen to what they say and allow it to count.

(2) *Make research accountable.* Never deceive those involved about your
aims and methods; negotiate these as the project progresses.

(3) *Share as much privileged/expert information as possible;* never assume
'informants' do not need or want to know what you know.

(4) *Make research accessible.* Feed back what you learn from it in a form
those involved can understand and make use of.

Evidently, these maxims are ideals, and some are more likely than
others to be followed consistently (thus it seems to me that (2) is
indispensable, while (1) and (4) may sometimes present problems). But
they do articulate a view of research which resonates better than traditional views with a feminist outlook which seeks to empower people, to
value their experience, to get rid of hierarchy and so on.

On reflection, I realised that these maxims for research could also be
maxims of democratic or feminist *teaching*. A lot of teaching has the same
faults as traditional research: it imposes questions on students irrespec-
tive of their concerns, it disvalues their experience, it effectively rations
knowledge; too often we as teachers do deceive our students as to what
our real aims are, if only by not making them clear and explicit. I began
to consider the differences between my experience in Southwark and
my everyday teaching. Having formulated these maxims in one context,
how far was I actually applying them in the other? I was forced to
conclude that it is much more difficult to do feminist teaching in a
formal institution, and in the section that follows I want to explore why
this should be so.

Language, power, politics and sexuality: teaching linguistics to first-year undergraduates

The young white women who make up the majority of my undergraduate students have as much to gain as the Southwark group in reflecting on language and their relation to it. Moreover, the English Department in which I work agrees that this is educationally desirable: all first years following a foundation course in English take, as a compulsory element of their programme, a five-week course with a linguistics tutor, called *Language, power, politics and sexuality* (LPPS). The last three weeks of this course examine the relation of language to gender, ethnicity and class. The format is that of a half-day seminar, and students write one essay which goes forward for assessment.

In seminars, the major activity is discussion, beginning from various written materials, both academic and popular. Students are encouraged to draw on their own experience in their response to their reading. We also show videos (including parts of 'Respect, please!') and do brainstorming exercises in the group (e.g. 'think of ten racist insults/negative terms for disabilities/grammatical solecisms'), and analyse cultural products such as newspaper reports. In other words, the methods used in LPPS are relatively informal and student-centred; they include many activities which were also used in Southwark and which I have used in other community contexts (e.g. workshops with women's groups). Yet although some students enjoy the course and report that they get a lot from it, it is obvious to me after teaching it nearly twenty times that many do not. Far from finding it empowering, they find it threatening or pointless. I almost never feel that positive sense that I felt in Southwark, of reality being changed. And in fact, by comparing the two contexts in more detail it becomes clear there are good reasons why, judged against the ideal of feminist teaching, one is so much more successful than the other. These reasons fall into two main categories: the first 'institutional', the second 'political'.

Institutional factors. By definition, a course like LPPS breaks my first maxim, that teaching should proceed from the students' own concerns. As much as I might wish that undergraduate students considered political matters relevant to them, as much as I can see that their whole lives are circumscribed by issues of gender, ethnicity and class, this is not how most of them perceive things themselves. Thus right from the beginning, my agenda is imposed. That it should generate a good deal of apathy and resentment is therefore not surprising – and these attitudes are only intensified by the political resistance which I shall discuss later on.

There is also a problem, as I have already hinted, with trying to do 'process-oriented' teaching (i.e. aiming to explore and change students' and tutor's perceptions) in an institution which is basically product-oriented. In the case of LPPS, the product – a compulsory assessed essay – is seldom far from the students' minds. This makes them reluctant in reading and discussion to waste time on anything they think is peripheral, or to voice views they think the tutor will not like (since she after all will eventually be assessing them). It makes them more interested in neat facts and tidy arguments, and above all it leads them to pursue 'the right answer'.

This quest leads us on to a third institutional problem, the authority structure of the seminar room. Young undergraduates have usually had years of classroom training in treating questions from teachers as 'closed', i.e. tests, *viva voce*, of knowledge absorbed, rather than invitations to explore one's own ideas, defend one's argument or just ask a question back. Higher education is supposed to help students unlearn this reflex, and student-centred teaching in theory makes this easier by breaking down to some extent the extreme hierarchy of the teacher-pupil relationship. I do not deny, of course, that students can become more assertive, but in my experience this is least likely to happen when the questions they are asked concern issues which are both contentious and personal (as in the case of sexual politics). The old defences of platitude and silence come into play. Nor do I believe that this problem can be overcome fully even by the most sensitive teacher. It is a *structural* problem whose intractable core is that you are the teacher and they are the students. In Southwark, as a white adult professional woman among working-class Black young people I was socially extremely distant from the group; yet the effects of that distance were nowhere near as potent as the ascribed authority I take on for my students. Obviously, in a course on language, I point the problem out; but I find it hard to solve. The consequence is that within the institution there is rarely the feeling of genuine, equal exchange which struck me so forcibly throughout the Southwark project.

Political factors. All the institutional factors that make feminist teaching about language difficult are reinforced by political factors. Since institutional constraints affect every course, it is politics above all which makes LPPS threatening.

Firstly, it is inevitable that a group of undergraduate students contains many shades of political opinion. If there is a consensus, it is apt to be anti-feminist (though 'I'm not a feminist' for these students may encompass some commitment to liberal equal rights; 'feminist' for them is synonymous with 'extremist'). This makes the average undergraduate group rather different from the Southwark group, who did share an interest in politics and certain views about it. In particular, whereas the Southwark group contained no explictly racist people, student groups usually contain overtly anti-feminist women. This presents a serious problem in 'listening to their experience and letting it count': especially since I am a woman myself, I feel more inclined to challenge their interpretations of female experience. Yet to do so reinforces the institutional problem of teachers' authority silencing students. A nice Catch-22 for the thinking feminist!

A second, overtly political problem has to do with the politics of academic knowledge. The ideology of higher education proclaims that true knowledge is value-free. Feminist analyses of (in this instance) language are not value-free: ergo they do not count as real knowledge. They are mere propaganda, indoctrination, bias. In the Southwark project, this point was not at issue – partly because the group had had little opportunity to internalise the notion of value-free knowledge, but also because research on the properties of patois is presented by linguists as a corrective to bias – that is, as unbiased, apolitical 'truth'. The same is not true of work on language and gender. My nonfeminist students resent 'bias' above all.

Conclusion

In this chapter I have been working with a concept of good feminist teaching as a process of 'releasing into language'. The implication is that we are releasing students from silence and inarticulacy – from their lack of space in which to discuss their experiences or of a framework of language and knowledge in which to place and interpret those experiences. This model is strikingly appropriate to the work I have done in community groups, but not to my everyday teaching in an institution.

I am led, in conclusion, to pose the question of the role of a feminist teacher in an institution whose ethos is far from being feminist. The question is all the more insistent where feminism appears in the mainstream curriculum. I know that in many institutions feminist teaching is confined to courses on the margins of acceptability, which therefore attract sympathetic students who find themselves alienated from prevailing views, and such students, together with their feminist teachers, create enclaves of language in the general state of silence. Their problems are real, but they are not the same as mine.

2

Women returning to study
Elaine Hobby

The most challenging part of my week when teaching at the Cambridgeshire College of Arts and Technology, a mixed Further Education and Higher Education college, was my work in Return to Study groups with mature re-entrants to education. It was in those classes, I believe, that my feminist ideas about teaching (that the teacher should not masquerade as the source of Truth, that women students should be strengthened and empowered) were tested and developed.

The groups varied in size from nine (too small for really effective small-group work) to over twenty (too large for the plenary discussions). Within any one group I faced a range of expectation from women wanting to take O Level to those who had dropped out some years before from the middle of a degree programme. I say 'women' because nearly all the students were female: some groups had no men at all and none of them had more than three.[1] A good number of students were foreign, some with a first language other than English, and almost all of them were white, perhaps reflecting the very white population of Cambridge. They varied in age from their late teens to mid-sixties, with most falling into the thirty to forty-five range. All of them felt they were at a point of transition in their lives: they had lost or were bored with their jobs; their children had started school or left home; they were approaching retirement.

The first meeting of each Return to Study group is nerve-wracking and exhilarating for all concerned. Women arrive tense, sometimes literally shaking with fear, believing themselves to be an exception: an exception for whom there is no place in education. For most of them, their last experience of education – whether in school aged fourteen, thirty or more years before; or in a college classroom in more recent times – was that they 'were not up to it'. Precisely because their experiences of schooling are not a result of individual failings, but manifestations of wider social structures, by the end of the first session of Return to Study their understanding of their own pasts had begun to shift. This change of perspective comes about not through the teacher – me – blandly assuring them that they misunderstand their own lives but by introducing from the very beginning the small-group discussion that is central to the course.

Small-group work is a remarkably successful technique popular in adult education because it encourages students to talk together, to try out ideas and develop discussions along the lines of most interest to them. Early in any course I make a point of leaving the room for a while whilst discussion is underway. This demonstrates to everyone, me included, that learning does happen in the teacher's absence. Arguably, in a feminist classroom the teacher should be involved herself in a small-group discussion: some feminist friends of mine make this part of their teaching practice, believing that holding back from the groups reinforces the artificial divides between teacher and students. Although I understand this argument, I disagree. There is in fact a divide between teacher and student: a power divide. Students pay to attend classes, where the teacher is paid. Students need academic references to gain access to Higher Education, and the teacher writes them. Students do not readily forget this division and I feel that the teacher should not require them to. If I join a small group, the students are bound to be influenced by my interests, deflected away from their own concerns. The teacher's task is to set the initial exercise or problem, and then to chair a plenary session where students feed back their main ideas to the group as a whole.

In keeping with these principles, the first meeting opens with women talking for a few minutes in pairs about their past experiences of education and what has brought them back into a classroom, and then introducing their discussion partner to the group as a whole. Right from the start, the classroom becomes a place where students talk, when for most of them education had meant listening to the teacher talk. As they hear about each others' pasts they also learn that they are not alone: that someone else in the room is looking for something worthwhile to do now that the children have left home, or is regretting having left school and got married too young. They realise that the room is full of women who feel that they have either forgotten how to think, or never knew how in the first place.

This insight is built on in the second half of the session, when students in pairs and then in small groups recall good and bad experiences of learning and analyse why learning to sew, perhaps, was pleasurable (it was taught lovingly and patiently at a time when they wanted to learn it), when learning trigonometry, perhaps, was not (the teacher ridiculed those who found the subject difficult, frightening them into 'getting by' or into silence). By the end of the first session, therefore, students begin to experience the same heady delight familiar to feminists from consciousness raising groups: elements of our lives that we have identified as purely personal are in fact common to many women. Their origin, therefore, is not some individual quirk, but is social, rooted in gender, class, race, sexual orientation; in the power-play that so often defines the dynamics of a conventional classroom. The students also begin to recognise that others in the class can be a source of support and shared analysis, not competition; a source of learning at least as important as any 'instruction' available from the teacher. I doubt if this collectivising of experience and abandoning of competitiveness would happen in a group made up wholly or mainly of men.

The course as a whole continues with a combination of small-group and plenary work, with the intention of developing these initial insights and empowering the students to make their next experience of education different. Course materials do not, however, remain wholly at this experiential level. In each session the students are set specific practical tasks, designed to let them find out together what they are really expected to do when told to 'read this book' or 'write an essay about this'. Students often say they were initially attracted to Return to Study because the course promises help with 'study skills': the advertising blurb specifically mentions effective reading, note taking and essay writing. Students arrive wanting to believe that their past experience of failure was a result not of their own badness, but of their not learning useful techniques: that the course will be a series of how-to-do-it sessions. To some extent they are right: you can learn to write an essay, just as you can learn to make a table, to manage a household budget, and undoubtedly some people will find these things easier than others. The difference is, we live in a society where no one is considered stupid if they cannot plan in advance what clothes three children and their father must have clean to wear in a week – a very complex task performed 'effortlessly' by many women – but in a society that thinks people stupid if they cannot write essays or pass exams. (Women not performing such domestic tasks might be thought 'bad wives', but their intelligence is less likely to be questioned than their femininity.) In the classroom, I adapt

Open University teaching materials specially designed to teach students such academic techniques. Students' problems are not a result solely of lacking technique, though. For many of us, our earliest schooling experiences were variations on rote-learning; our essays and exams apparently a test of our ability uncritically to regurgitate the details we have been taught. To succeed in education, students need not only to learn techniques, but also to understand that facts stick in our heads best when they make sense in relation to something else. By the time they approach Higher Education, at least, what is being demanded of them is to draw out themes and trends: that is, to develop ideas and connections.

It is at this point that the feminist element in the course's structuring becomes most clear. I have found that women who have dropped out, or been ejected from the education system often believe their 'failure' is due to poor memory or bad technique, when what is more crucially lacking is the self-assurance needed to construct academic arguments. Making generalisations of the kind required in Higher Education is, I believe, more difficult for women than for men. Not only are women, quite properly, chary of accepting 'truths' about 'mankind' which we are told apply to us too but don't seem to; women also tend to back off from the implicit arrogance of generalisation. It is much more self-assertive (more arrogant, more frightening) to offer an opinion about the general drift of a text or argument, than to recall some statistical or factual data it refers to. The task of Return to Study is therefore not just to teach women the study skills they were not taught at school. It is also to help them develop the confidence they need to do something more difficult than the thing they thought was the problem: they need to learn to not be afraid of making academic generalisations.

When getting things wrong is punished with ridicule from the teacher – a common earlier experience of second-chance students – it is not surprising that many women fall silent. The non-competitive ethos and small-group work of Return to Study is crucial in changing this, since through the course women discover the pleasure of making leaps of intellectual daring. This is not to say that the point of the course is to make women 'think like men'. Students are not left to make this change of self-perception alone, each learning to be 'tougher' under the teacher's watchful eye. The women develop their own support networks within the group, each being helped by others to recognise the common cause of their lack of confidence. A particularly successful part of the classroom dynamic is something that arose almost by accident, as a joke I made to tease a woman who always deprecated herself when offering an opinion. I suggest that the class operate a 'swearbox', and that women be required to pay a fine every time they put themselves down. Although no actual fine system has ever, of course, been operated, students were quick to latch on to this idea and use the threat of the swearbox to make one another more conscious of the extent to which they undervalued themselves.

There is insufficient space here to describe in detail all the teaching materials I have used with these groups, but a couple of examples will be useful. Many exercises are adaptations of distance-learning materials, some of the best of which are produced by the Open University. Over the weeks of the course, students experiment with reading, note-taking and essay writing. One of the most stimulating sessions has proved to be a discussion of William Perry's 'Students' use and misuse of reading skills' (1959). The article concerns Perry's endeavours to improve the effectiveness of students' reading, and describes the various experiments he undertook to diagnose the source of study difficulties. He analysed his students' reading habits, discovering how purposeless and directionless their reading often was, since it tended to concentrate on the accumulation of facts rather than on grasping the overall argument of a text.[2] The experiments Perry describes include one in which students were given an impossibly short time in which to read part of a book, and then asked questions about it. He found that students who are 'ineffective' readers read from the beginning and fail to finish, not daring to flick through the text and discover that it ends with a summary of its general findings: a far more useful section of the book for their purposes than the more detailed factual information that precedes it. I use this essay in a session where I ask students to read and summarise it, deliberately giving them far too little time to read it in detail. Before their time is up they have usually reached the section where Perry stresses the need to have the courage to glance through to the end. Always, the realisation dawns at this moment (because Perry's article, too, ends with a helpful summary) that they have been making the same errors as Perry's 'poor readers': that they have been schooled into the belief that to read the end first is 'cheating'. This realisation has always been accompanied by much laughter, not all of it embarrassed. The discussion that follows this exercise takes up the issues raised by students themselves: that what they lack is not 'reading technique' but confidence in their own ability to find what they are looking for in a book, and recognise it when they see it.

Inevitably, this exercise awakens further memories of schooling, providing students with more data to make sense of their own past. The subsequent session, always, is an exercise in which students are required to grasp and summarise a book's content within twenty minutes. In the process of trying to complete the task they find out in practice that a great deal about a book can be gleaned in that time: enough to make a subsequent detailed reading of it unnecessary, if the book is clearly irrelevant to their study project; or to make the next reading more analytical and productive because they have a better sense of the author's overall thesis. Risk-taking in the form of jumping ahead and making judgements can be experienced as rewarding. Ideally, too, as the students pool their impressions of texts, making errors or having differences of opinion can come to seem less terrifying. By the end of a small-group discussion of a text, everyone is likely to have modified her impression of it, and no one will have been mocked. There is also a practical side to this, of course: many women with children and with or without husbands have little time of their own, very little time in which to study. Often they are anxious about the strains that their returning to study might place on their families. If they can find ways of making their reading efficient they are less likely to be frightened off from the attempt in the early stages.

Using this sort of material has proved to be very successful: more than half of the students attending these classes have continued in education, many of them gaining direct access to degree courses when they present the written work they have completed for me. Those who do not continue in education have none the less commented that the course has given them new energy and confidence. One woman, for instance, said on joining Return to Study that what she was really looking for was a better grasp of paperwork, so that she could stand up against the male domination of a local club she belonged to. She came along to the last meeting of the class jubilant, having attended her organisation's national conference. Fed up with the patronising way men there had referred to women members making tea and doing the fund-raising, she had stood up and attacked them for their sexism. Afterwards, she told us, many women at the conference thanked her for saying the things they had not had the confidence to say themselves. She was sure it was Return to Study that had made this possible for her.

The Return to Study classroom, then, is a very different place from more traditional Higher Education work. Freed temporarily from competitiveness and actively encouraged to view their own and others' experiences as important, women begin to feel hopeful that next time things will be different. Because they are women, by and large they are responsive to one another's needs and sensitive to each other's insecurities: they encourage each other in speaking up in class, writing essays and applying for further courses. When I started this teaching, I was afraid that in pursuing a basic feminist aim – making it possible for more women to enter Higher and Further Education – I would also be doing my students a disservice. I feared that the Return to Study experiment might be too cosy, leaving students ill-prepared for the brutish world of academe. As it turns out, my fears were misplaced. Several women who have gone on to study for degrees have delighted in telling me about their undermining of the oneupmanship they have seen in some of their classes. Having thought through their own educational experiences, they know how teachers can maintain authority by humiliating or embarrassing students, and are quick to spot this when it happens. They are no longer likely to be bullied into silence, since the co-operative spirit of Return to Study encourages them to form alliances with their fellow students and resist such teacherly tricks. My students are tougher, and more creative, than I had given them credit for.

I have also come to realise that another element of my teaching practice is helpful to students when they make the transition to mainstream classrooms. When I first came out as a lesbian to my students I explained this decision to be open as something that I was doing in the interests of my own integrity, and to make things easier for my gay students. I have developed a patter in which I explain to new groups of students why I tell them about my lesbianism: that if I don't mention it I am assumed to be straight, and that part of the oppression of gay people lies in the fact that the majority act as if we don't exist. I explain that since about ten percent of the population is gay, all of us know gay people who keep their sexuality a secret. It is in the interests of gay students, especially, that they see an openly gay teacher being accepted by their peers, once the initial shock of hearing the word 'lesbian' spoken quite openly is over. As I say, at first this was a statement I made for my own reasons, not seeing it as having specific pedagogical usefulness. After two years' teaching in many different classrooms as an out lesbian, I am beginning to understand that my openness has various effects, most of them positive. With Return to Student students, I believe, it is the clearest demonstration of the ways in which this classroom is not like the majority of those they will later encounter. They do not expect their next classroom to be as non-competitive or as open to student direction as this one is, any more than they expect their next teacher to be an out lesbian (though, roll on the day for both!).

I have found my Return to Study teaching to be the most educational experience I have had. Before I understood it I had read theoretical material concerning the 'pedagogy of the oppressed', classroom dynamics and gender and schooling, and been involved in Adult Education with the WEA. Return to Study teaching, however, makes the methods and experiences of teaching and studying central to what goes on in the classroom. In listening to students talk about past good and bad experiences of learning, I have been forced to re-examine my own history as a pupil/student, and my practices as a teacher. By putting myself on the line and telling students that if they don't understand what I am saying, I am not doing the job I am paid for, I have opened myself up to the (sometimes angry or urgent) demands that students can make for clarity. By learning to teach these students how to write essays, I have come to a clearer understanding of the difficulties my other students face in making their point clear, either on paper or in discussion. I have learned to see how much women's academic work is undermined by lack of confidence, and become more explanatory in my insistence that they take risks in their work and try things out. Above all, perhaps, I am being weaned off the need to feel all-powerful and all-knowing in the classroom. The best way to encourage students to feel safe to say 'I don't know' or 'I don't understand' is to say those things myself.

Notes

1 If it had legally been possible, I would have made the groups women-only, as the men (with few exceptions) tried to dominate discussion and were less skilled at co-operation and giving support.

2 Perry's students, far from being the discriminated-against who make up Return to Study groups, were Ivy League freshers. The fact that he found similar problems amongst such students indicates that the problems I focus on here are far more widespread.

3

Biting the teacher's apple: opening doors for women in Higher Education
Susan Sellers

This chapter has roots in a number of different teaching experiences. In 1981 I was a student on an experimental Postgraduate Certificate in Adult Education at the London Institute of Education. Part of my teaching practice for this course involved women-only 'Access' and 'Threshold' courses organised in conjunction with Paddington College and the University of London. In 1983 I joined the Centre d'Etudes Féminines in Paris where I became a member of a research seminar organised by the Centre's founder and director Hélène Cixous pioneering a radically different approach to 'feminism', teaching and the literary text. In 1986 I was asked by Ied Guinée and Renée Hablé of the Institute of Andragology at the University of Amsterdam to take part in a research project on 'women and learning' with a view to adapting the work of the research seminar at the Centre d'Etudes Féminines in ways appropriate to women returning to full-time education. Finally, in September 1986, I was a participant on the Development of University English Teaching (DUET) conference organised by the University of East Anglia. This conference provided additional perspectives to the teaching of literature, as well as the chance to experience in practice some of the situations and ideas I describe here. I would like to dedicate this chapter to the work of these various projects which, in different ways, strive to open doors to students and ways of thinking normally excluded from our rigidly hierarchical, patriarchal system of education.

I will divide the bulk of this chapter into two parts. First, I will give a brief introduction to the work of Hélène Cixous at the Centre d'Etudes Féminines, going on in the subsequent part to list some of the implications of Cixous' work for the teaching of literature, and showing how the practices of 'études féminines' were applied to a group of mature women students returning to full-time education as part of a research project co-ordinated by the University of Amsterdam.

Why 'feminine'?

I begin with a brief description of the work of Hélène Cixous at the Centre d'Etudes Féminines.

The use of the term 'feminine' to describe the work of the Centre d'Etudes Féminines derives from the notion of an alternative response to the laws which govern patriarchy. Drawing on Freud's model of the Oedipus complex – which Cixous sees as a useful metaphor for the processes by which the anarchic, desire-driven human infant is brought to assume its adult role – Cixous posits two different types of response to phallic law. One is the 'masculine' response outlined by Freud, a response which interiorizes the threat of castration to remain circumscribed within it, accepting its attendant prohibitions, and system of definition based on suppression. In her essay 'La venue à l'écriture',[1] Cixous illustrates this 'masculine' response with reference to a short story by Kafka 'Before the law'.[2] In Kafka's story a man from the country arrives before the law and asks the doorkeeper for admittance. The doorkeeper's reply is a non-committal 'not now', a reply that is repeated at periodic intervals as the countryman settles down to wait. The years pass, the countryman grows old, and still he is denied access to the law. Eventually, towards the end of his life, it occurs to the countryman to wonder why – in all the years of waiting – he has never seen anyone else try to enter the door of the law. He asks the doorkeeper. The doorkeeper's reply – the final closing of the door, his door – illustrates, Cixous tells us, that the power of the Law is the power of allegiance we give to it.

Cixous contrasts Kafka's story with the story of Eve in the garden of Eden. Unlike the man from the country, Eve refuses to take the word – God's Word – as law. She transgresses the interdiction, risking the incomprehensible threat of expulsion and death, giving in to her desire to taste the forbidden fruit. Despite the conclusion arrived at by the Scriptural Fathers, Eve's 'feminine' response is – Cixous believes – the prerequisite for knowledge, creation and art.

Two ways of telling the alphabet

There is a scene in Virginia Woolf's *To the lighthouse* in which Mr Ramsay, Philosopher, Patriarch, Champion of Logical Discourse, paces the terrace outside his house, thinking.³ Sitting facing him in the window are his wife and young son. As he walks backwards and forwards across the terrace, Mr Ramsay concentrates his attention on the progression of his thought. He moves from A to B to C to D all the way to the letter Q. Now very few people, the text tells us, get as far as the letter Q. The description situates him quite clearly, his advancement in relation to his wife's gaze, dependent on her watching him, on her acting as a mirror to reflect back to him the image of the hero he would like to be. Stopping in front of the window, Mr Ramsay prepares for the next step, the valiant stride on to R. He makes a great display of his courage, in fact, just in case his wife fails to notice him, just to make sure she looks up at him from her knitting, he sings a stirring marching song, a military tale of battle and splendour. But he can't make it, great philosopher that he is he can't make the next stride on to R, he is forced to dig his heels in at Q, abandon his dream of conquest, his attempt to master R, which is, of course, his own letter, his own signifier, his own personal phallus.

But there is another element to this scene. Watching Mr and Mrs Ramsay is the painter Lily Briscoe, who is also searching, also striving to find an answer, but whose understanding comes in a sudden flash – a sudden, visionary glimpse of the whole rainbow of letters together.

These scenes from *To the lighthouse* illustrate a number of elements of 'études féminines'. They contrast Ramsay's 'masculine' way of thinking (with its linear progression, its dream of mastery, its appropriation of the other in order to achieve its end) with that of a radically different approach – Lily Briscoe's 'chaotic' vision.⁴

Revaluing differences

The keynote of 'études féminines' could be described as the valuing of differences – the refusal to appropriate or subjugate another in order to construct the self in a position of mastery.

This valuing of differences has implications both for the way a group is structured, and for the way a text is approached.

Towards a new group politics

The dismantling of the student/teacher hierarchy. The structure of Hélène Cixous'
research seminar illustrates her attempt to initiate a 'collective' approach
to research which refuses the traditional hierarchy of 'student' and
'teacher'. A research programme is put forward at the beginning of the
academic year which participants in the seminar are then free to use as a
starting point for their own investigations. Participants may choose to
work on 'prescribed' texts in relation to the proposed theme, or to
introduce their own choice of texts in relation to this theme, or to follow
different directions suggested to them by their reading.

In Amsterdam, the attempt to move away from traditional hierarchies
led to initial feelings of insecurity within the group. Many of the women
felt the lack of a 'teacher' increased their anxiety at returning to full-time
education and were anxious to reinstate this role. Some felt that the
absence of a clearly-defined 'group leader' made it more difficult for
them to speak, since they wanted to be asked to do so in order to be able
to contribute. Resentments began to develop as some members felt that
other members were dominating group discussion. It was generally felt
that the group's resources (including those of their 'teachers') were not
being used in the best way, and that a structure needed to be developed
in order for each person's contribution to have a place. Accordingly, a
compromise was worked out whereby participants took it in turns to
assume the role of group 'facilitator'. The tasks of the facilitator were
defined as keeping the group to the work programme and time boundaries the group had agreed to adopt. This system of rotating the role of
facilitator led to interesting discussions on the nature of the power-role.
Many of the women felt they would not have dared to occupy this
position if they had not been 'required to' by unanimous vote. Most
were surprised at how well they were able to carry out the role once its
tasks had been defined and the necessity for it acknowledged by the
group as a whole.

Taking time . . . The difficulties experienced by some members of the
Amsterdam group in speaking, and the resentments that arose whenever
it was felt that other members were taking up too much of the group's
time, were resolved in an adaptation of the organisational structure
pioneered by Hélène Cixous at the Centre d'Etudes Féminines. Cixous'
own research seminar is organised around offers of oral presentations by
individual members of her group. These presentations are then listened

to by the seminar. There is little discussion – the 'exchanges' take place through each person hearing the specific questions and paths a speaker has chosen, as well as the points of difference and similarity with their own work. This practice was tried in Amsterdam in a slightly more dogmatic form. In the initial sessions of the project, when the emphasis was on participants thinking back over previous learning experiences to try to evaluate patterns of 'failure' and 'success', time was divided equally between members of the group. Each member thus had an equal share in the group's time and attention, which she was free to use in whatever way she chose.

. . . to listen. Listening – which is a major feature of Hélène Cixous' research seminar – also became an important point of practice in Amsterdam. Interruption was found to cause a speaker to deviate from the telling of her own story, since another's question could sidetrack or lead her to proceed in an entirely different direction. In the initial stages of the project (where the emphasis was on each member of the group learning the lessons of her own 'learning autobiography'), the free flow of discussion was suspended in favour of a situation in which different stories could be placed alongside each other, allowing each member of the group to find the points of interconnection and comparison with her own. This suspension of discussion in the initial stages of the project avoided the trap of trying to find a common denominator for the group's experience, enabling the differences between the stories to make themselves fully heard. It also meant that members of the group were free to listen in a new way. Since the onus was no longer on the group to intervene, members were free to attend to the listening of each other's stories without feeling that their silence could be construed as lack of interest, understanding, or ability to comment and advise.

The value of attentive 'listening' was demonstrated by an exercise tried during the 1986 DUET conference. The aim of the exercise was to enable participants to reflect on the nature of the preconceptions we all of us bring to our reading of a text. The first part of the exercise was as follows. The group was divided into pairs. Each member of the pair was given two minutes in which to speak – without promptings or interruptions – about their personal values. The silent member was asked to listen, noting down the main points of what their partner said. After changing roles, each member of the pair took it in turns to read back to their partner what they had written down. The silent member's participation then became apparent. Not only was each member of the pair given a resumé of what they had said (often difficult to achieve, particularly when – as here – one is asked to consider one's own motivations and personal priorities), but the resumé often served to highlight for the speaker points they were not conscious of having stressed. Most of the participants in the exercise found the task of speaking to an attentive audience helped them to focus and say things they would normally have found it difficult or even impossible to express.

In Amsterdam, the adoption of time-sharing and the attentive listening to others led to a different group dynamics. Silences became an integral part of group sessions. After experiencing these silences some members found it difficult to imagine how they had been able to think in the frenzied pace of previous classroom exchange! In fact, 'ordinary' types of exchange were never excluded from the project. In the initial stages – when discussion was suspended from group sessions – members who wanted to comment on or discuss another's work tended to group together informally – during coffee-breaks, for example, in one-to-one or smaller group breakdowns. This practice of attentive listening during timetabled sessions, with discussion and exchange taking place on a more spontaneous basis away from the main group, continued even when the group moved on from considering their own learning experiences to reading texts, and 'discussion' became an integral part of the main course.

The need for an external system of reference by which to measure progress versus the refusal to sit in judgement on another's work. As the members of the Amsterdam group gradually acquired confidence, both as individuals and in terms of their sense of security within the group, and the activities changed from the initial exercises designed to evaluate personal learning experiences to reading and writing about texts, the question of marking arose. As was the case with the attempt to abandon traditional student/teacher hierarchies, the attempt to adopt the non-judgemental practice of Hélène Cixous' seminar created problems. Many of the women found our refusal to sit in judgement on their work one of the most difficult aspects of the whole course. Although many of the women who volunteered for the project came with labels of 'failure' inherited from previous learning experiences, many found it difficult to accept that there would be no new system of right or wrong, good versus quite good, 4 versus 8 out of 10. Most hoped that the course would provide them with an alternative scheme of marking based on a new evaluation of their abilities and modes of expression. One argument carried particular weight. Almost all the women in the group hoped to go on to study for a literature degree and argued that they would therefore need to be able to write the type of essays that would satisfy the university examiners who – despite all our attempts to deconstruct this role – would nevertheless continue to sit in judgement upon them. Two exercises helped here. One was to discuss the criteria the group felt operated when 'exam-type' essays were being marked; the second was to ask members of the group to mark their own and each other's work in relation to these criteria. The exercises had a number of positive results. It quickly became apparent to the group that writing the type of essays they decided were needed to impress the university examiners did not necessarily or even often reflect their experience of reading, and that whenever these criteria were shifted around (as, for example, when a particular theory was being discussed by the group and it was agreed that a new set of criteria would be needed for essay marking to conform to the applications of this theory) the A grade essay of a previous set of criteria could turn into an E grade essay and vice versa. Participants thus gained an insight into the marking process – learning both how partial and how fallible it can be. The exercises also gave the group renewed confidence for writing, as the stigma of having had one's work marked 'a failure' or 'not good enough' began to lose its sting.

These exercises did not, however, tackle the question of how to measure individual progress. One of the most successful attempts to deal with the need to measure individual progress against a shared scale of reference involved the adoption of a 'collective' marking scheme. For this, each member of the group was required to comment on the work of all the other group members. Here a different problem to that encountered in the early sessions emerged. Whilst most of the participants now found it relatively unproblematic to comment positively on another's work, many still found it difficult to voice 'criticism' – points they had not understood, or which they felt had not been sufficiently worked out or thought needed further development. To get round this problem, a system was adopted whereby each person in the group was asked to respond first with a positive comment to another's work, then with a suggestion for improvement. As an alternative to the voicing of comments in group sessions these were sometimes written down immediately after a presentation and handed to the speaker. These written comments proved particularly helpful as participants were gradually encouraged to evaluate their own 'progress' between pieces of work.

A 'feminine' way of reading and learning: études féminines and the literary text

In Karen Blixen's *Out of Africa* one of the characters – Count Schimmelmann – tells the author that animals only begin to exist once they have been named and classified – caged – by man.[5] The Count's view (which includes the colonisation of Africa and the creation of unequal relationships between master and slave, white and black, man and woman) is juxtaposed in the text with alternative procedures of 'naming' which seek to celebrate rather than annihilate or capitalise on differences (p. 316). In an essay entitled 'Extreme fidelity' (Sellers, 1988) Hélène Cixous explains why the literary text is the subject matter of 'études féminines'. The 'poetic' text is, she argues, freest from the power relations implicit in logical discourse, and therefore allows for the inscription of those elements which are normally repressed. It is the site of inscription of different 'economies'. The examples of these different 'economies' enable the reader to work on his or her own 'life questions' by describing attitudes to the fundamental conditions of life (severance, loss, bereavement, death, love, etc.), keeping alive the possibility of 'femininity' as an alternative to the suppression and appropriation of the other.

These premises entail a number of implications for reading.

Working collectively. Perhaps the most important feature of the Centre d'Etudes Féminines is the emphasis on collective working. In a volume entitled *Writing differences*, Hélène Cixous justifies this practice both in terms of the role of others' thinking in the development of our thought and as the only way to ensure each contribution is heard.[6] No single reading can ever be definitive. These 'collective' readings – comprised of a collective multiplicity of individual questions and paths – are thus, Cixous insists, our closest approximation to a ('feminine') re-creation of the text.

A question of perspective. In Karen Blixen's *Out of Africa* there is a story about a donkey called Molly which all the African estate workers call 'Kejiko' or 'the spoon' (p. 255). When Karen Blixen first hears her African driver using this name she is very surprised and asks the driver to explain why. Eventually, and with some reluctance, the driver tells her that they call the donkey 'the spoon' because the donkey looks like one. Now Karen Blixen, who has come to Africa with all sorts of preconceptions and who is as a result having quite a hard time, finds this totally incomprehensible. As far as she's concerned the donkey doesn't look anything like a spoon. But the story stays with her: she keeps coming back to it, puzzling over it, still unable to understand, until one day she has to drive the donkey cart herself. And sitting in the driver's seat, looking down on the donkey's round haunches and narrow shoulders, she realizes that the donkey looks exactly like a spoon.

This story illustrates a number of points about a 'feminine' reading of the text. It illustrates the need to find the right perspective in order to understand – a perspective that neither suppresses nor appropriates the other's difference.

The question of finding the 'right' perspective to a text resulted in a number of innovations in Amsterdam. One of the first texts to be studied by the group was a sonnet by Shakespeare. Many of the women in the group admitted to feelings of intimidation at the thought of reading Shakespeare because of adverse memories of reading him at school. They found it difficult to tackle the various exercises we had devised for them, exercises aimed at getting them to explore a whole range of textual perspectives, from a general overview of the sonnet's shape and form to detailed examination of its graphic layout. In order to get round these feelings of intimidation we subdivided the main group into smaller units of four, then presented each group with envelopes containing cut-up fragments of the text. Once we had physically cut into the sonnet in this way we tried a different series of exercises that included asking the group to 'brainstorm' the thoughts that came to mind as they looked at the fragmented text,[7] presenting dramatic presentations on selected aspects of the sonnet, and re-writing the sonnet in various ways (replying to Shakespeare in letter-form, writing about experiences connected to the sonnet, attempting to reproduce the verse metre, etc.).

Kejiko's story also illustrates the nature and effect of the preconceptions we each of us bring to our reading. Exploring these preconceptions was one of the themes of the 1986 DUET conference and some of the exercises devised there were adapted and tried in Amsterdam. One of the most successful of these was asking group members to sit and reflect for a few moments at the beginning of a session on their 'journey' to the class. At the end of the session we asked the group to think about any connections between their journey (an argument, patterns cast by sunlight, worries about children, worries about work, etc.) and the things that had happened during the session. Some of the interconnections – such as the discovery that an argument before the class had led to a new reading of a (previously unperceived) power relation implicit in a poem – provided a useful basis for further exploration.

The reading journey: starting from the self. In an exchange at the end of *Writing differences* Hélène Cixous compares the activity of reading to a visit to a foreign country. Just as a journey to a foreign place entails our 'noticing' certain things and not others, so – Cixous argues – our reading of a text bears a complex relation to our individual 'life questions', needs and desires.[8]

A relation to theory. This acknowledging of the questions, needs, and desires that come into play as we read connects to Cixous' refusal to apply literary theories that serve to distance the reader from the text, or construct the reader in a position of mastery. This does not, however, mean the rejection of literary theory,[9] but the use of theory as one element among many in the constant process of readjustment a 'feminine' relation to the text entails.

Differences of response. Just as the return from a visit to a foreign country involves our sharing our experiences with others, so our return from the 'journey of reading' entails the translation of our discoveries in a way that makes them accessible to others. During the 1986 DUET conference experiments were tried with alternative forms of expression to that of the literary 'essay', and these experiments were extended and repeated in Amsterdam. Drama, mime, an informal reading diary, as well as various types of creative writing were all used with positive effect. Most of the women who took part in the project found the experience of these alternative 'writings' liberating, providing them with renewed confidence to tackle the type of essay they would eventually be required to write for a degree. Since the university system remains generally hostile to the inclusion of 'writings' other than those that follow the question-answer format of conventional discourse, this confidence seemed a particularly important (if frustrating!) result.

Notes

1 In *La venue a l'écriture*, with Catherine Clément and Madeleine Gagnon (Paris, 1977).
2 The reference here is to the short story which Kafka wrote in 1914 as part of *The trial*, English edition translated by Edwin and Willa Muir (15th edition, New York, 1977), pp. 213–21.
3 See *To the lighthouse* (Harmondsworth, 1964), pp. 40, 41 and 237.

4 I am interpreting Lily Briscoe's 'vision' in the light of the distinction Woolf makes between two different types of thinking (see *To the lighthouse*, p. 41).

5 See the section entitled 'In the menagerie', *Out of Africa* (Harmondsworth, 1954), pp. 258–61.

6 See 'Conversations' in Sellers, 1988, pp. 141–54.

7 This exercise was also tried at the 1986 DUET conference.

8 See 'Conversations' in Sellers, 1988, pp. 146–7.

9 Freud's theory of the unconscious, and the post-structuralist analysis of the power relations implicit in discourse, are two examples of theories Cixous uses to provide insights into the reading process.

Valuing women's experience

Introduction to
Part Two

'Starting from the self': at the end of her essay in the previous section, Susan Sellers uses the work of Hélène Cixous to discuss feminine modes of reading and alternative modes of writing which begin with our own individual 'life questions', needs and desires. In this section the idea is taken up literally in three essays on various uses of autobiography in feminist teaching.

Autobiographies, diaries and letters constitute some of the earliest forms of sustained writing we have by women, but as texts they occupy an uneasy position on the fringe of the literary canon. And while they are dismissed as 'not really Literature', it is simultaneously possible for novels and poetry by women to be considered in a patronising way as 'merely' autobiographical. Yet all of us who have taught courses on women's writing or on feminist theory and criticism know that female students are regularly and joyfully 'released' into a different perspective on academic study by the novelty of being able to bring their own experiences as women to bear on the texts they are studying: the sense of exhilaration this can give is evoked many times in this book.

Just as in the seventeenth century autobiography was the way in which British women entered the world of letters, so in our time women's own lives can be seen as holding the key to their access to the academic study of reading and writing. Women are currently engaged in rediscovering and re-evaluating female autobiography from the past as well as in exploring the relevance of their own autobiographical experiences to their reading and writing of literature.

As two of the essays in this section demonstrate in quite different contexts, women's lives are different from men's lives. Louise Stewart and Helen Wilcox record the ways in which students were both intrigued and baffled by the unfamiliar procedures which Margaret Cavendish, Duchess of Newcastle, follows in her *True relation of my birth, breeding and life* (1656). She denigrates her own text, calling it 'scribbling rather than writing'; she eschews formal structure in favour of a rambling, impetuous flow of long sentences linked together rather casually and full of contradictions and qualifications. As Stewart and Wilcox comment, 'Many in the group were uncertain whether to condemn this as a lack of discipline, or to discern in it the multiple interwoven strands of women's lives as opposed to the linear pattern of male autobiography'.

Maggie Humm uses similar domestic or feminine metaphors in talking about women's lives as a 'patchwork' or 'web' of experience rather than a programmatic narrative. For her, a close reading of the autobiographies written by students of both sexes as a qualification for their entry into higher education, revealed that 'The differences between men and women showed up both in their life stories and in the way they told them.' Men's lives were indeed viewed by themselves as linear and coherent, focussed straightforwardly on educational and career objectives, while women's lives were presented as much more uncertain and shifting, 'always part of the lives of others', just as Margaret Cavendish ultimately places herself as daughter of one man and wife of another.

Ironically, even here, in what might seem to many of us in higher education a very enlightened assessment procedure, women are again in danger of being judged as failures, their experiences undervalued and their writing dismissed as incoherent or inappropriate. Maggie Humm makes use of the work of Pierre Bourdieu and of feminist criticism of autobiography to establish alternative modes of analysis, discovering, like Deborah Cameron in Part I, that she must problematise her own research project.

All three essays in this section make extensive use of the work of students who are clearly active participants in their own education, not passive consumers of what their teachers provide. Moira Monteith puts the emphasis on personal as well as collaborative response as she describes her teaching of the autobiographical texts of Maxine Hong Kingston, a Chinese American woman, in an attempt to break down some of the barriers set up by the more formal modes of literary discourse and to evoke the more egalitarian, co-operative atmosphere of the creative writing class. As she points out, the reading of literary texts performs for many mature students the function of an 'access to study' course, but there is usually little room or encouragement for them to bring their own experiences of both life and literature to bear on their academic studies. For women in particular it is important to examine the dislocation between social and personal experience, to discuss texts which raise these issues, and to permit responses which give us more opportunity to 'write ourselves'.

4

Subjects in English: autobiography, women and education
Maggie Humm

The subject of English is always the site of subjectivity. Academics try to train students to translate subjective readings into the critical analysis of texts, and students, in their conscious perceptions of that experience, become student 'subjects'. Little is written directly about this process because the dialectic of personal change and critical expression is not a usual part of academic writing. This is because 'English' depends on students agreeing with staff what can count as English. Meanings are not in English texts but in interpretative strategies that students learn to use to produce texts.

Writing an autobiography can give students that sense of a narrated identity. It is a sense we often forget to include in the *content* of academic courses. In her *Signs* review of recent feminist scholarship on women's life histories, Susan Geiger argues very well that life history writing provides a deeper understanding of women's consciousness since it overcomes the hierarchical relation between the researcher and the researched and because it centralises women's social experience and perceptions.[1]

In Higher Education, the School for Independent Study at North East London Polytechnic can probably lay the strongest claim to a tradition of incorporating autobiography into course material. For over ten years now, all new students have written autobiographies as part of their course planning in a contract system of learning. The autobiographies take the place of unattained A levels and are credited, or validated as a student qualification for entry into their self-designed course. Students are asked to examine both their past life and their need for achievement and to channel these into educational paradigms. To encourage students to link an inner 'mode' of retrieval and recovery with a public account of their future education is to encourage diversity. In particular Black and gay students can be recognised as creators and subjects and allowed to define for themselves what is normal rather than being a distant Other in the blinkered world of Higher Education.

However, even in a liberal environment like NELP, educational paradigms absorb radical intentions. Students have to organise the discourse of their past into a rhetoric 'appropriate' to Polytechnic bureaucracy. Perhaps, not surprisingly, this contains a hidden agenda of sexism since more autobiographies by women (with their confused, but very moving, accounts of mothers, childhood and caring relationships) than those by men, are judged 'unsound' by the School's validation procedures. Over eighty per cent of male autobiographies 'pass' validation compared to just under sixty per cent of female autobiographies.

At first then, I felt that as I was a feminist and because I wanted to help women make valid their subjective voices it would be a simple project to uncover educational sexism by describing its corruption of women's language. And that this would be feminist research. My starting point was to find out how and why women were more circumscribed by the process of writing than men. My initial research 'design' was to compare interim autobiographies with those eventually accepted by the School since validation requires students to make educational aims an integral part of their life history.

At first sight the problem of what was and was not relevant seemed straightforward. The differences between men and women showed up both in their life stories and in the way they told them. Men made their lives into patterns of self-chosen events set in a rational pursuit of well defined education goals. Women's lives were always part of the lives of others. Rather than insisting on personal strength, women's identities were part of what Margaret Mead has called 'significant others'.[2] These differences were echoed in the very syntax and vocabulary that men and women used. Women's voices were diffuse. Men already seemed to possess or to recognise the restricted mode of autobiographical discourse which tutors were happy to accept as a norm for course approval. Tutor comments of 'make more coherent' and 'clarify objectives' were clearly suspicious of autobiographies which explored childhood in more detail than the later stages of career and education. Autobiographies, in other words, written by women.

Rita changed her 'unsupported' autobiography quite dramatically. Her interim account had a successive randomness focusing on the people around her rather than on herself. Because she left the Caribbean as a baby and was an only child, her relationship with her mother was very significant to her and so too were her nursery friendships with other immigrant children. Often Rita's sentences were discontinuous, omitting pronouns in a succession of key words like 'tense', 'loss' and 'difficulties'. In the re-written version Rita dropped all references to early childhood and maternal warmth in creating a picture of a developing professional looking to a future training rather than to a past community. Rita's second version may be less valuable to her and to the reader as autobiography but clearly sets an agenda for her programme of work. The problem, however, is that women students like Rita are misled into valuing autobiography since the School cannot accommodate it educationally.

So Rita's account had given me my initial hypothesis which, I feel now, was too simple a view. It was too close to essentialism. It seemed to imply stereotypes of male and female writing. In 'Who remembers what?: gender differences in memory', Elizabeth Loftus and others researching autobiographies cite evidence that 'while sex differences in autobiographical memory recollections were observed, they were not particularly pronounced.'[3]

Nor did my hypothesis take account of student needs. How and why did women and men students manipulate their subjectivity into these distinct gendered objects if a gendered antithesis in writing and memory can be regarded as a false one? Revealing sexism in abstract is all very well, but in this as in most other activities there is some distance between theory and practice. Yet Loftus et al. do end their research with a persuasive and resonating notion. They suggest that the differences between men's and women's memories 'are more indicative of their memory preferences than their memory abilities' (my italics). The question to ask, I realised now, was what it could be about women's needs, or preferences, as represented ideologically in the lives they wrote that caused such educational allodoxia, such false recognitions in the School's judgements. Perhaps then the scripted iconographies of women's lives would cease to be so educationally powerless.

To provide an adequate answer, one that acknowledges that we are more than 'just' or 'essentially' women, I thought to recast the terms of my understanding of autobiography as a process. In an essay called 'Brecht and discourse', Barthes compared Brecht to a Paris dressmaker since both use bell pins in their work – the dressmaker so that she can find her pins when her sewing might be too perfect, Brecht so that he could separate the perfect 'fabric' of language by the insertion of links

and transitions.[4] I wanted to use 'bell pins' in my criticism about autobiography – in other words to try to incorporate the force of the making of
autobiography into my account of it. I felt that my research then must be
like the women's autobiographies that I was reading. It must not use only
one 'acceptable' mode of analysis.

Feminist research is often suspicious of a self defined through public
activities. We seem to desire accounts in which emotions give a special
and unmediated access to some 'truth' about identity. Trying to avoid
this fallacy I turned to the theories of Pierre Bourdieu,[5] who tells us that
writing involves 'categories of experience' which control our responses
and memories, the meaning we give these, and our ways of writing and
choosing social options. Bourdieu suggests that power relations are
present in people's minds in the form of these categories. He uses the
term to explain why the legitimate mode of perception, the way of telling,
is therefore such an important prize at stake in educational or social
struggles. In other words the actual categories of autobiography are
involved in a power battle.

Bourdieu conceives the social space of education to be a collection of
fields of perception drawn from economics, culture, education and
family background. He suggests that our power as agents in this space is
increased by the number of positions we occupy in different fields, since the
way we write or speak is the product of previous symbolic struggles.
Many women students lack experience of the multiple sites of career,
work, and training. They occupy the domestic space described in their
autobiographies and from that base their power in education is slighter
than it might be. It is not that these lives are one-dimensional but the
multiplicity in that site is not recognised. Women are, therefore, less
likely to pass through any educational gate-keeping mechanism which
closes off the field of the domestic. Also, at the risk of crude oversimplifi-
cation, what is more distinctive about this metatheory is Bourdieu's
description of an individual's language as his or her framework of power
or powerlessness in the social space. Bourdieu argues that language
reveals 'time'. The time taken to acquire symbolic experience, 'cultural
capital', including these 'appropriate' languages, determines distance or
proximity to the power base of any social space. Since women traditionally take longer to acquire cultural capital in education, this would
make them distant from power.

Where Bourdieu is most fertile, in other words, is in this notion that
the true nature of the social space is expressed in the distribution of
agents within it by sex. This is because our different relations to culture

stem from our different *modes* of acquisition and the most crucial distinction in acquisition is that between the *domestic* (or acquisition in a family context) and the scholastic/career or acquisition at work. Access to the 'profits' of a social space, or entry into higher education, Bourdieu says is determined by the *set* of distributions, not by the language of one field alone, by time *and* by mode all of which might disadvantage women. Especially since education, Bourdieu claims, is the key site where the price of these competencies is determined.

I find Bourdieu's analysis particularly valuable because he draws political conclusions from connecting autobiography directly to life experience. We can add the technique of literary criticism. Feminist criticism of autobiography – for example, Estelle Jelinek's collection (1980) – has contributed a more precise syntactical analysis of literary form. Literary theory familiarises us with autobiography as the realisation of a text as well as with a life script. This is particularly useful when reading student writing since in their retrospective self-analysis psychological need becomes conflated with compositional needs set by the School which are at cross purposes to those demands.

All this was dramatised for me in a cry from Anastasia, born in Dominica and confused about where to locate her identity. 'I am unable or unwilling to *look* at myself'; she felt psychically swamped when comparing her career failures in England with the apparent success of those friends who stayed. To write an autobiography in education is to negotiate with the overt question: 'How can I make my definition of education narratable?' Anastasia's literal social and psychic displacement from Caribbean 'fields of perception' narrows her choice of educational meanings.

One of the main moments in all these women's autobiographies occurs in the choice of a beginning for the life they describe. Autobiographical beginnings are the one place where gender divisions and values are most clearly visible. It is where the term 'memory' is found resonating between its gender and cultural categories. Any beginning (especially of a heuristic pattern in time, but I will come back to that question) will shape future educational expectations.

Women carry with them their childhoods. As a time of feeling it is brought forward again and again to shape responses to much later social and educational experiences. Mary begins her life with 'my great grand parents, who were of the Spiritualist religion, fled from Germany to England because of political activities'. Denise chooses to start with her birth in Ireland described in vivid detail: 'Mother haemorrhaged severely as the placenta was not fully delivered. A suitable blood donor was hard to find and rumour spread through the town that she had died.' With frequent house moves Marisa, at the age of four, thought she must be a gypsy. 'When we first moved to Milan I was four and a half years old and I used to spend the week sitting at home on my own after I had rejected the woman who was looking after me.' Women use the tension of childhood experience as the basis of adult analysis. The energy is palpable. Elizabeth was 'petrified of the unknown, for example people, water, dogs, cats, shadows, balloons'. But that fear gives her a perception of the psychosocial dynamics of family life. 'I think a strong possibility was that both my parents were anxious and I was able to pick this up from them.'

Male students seem never to admit childhood. They enter their 'real' worlds at fifteen or twenty. Paul, a future minister in the Falklands, starts 'I remember little of my primary schooling.' David remembers childhood as 'full of happiness of the kind that a financially secure marriage produced' only as the site of his father's career. Geoffrey, as an evacuee, might be said to be dislocated from Bourdieu's 'fields of experience', but very quickly he can make a masculine separation from family anxiety. 'The free time this state of affairs afforded had its compensations and I gathered quite a large collection of birds' eggs and acquired a knowledge of their habits that I would not otherwise have obtained.'

Like all good Lacanian subjects, men write autobiography as access to a future: 'The course is an ideal opportunity for me to restructure my life.' Women prefer to retrieve a past. Tutors encourage students to delete 'extraneous' early memories because these *are* difficult to translate into educational paradigms. But since it is mainly women who begin at the beginning such a mandate denies women more than men identity and ideology. An ideological consciousness is not only a structure of feeling that comes from the relationship of people in work, privileged more by men, but it is also an understanding of the world in childhood. In my own 'history' I take my fear of institutions back to a memory of the caged hospital bed thought suitable for a two-year-old who, for a whole week, lost along with her tonsils any sight of her parents. Women's longer life-span then is not only one of demography but a transformation of the concept of memory.

If we read autobiography from the students' subjectivities we begin to use more complicated modalities in reconstituting memory. Women's autobiography teaches us that memory can not only be 'symbolic capital' but is made up of images whose social reference points are not simply objectively there but come through the physical context of the recollections. But rather than seeing women *denied* access to a speaking voice we might commiserate with men, forcing themselves to live in a 1984 world of dislocated memories they are desperately trying to conscript.

The texture of women's experience is one where emotions are recollected very physically. Women are continually diving into emotional waters. To Kirsty 'people frightened me, they were loud and too crude in comparison with my parents or so it seemed. We were working class but we were different in that we were not "East End" working class.' Men lack this physical awareness or refuse it access just as they refuse their childhoods as 'categories of experience'. Mark, unusually for men, did admit to liking wild flowers but he makes his pleasure become a botanic quest, 'hunting Hampshire for a single specimen'. Women seem to write from within and this 'within' is not symbolic but literal – a sequence of alive and vivid scenes. If we adopt Bachelard's term[6] what we are dealing with in women's autobiography is a rhythm in a 'system of moments' which become our touchstones of evaluation.

This system of moments is irregular rather than orderly. The narratives of women's lives are often not progressive or heuristic but disconnected and organised into self-contained scenes rather than a connecting plot. There is no masculine linkage of Bourdieu's 'sets of distributions'. For example, Jan, from Jamaica, describes being 'very, very myopic' as a child and found that 'it took a lot of persuasion before the teachers believed that I really couldn't see the board'. The pain of that problem lives on in her inability to disentangle from the scene. She returns again and again in her writing to interrogate the school system rather than give us a clear chronology of her life. Denise's life lacks a strict chronology but has a very affective logic in her strange and witty comments on her subjectivity. 'Concepts that depress me: a non-neutral Ireland, giving up smoking, the second law of thermodynamics, a blight on green beans, moving statues.'

To make one's life have an objective demands that one perceives that life as coherent. Rather, women's autobiographies exploit a rhetoric of uncertainty about themselves and about the role of women, and record feelings not accomplishments. Linda Anderson suggests that this use of form as 'potential' rather than plot reveals anxiety (Anderson, p. 60). Not only was the *content* of these autobiographies gender distinct, but there was too a significant difference in organisation in the way women pursue an infinite variety of issues linked by place rather than thematisation.

Over the last weeks, writing this, I have thought about my own inability to put any headings on my notes until after I have written or to begin a paragraph with what I want to say rather then helplessly arrive there at the end of the track.

Men made conceptual bridges between the public personas of career or leisure and psychological feelings. These linked 'fields of perception' give a positive and linear sense of identity. Paul gives his life firm titles: 'Childhood 1939–1955; Early employment 1955–1958; National Service and Bible College 1958–1960: agony and ecstasy' (although very little emotion is here); 'Southampton 1963–1967: growing into the real world; The Falkland Islands 1967–1971: my most formative years'. Paul gives each section a retrospective summary 'Looking Back'. David preferred to sign all his different sections with his full name. Leo even used gold address labels. The excess of signatures is the sign of male students' anxiety. But such anxieties stay out of their retellings. Do men make strong marks in autobiographies because they can make social marks in their lives? Or should we remember Freud describing a masculine identity as one dependent on a necessary forgetting?[7]

To return to Barthes, he makes this difference into a war of language between 'encratic' language which is diffuse and conversational and 'acratic' language whose strength is systematic (p. 107). Assuming for the moment that features of adult writing *are* consistent with the acquisition of gender identity in childhood, we should not be astonished that 'encratic' women need conversations with Others more than 'acratic' men. The most important conversation is with our mothers. Although there was a total absence of mothers in the tales told by men, women use a category of matrilineal perception. For Agnes 'it was a real shock seeing my mother so unstable and weak. I choked up with frustration. I wanted to be independent and get on with my own life but I felt I was not being allowed to'. Agnes's perception is formalised by Nancy Chodorow (1978) whose argument centres on the shared gender identity of mother and daughter and the difficulty daughters experience in perceiving their mothers as separate from themselves. Parting from her mother as she left Zimbabwe was Marjorie's 'saddest moment of my life' and, full of matrilineal consciousness, she began to train in England as a nurse 'with a special interest in mothers with puerperal psychosis.' An only child myself, reading Marjorie's account gave me an instant empathy with my mother. After childbirth I entered an incredible post-partum experience of fresh and bright memories of my mother, dead since I was twelve, and my early childhood. The physical memories quickly became practical childcare in a wonderful world of what seemed to be psychic possession.

Sadly the scenes lasted only for about three months ending perhaps at the moment of my own apparent competency.

Marisa might be Chodorow's signifier. 'I didn't want to lead the life my mother was leading and I used to end up feeling either guilty or inadequate'. Of course feminism has valorised mothers. Yet we might read the mnemonic of mothers in these autobiographies less as accounts of 'real' women and more as processes women use to inscribe into education an ideology of caring. Pat's childhood is a world of male psychosis. 'My older brother broke my leg when I was three and cut off one of my plaits when I was nine. I lost my front tooth when I was banged on the head on a school faucet by the boys.'

Women save themselves by strong attachments to one or more women who are role models or reciprocate their love. Helen loved Miss Smith her teacher who 'used to wear different coloured scarves for different moods. For example, when she wore red it meant that she was in a dangerous mood and that it was better for us not to say or ask her anything'. Helen's friend Carol 'stopped me from becoming totally isolated' after the death of her mother. Helen even invites Mrs Mac, a next-door neighbour, into the space of her autobiography because 'she listens and teaches me to listen'.

For men, relationships are often chosen 'contracts'. Tom claims not to 'regret' his choice of girlfriend although 'having to visit my future wife in Watford meant I was unable to run in the Brighton, London, Brighton race'. Defensively he knows 'that it is difficult to deny the actual experience of becoming friends' with other people but they remain anonymous contributors to his banking career. According to Bourdieu a group exists when it begins to see itself in representation. Tom the bank employee and the other male students could use the symbolic language of institutions in a way that seemed difficult for women.

Men and women's 'categories of experience' seem almost diagrammatically distinct. Women existed in a three dimensional game of tic-tac-toe, bouncing between relationships at a tangent to the linear school to career of men. Yet both kinds of category may be equally heuristic. For example, Enid, who 'could not hide my feelings', became a psychiatric nurse in order to help patients 'express their feelings'.

What has emerged from this journey through the lived experience of a group of students? What can be meaningful, with regard to autobiography or to the development of the School's contract system of education? The School clearly presupposes in its validation procedures that autobiography can give students a developed sense of their individuality, a self-conscious 'I' being able to perceive itself as the controller of its life history and social world. Yet, for many women, speaking of ourselves publicly and creating an educational continuity are often ideologically contradictory. In broad outline it is not a single woman's voice we hear in her autobiography but that of a family.

But rather than approaching women's autobiography as a catalogue of barred access to a 'real' world of education we should be talking about educational structures not in terms of repression but in terms of their constituting influence on women *and* men. Autobiography would become negotiation – between the student's subjective self (modified by the constant internalisation into one's self of the interpretation of that self held by other people) and the expectation of self presentation held by the School.

It is important to make a 'distinction' between institutionalised mysogyny and men as individuals (like women with unconscious internalisations of a social self), just as it is important to make a distinction between black students and white students and between gay and heterosexual. We could see subjects themselves as sources of signification rather than judging *only* their social responses to education.

In other words, if students could present their autobiography as *process* rather than text, the 'social space' of the School could use 'role models', 'mothers', 'physical' dramatisations of social events; projects about childhood as part of course material rather than relying on an outdated pattern of life planning. We would need a new critical language, a new validation technique. Inevitably a vocabulary of 'patchwork' or 'web' as a checklist of criteria rather than educational objectives might be more difficult to use than a strong linear chronology.

But unless *all* students and staff, men and women, Black and gay attempt to understand in autobiography the processes which control us, I will continue to feel when reading male autobiographies as Humblot, the reader for Editions Ollendorf, felt on reading the manuscript of *Swann's way*: 'I don't know if I've gone completely blind and deaf, but I can't see any interest in reading thirty pages on how a Gentleman tosses and turns in bed before falling asleep' (Barthes, p. 281).

Notes

1 Susan Geiger, 'Women's life histories: method and content', *Signs*, 11, no. 2 (1986), p. 350.
2 See Margaret Mead, *Male and female* (New York, 1949).
3 Elizabeth Loftus et al., 'Who remembers what?: Gender differences in memory', *Michigan Quarterly Review*, 26, no. 1 (1987), 'Women and memory: a special issue', pp. 64–86.

4 In Roland Barthes, *The rustle of language* (Oxford, 1986 and New York, 1987).
5 Pierre Bourdieu, *Distinction: a social critique of the judgement of taste* (London and Cambridge, Mass., 1984), and 'The social space and genesis of groups', *Theory and Society*, 14, no. 6 (1985), pp. 723–43.
6 See Gaston Bachelard, *La formation de l'esprit scientifique* (Paris, 1970).
7 Jeffrey Moussaieff Masson ed., *The complete letters of Sigmund Freud to Whilhelm Fleiss* (Cambridge, Mass., and London, 1985).

5

Too personal a response?
Women's collaborative reading
Moira Monteith

Recently I have become concerned about the nature of literary study as seen in most Humanities programmes, that is, as a discourse to be entered into and handed on.[1] I've noticed how students become particularly anxious when they perceive that conflicting presentations of literary discourse are offered by different lecturers. Also, I find myself more and more unequal to the task of arbitrating the 'discourse' when literary studies is increasingly seen as peripheral (in terms of degree study) in most higher education institutions, yet reading literature is highly important and significant in the educational development of many mature students. (Indeed it often performs the function of an 'access to study' course.) Such readers' own experience ironically is often at odds with the values made explicit in the proffered discourse. It seems reasonable therefore to legitimise students' own entry to the text, their individual reading, at least as one part of the course.

In this brief chapter I examine the response of two groups of students[2] to a particular text, their perception of it mediated partly by a group discussion which I chaired and partly by their own experience in terms of their own lives and previous reading. 'Chaired' indicates the nature of the discussion. Everyone was encouraged to give opinions but I organised the discussion in that I tried to ensure a fair hearing for those less able to get their point across, encouraged those more hesitant in giving voice, and moved the discussion on if I thought it was becoming repetitive. No doubt I signified my agreement or otherwise with certain points of view though I tried consciously not to make my opinions too obvious. I then asked the students to write about their response to the text discussed in terms of their own experience.

The students seemed excited by a collaborative approach which admits individual perspectives, though two students disliked the text selected and this possibly inhibited their expression. Maybe all of us were cheered at the thought no one would be wrong. Failure to perceive the 'correct' signification (correct for that class in its time and space warp) can be disheartening to say the least.

I have found that such a writing activity emphasises the problematic nature of textual meaning, encourages an examination of the relationship of author and reader, and makes clear the varying levels of response/stages of reading. It validates these stages while simultaneously indicating that we are indeed centring our writing around one collection of words. Subsequently, the group can begin, if it wishes, to generalise from those responses, thus forming a collaborative reading. And writing as an activity is a positive, creative act (criticism is often seen in an ambiguous even negative light) which in itself contributes to the efficacy of later discussion.

I chose Maxine Hong Kingston's two stories, 'No name woman' and 'White tigers',[3] since they offer valuable insights into women's experience generally, at the same time delineating a perspective (Chinese/American) different from the experience of any of us, which allowed us to distance ourselves from the text. We therefore had a dual focus, a connection with our own experience (though this turned out to be much more varied than I anticipated), plus a longsighted view of cultural attitudes which might at first glance seem quite alien. The two pieces are also remarkable for their incisive undercutting theoretical edge. In these two stories Maxine Hong Kingston gives straightforward accounts, vividly and exquisitely told, of two fictions handed down in her family. One concerns the death of an aunt who drowned herself and one is the mythic story of a female warrior who avenges the wrongs her family has suffered. In the first Kingston hypothesises as to the behaviour which may have led to her aunt's death and in the second contrasts the model of the warrior training and fighting with her own experience. In both, the autobiographical experiences are carefully scrutinised. The sense of enquiry is all important.

In writing of her own experience Kingston qualifies the account by referring to the demarcation between each person's own experience and that of her culture. 'Chinese-Americans, when you try to understand what things in you are Chinese, how do you separate what is peculiar to childhood, to poverty, insanities, one family, your mother who marked your growing with stories, from what is Chinese?'[4] Awareness of this dislocation between personal and social knowledge is both a psychological event for all of us and a continuing situation in life. Since so much of women's experience has, like incest, been hidden, this hinge between the social and the personal is highly important. If we are to achieve the community ethos which seems to exist as a wished-for dream in women's writing[5] rather than a historical reality, we must discover what experiences we share with other women and what might be different in our own case. Women are fundamentally dislocated by the pressures of gender cutting across those of race and class so it is very relevant to look at our own autobiography alongside those of other women and examine our own interpretive readings alongside those of others. We can then consider what might be our own response and what might be that of women in general or as a group.

The students and I discussed the taboo opening of 'No name woman': 'You must not tell anyone,' my mother said, 'what I am about to tell you . . .', the nature of a suppressed text, the failure to communicate women's experience openly. We looked at the complicated mixture of language: what we assumed to be immigrant talk 'seventeen hurry-up weddings', the poetic design of some sentences, 'Like a great saw, teeth strung with lights, files of people walked zig-zag across our land, tearing the rice', the rhetorical address to Chinese-Americans (and where that places us as readers), and a denigratory phrase that jerks us into the present though referring to ages-old pornopleasure, a 'tits and ass man'.

We considered the practice of hypothesising about our immediate pre-history. Kingston queries whether the aunt's adultery occurred because she had been trained to submit, wanted a private as well as a communal life, could have had a romantic disposition or sexual desire. She changes from a sympathetic casting of the aunt's behaviour to the suggestion that she was a 'spite suicide, drowning herself in the drinking water . . whose weeping ghost, wet hair hanging and skin bloated, waits silently by the water to pull down a substitute'. The original text was an oral warning by the narrator's mother to restrain her daughter's sexuality. Its function has been altered, rewritten but not closed.

'White tigers' centres on the notion of paradox, implying that often this is a fundamental characteristic of women's experience. If we are given models of female endurance or courageous exploits we are at the same time given instructions to behave well, be obedient, not attempt to take over privileges considered to be male prerogatives. For some the paradox is fulfilled (as in the case of the narrator) by being 'bad' and disobedient, because such qualities are nearer those of the male heroic who fights injustice and confronts evil. The myth tells of a Chinese girl trained by an old couple to be a warrior and avenge her downtrodden family. However although she is accepted by her own and husband's family as a female liberator she wears male armour and hides her sex on pain of death. The myth ends with domestic reconciliation, with the woman swearing obedience to her mother-in-law. The story continues with the illustrative paradox of the narrator's own experience. Kingston makes conscious use of the sense of dislocation to indicate the anger that results from the experience of paradox. She deliberately uses the disjunction that Virginia Woolf deplored so much in *Jane Eyre*[6] to indicate clearly and positively the alienation and anger that follows the mismatch of model and experience. She was unable to kill gloriously (actual killing was 'slum grubby'). Her assertiveness often seemed futile. Her revenge is the display of words, a parallel with those tatooed on the back of the warrior woman, an act of disobedience against the male organisation of society.

The students were asked to write about anything in their past experience which they felt connected with either of the pieces we had read and discussed. Most were concerned with secrecy in the family and this usually centred on illegitimacy or what seemed to be any kind of abnormal family structure, the father living elsewhere for instance. It was abundantly clear that most students knew of a secret 'abnormality', and since it seems unlikely that students should be remarkably different from other people, it follows that we keep secret what is very common. They speculated on the pressures that control women, and several commented on the role women play in suppressing each other, from insisting on the norm of marriage for everyone to teachers who reward or punish specific kinds of behaviour. Three looked at the problems of cultural divide, and one woman wrote of her own experience of 'the haunting of the living by the dead'. One woman felt she could not write about the trauma of her childhood at all and wrote about life in the services – she obviously enjoyed being a woman warrior, 'not from patriotic reasons, but as an escape from an unhappy homelife'.

There were a great many aunts (certainly a feature that did not come up in the discussion at all), and aunts that weren't aunts but someone else's (secret) illegitimate daughter. Families are misrepresented in stereotypes and certainly in literature[7] but it seems no accident that it is Maxine Hong Kingston's aunt who is the focus of the story. An aunt is close enough for the warning to be real and common enough to be dangerous if accepted as a numerous, transgressing minority.

I include some brief extracts of the students' writing since it is unfortunately impossible to include all their work. I have grouped them under specific headings because that seemed to be how they wrote.

Concerning secrecy

. . . of being where you must be although not feeling as though you belong. And there is the silence – you do not speak because you know what the other person's response is going to be – and when you do speak it is to create something (a world or a childhood) entirely different from reality.

I kept the secret, and I did often think about it, particularly when I saw the family acting out the charade of who people were, or should I say, in reality, were not. I think it gave me a small sense of power.

I never realised how important individual members of a family are until I became aware that one of mine was missing.

I knew mothers cried. I had seen mine cry often when my father hit her. She always told me that I must never tell anyone at all . . .

The other terrible secret is about his mother. She used to 'see' to the local ladies who had unwanted pregnancies. There. I've said it. I think this revelation even shocked my emancipated mind. I know someone did these things but my grand-mother! Ugh!

This disgraced, almost forgotten, never discussed vibrant person pasted into a dissembling family album . . .

Control

'You will never get to grammar school,' said the teacher, slapping the back of my legs with the flat of her hand . . . I carried those strokes for twenty-four hours and they remain with me as part of my psyche now.

The most devastating event I can remember from my childhood was failing the eleven-plus examination. It was not the failure itself but my mother's reaction to it . . . she screamed and sobbed . . . After the initial reaction the attitude was not to mention it again and attempt to never admit to outsiders that she had a daughter at the local 'Secondary Modern'.

I think that for my grandmother beauty and virtue were indistinguishable and it maybe that the consequences of her belief were disastrous for my aunt. Whenever my aunt behaved assertively or in an experimental way, my grandmother admonished her not for unkindness or inconsideration, but rather recriminated her for ugliness: 'Don't behave like that, it's ugly!' or 'Don't do that, it doesn't become you.'

'If you go all round the orchard you will end up on the crab apple tree.' This was a favourite saying of my mother's when I was in my teens and starting to take notice of boys.

It is women who castigate wrongdoers, mostly verbally, rather than men, women who bring their daughters up on all these unspoken myths, even in this day and age denying daughters the freedoms they automatically grant to their sons . . .

'Right' was in being a virgin on the day of marriage and being true to only one man. 'Wrong' was the opposite.

Cultural divide

I think all women are warriors, our fighting is against injustice.

I also think constantly of words 'chink' words and 'gook' words that do not fit on my skin.

If I protested (at Hebrew lessons) I was told 'But you must be able to follow the Service, dear.' If I could hear it above the whispering in the gallery where the women sat . . . when the volume became too much for the men doing the serious stuff down below, the rabbi or one of the 'guardians' would look up and shush us and the gabble became a whisper, only to rise again before long.

Being Irish/American is not as visible as being Chinese/American, but it is a definite psychological state. I could not write, talk, think of my family and childhood without these myths.

Belonging to two cultures strikes a personal chord. I doubt if I would have written this otherwise.

Haunting

I was a person with a tragic background, somebody who was not normal.

The myths of our ancestors are strong and confusing.

A memory of my mother curled into a embryo ball on the kitchen floor, a helplessness, a dissolution. Sometimes I wish my father dead . . . Rejection lies like a mountain of snakes between us.

Illegitimacy

In a house full of people it was easiest just to call all adults 'Aunty' or 'Uncle' and all children 'cousin'. That way it didn't matter that Ann didn't have a father.

My first reaction was sympathy for Margaret, really because of having to live all her life never being able to be who she really was . . . Women have to bear all the responsibility for being 'good' was something important said in the passage. My Aunt Gladys's lover eventually disappeared, I guess, but she had to go on pretending.

Men were often entirely excluded from: discussion, decision, action (after the procreative act, that is!) and care of babies, and this was particularly the case in the matter of illegitimacy.

(Keeping the father's name secret) was something of her own, and being back under the jurisdiction of her mother she could feel that, despite having the baby, she had that secret as her own.

. . . the illegitimate child of my very young mother who was at that time aged fifteen . . .

Responses

Reading it was like opening Pandora's Box. I want to weep for my daughter and for the pain and hurt our tardy family secrets have caused all my children, but especially her.

Although the cultural background was so different to mine, the main issue in 'No name woman' was, in point of fact, a very general issue, and related to experience from my own life.

It is important to know that surface images, stories, voices, are only surface. Beneath the initial impression, lies a morass of reasons, of emotions. If these remain unseen then all you have is surface, and as such is untrue.

What is lived through in our imagination becomes as much part of ourselves as that which is lived through in reality (I think).

Writing has not developed my original response to the text but in reverse, it has helped me perhaps to understand the reasons for the difficulties I experience in comparison of the text with a minefield implies a continuing process, the effects following on as the text goes on exploding. Another reading completely paralleled the original by divulging her own secret, a grandmother who helped with abortions. And of course one felt her writing was her response since the text had evoked her own family secret. These responses are structural rather than thematic. They relate to the suppression of experience, the knowledge of secrecy. The reading (and writing) has become a collaborative unlocking of the text.

All the writing related to a fairly narrow thematic band, perhaps because of our discussion though I doubt that as a reason. For instance, the concepts of secrecy and control were not so emphatic in our talk as in the writing. All readers recognised the text as our central focus.

Some literary theorists believe there is a general level of literary competence in literature students paralleling the kind of linguistic competence we all have as speakers.[9] I would prefer to say there is a level of literary awareness which we have acquired through our reading, and from viewing TV and films and from the stories we have grown up with from our families, the school playground and work. We respond to the text because we perceive something in it which relates to us. These first responses are often emotional and usually discarded in favour of more sophisticated readings moderated by the institutional context. In these later readings the personal and emotional responses are neglected in favour of what is perceived as theoretical and objective. I suggest that there is no need to ignore these primary responses though I am not suggesting that they should be privileged above subsequent readings. Nevertheless they are part of the process of reading and should not be completely negated. In my experience readers are highly selective in what they write in response to a text. This would indicate that such writing exercises reveal part of the interpretative process normally accomplished more swiftly in the mind and are not merely a stimulus for casual reminiscence.

Of course there is the question of choice of text. What would happen with a text that is less emotionally involving or one which would be very negative reading material (for example, Norman Mailer)? If we take into account the transformative energy of the literary text (and I don't know why we discuss literature if we don't assume it has some) then our choice of text will vary according to the potential readership. The two pieces by Maxine Hong Kingston are important because of their archetypal relevance to female readers and their effect in encouraging them (as was obvious in these two student groups) positively to break the code of secrecy and reflect upon the constraints of their past.

The writing also led to an increased respect for Kingston's writing techniques. It has been fashionable to consider the text without an author but when we read texts that relate in some ways to ourselves we accept that there is an author, another woman writing of experiences with which we can connect. Similarly our own written response is structured (authored?) by our experience although as a piece of writing it can be examined without any reference to us. The relationship between author and text is perceived in rather more of its full complexity in such reading responses.

Finally there is the autobiographical nature of such writing. I think there can be no doubt that we are in such responses 'writing ourselves'[10] as well as producing a reading of a text.

As a child I used to watch my father shave. Stripped off to the waist, contorting his face to himself in the mirror, I found it amusing. One day I noticed a small scar on his back an inch or more long but old and faded. I asked him what it was. He told me of the tropics of Malaya and guerilla warfare. A mad crazed communist had stabbed him. He was so brave.

As I grew older my quizzing became more sophisticated I suppose. By now he was a communist too, his *Boys' Own*, *Eagle* story didn't ring true and I knew he was a storyteller/liar. With a tear in his eye, he told me how his mother had thrown the carving knife in temper. The blade had stuck through his small back missing his lung by a fraction.

I was shocked. I loved my grandmother.

My grandmother, a young woman then, was terrified. She, my father and his brothers and sisters knew the consequences of this awful incident. They all lied at the hospital where he was sewn up. For her protection and the families' survival it was forgotten, blanked out, an awful secret.

I don't believe she alone threw the knife. They all had a hand in it. Her drunkard husband, the rent man, the poverty of five children for her alone to deal with and her dead babies. All with her at the kitchen table, with the carving knife.

I loved my grandmother but this story made me love her all the more.

Notes

My thanks are due to all the students who joined in this reading: Claire Andrews, Molly Chaplain, Ruth Chapman, Audrey Church, Noma Clare, Christine Cull, Linda Denial, Kathleen Duggan, Eileen Eastwood, Carole Evans, Pam Flavell, Sue French, Angela Lawrence, Susan Mabbott, Hadie Mansfield, Marjorie Marples, Kathleen McMillan, Christine Spencer Polick, Ashoka Sen, Freda Scrivens, Jenni Smith, Gillian Smith, Geni Wolton.

1 See Eagleton, 1983, p. 201. I have used a male critic here because it seems appropriate

6

'Why hath this Lady writ her own Life?': studying early female autobiography

Louise Stewart and Helen Wilcox

The authors of this chapter confess unashamedly that, like Margaret Cavendish, we prefer 'to write with the pen than to work with a needle'.[1] As a tutor and former tutee on the undergraduate women writers' course in the English department at Liverpool University, we are collaborating in order to explore, from both sides of the staff/student divide, the delights and difficulties of studying women's writing. Our theme is autobiography and is explored through an autobiographical exercise of our own, in our recollections of setting the women writers' course into motion and of our participation in it. To write about the memory – shared, individual and institutional – of those experiences also mirrors the refreshingly personal and autobiographical nature of much of the discussion in the seminars, and especially in the early part of the course which dealt with seventeenth- and eighteenth-century women's memoirs, journals and letters. Later in the chapter we will focus our discussion on the reading of one of these works, Margaret Cavendish's *True relation of my birth, breeding, and life* (1656).

The remembrance of the course is aptly plural, incorporating not only our dual recollection but also the communal perspective in the context of the department; the memory belongs to both a personal and an institutional history. This blend of the personal and the political, often considered to be characteristic of feminism, is also fundamental to autobiographical writing, which gives public meaning to that which is primarily held to be a private concern. In 1982 our first attempts to 'go public' and establish a new women writers' course in the English department syllabus were defeated. When the proposal was accepted the following year, this was not without reservations in the department; the original title, 'Women and writing', had to give place to the (apparently less controversial) 'British and American women writers', perhaps to reassure staff colleagues that the focus would be on texts rather than more disturbing general 'issues'. This pioneering course, perhaps understandably and rather gratifyingly, provided a 'shock to the system'. Reactions among staff and students were varied and vocal, though occasionally predictable: 'Is it a "proper" subject?'; Women's literature is already there in our courses and it would be wrong to separate it', and so on. Among Helen's colleagues, academic and personal suspicions combined when it became clear that the option would be popular, at the expense of other cherished courses. The association of popularity with what is 'fashionable' was intensified in the context of a women's course, owing to that particular identification of fashion with women and our assumed susceptibility to it in society. This gave passing credence to those who thought that the subject was merely part of a temporary phase and not serious enough for a university curriculum.

The course, being optional, was 'sold' to the students in the familiar format of an introductory lecture, but this advertising session, because of the course's newness, proved much less polished and more honestly informal than many of the others. There was a refreshing openness in it to which the students responded. One of the questions asked of Ann Thompson and Helen (who jointly founded the course) was whether it was advisable to be a feminist if intending to take this option. Ann's answer was 'Yes' and Helen's 'No', both with reservations; and with that the tone of the course seemed set – it was an exploratory journey, beginning without a fixed sense of its conclusions. The texts would open up a debate in which students felt they could participate, free from the sometimes frustrating sense of tutor/tutee hierarchy often found elsewhere. The course introduced new texts which, not having previously been considered appropriate fodder for the academic mind, came to us free from the usual wealth of criticism. These were texts which both tutors and students may only have been reading for the second time; thus the sense of tutor knowledge and student ignorance was at least temporarily diminished. This led to a more relaxed atmosphere in the seminars which may also be linked to the fact that, although the course had not been advertised for women only; in that first year we had no male participants. Most women had experienced discussions dominated by competitive male peers, and the new atmosphere of co-operation and collaboration (including working together on papers) was a positive change from previous educational emphasis on personal achievement. That peculiarly aggressive brand of individualism was one area of the 'personal' we wished to do without.

Because the seminars were less competitive and more relaxed, the debates within them began to involve speaking about ourselves. For many it was the first time that personal reactions to texts or associations with them (in a sense, our 'autobiographies') did not seem out of place in an academic context. Because students felt less compelled to force literary conclusions, most were more willing to make comments, to interject and question, and to suggest new or old favourite texts for discussion. Suddenly books which had been read and reread for pleasure could be valued and discussed critically. By becoming involved in the structuring of the course in this way, tutees identified with it more readily and a strong sense of personal investment developed. While this could work positively, greater involvement might also mean greater disappointment if the course should fail in some way to meet the high expectations generated by the early euphoria. Because of the newness of the course the tutors could have no idea of the way in which students would respond; with hopes running high, Helen felt a great sense of responsibility for whether the students would be both satisfied and challenged by the course. Meanwhile, external pressures weighed on staff and students alike as our peers in the department looked on, waiting for us to sink or swim.

One of the problems faced by students on the course was an increasing sense of working in a vacuum. There were no former students of the course to talk to, and there was concern as to how assessment would be carried out, which threatened the relaxed atmosphere of the seminars. While all students on optional courses had to sit a three-hour exam at the end of the year, those on the women writers' course had no previous papers to look back upon and very little sense (so far) of the perameters of the subject. On the other side of the fence, Helen and Ann found the exam paper particularly difficult to set. While the possibilities were limitless, it was clear that setting the questions would also be setting a precedent and establishing, in a potentially limiting way, a tradition.

The course study began in an early period familiar to Ann and Helen, both Renaissance specialists, but we were working on women writers whom none of us had taught or studied before. This unknown area was made more challenging because we were looking at autobiograpies – another vacuum for the majority of us who had not previously dealt with that genre as a subject for literary criticism. The decision to begin with early diaries or autobiographies was to give primacy to a 'women's' form, as well as to keep to chronology. Incidentally, for many students it was quite a revelation to discover that there had been women writers before the Brontës, the point at which many studies of women's literature begin. The newness of the texts for students, and the challenge of teaching them for tutors, were both unsettling, though ultimately in a positive way. These works came with no useful guidelines as to how to read them, and offered no easy answers. Unfortunately this did not necessarily mean that we were reading in revolutionary new ways, for prejudices and familiar formulae were hard to avoid. Both of us felt uneasy at different stages in the study of the autobiographies and unwillingly reverted to customary strategies in our attempts to deal with this unfamiliar genre. While Helen fought against a compulsion to read the autobiography of Anne Halkett as a novel, Louise first read Ann Fanshawe's autobiography as factual, skipping over the true character of the piece in a search for historical detail.[2]

So how did we cope with discussing Margaret Cavendish's *True relation of my birth, breeding, and life*, one of two seventeenth-century autobiographies which the group read for one seminar? We had a mere three-quarters of an hour in which to come to terms with this fascinating and distinctive work, and, first of all, there were important minutes to be spent considering how and in what form the text had landed in our laps. We were, typically, catching the text at three removes – reading a photocopy of a nineteenth-century edition of the autobiography, where it appeared as an appendix to the biography which Cavendish wrote of her husband, the Duke of Newcastle (the work by which she has, until now, been best known). We were lucky to have even that third-hand text: as the nineteenth-century editor pointed out, women's lives tend to pass 'unnoticed except by a few black-letter literati' (264). It was tempting to begin the seminar by sharing Russ-style frustration and disbelief at the 'suppression' of women's writing (see Russ, 1983), but easy assumptions about the distortion of reputations can be misleading. We had to note that Cavendish's *True relation* was not repressively preserved in manuscript, but was in fact published in 1656,[3] a bold move unique among the early autobiographies we considered in the course. However, when Cavendish's account of her husband's life was later published, she withdrew her own autobiography, in deference, presumably, to his greater status in public life. It was clearly worth our while to pause over the publishing history of our chosen text: it highlighted for us the peculiar tangle of defiance and modesty which marks most female autobiography, and Margaret Cavendish's in particular.

Our discussion was then structured by introductory comments from

Louise and a fellow-student, Kathy Fitzgerald. They had been 'allotted'
one work each but had chosen to work together on both – a collaborative effort which grew quite naturally from the spirit of the course. What
emerged from Kathy and Louise's preliminary analysis, and still predo-
minates in our shared memory of the seminar, was the surprising pleasure we all found in the reading of these texts. But what was the basis of
our readerly pleasure? For some in this English honours group it was
the first chance to apply so-called 'objective' analytical skills to a text so
thoroughly subjective and obviously centred in the facts of one woman's
life. For others, the enjoyment stemmed from the character portrayed by
Cavendish – complex, colourful, 'singular' as she herself described her
nature (304) – and from her conversational style. For others still, there
was the fascination of finding that, despite inevitable differences of
period and class, writer and readers had much in common as women
coming to terms with family relationships, social responsibilities and
selfhood. Reading female autobiographies led to the breakdown of
barriers of time and literary expectations, as well as easing inhibition
within the seminar group itself.

But for many in the group, the thrill of the reading was limited by
baffling uncertainties. Fundamental to these was the question of why we
were studying Cavendish's *True relation* at all. Where had it come from?
In the absence of a canon of female literature, or of autobiographical
writing, the matter of whose prejudice, whim or enthusiasm had given
the text this status in a literary syllabus was suddenly an issue for discussion. This must be a good thing – and indeed it seemed to lead to healthy
enquiries of a similar sort about the content of other courses – but at the
time it further contributed to the bewildering sense of journeying
through uncharted terrain. The course appeared to be celebrating
absences: not only the lack of received critical opinion mentioned earlier, but none of that reassuring, if ultimately stifling, academic familiarity.
The text itself contained denials of its status as worthwhile reading.
Could it be that, ironically, we had begun to read Cavendish's *True relation*
for the very reason we wished to reject – because she was the wife of a
famous man?

When it came to the process of analysing the text, there were further
difficulties: we found ourselves seeking a formal structure, expecting,
perhaps, the imposition of conscious artistry. Cavendish's autobiography instead gives an impression of spontaneity, with its rambling sentences and the habit of introducing a new topic apparently at random
with the phrase 'As for'. Many in the group were uncertain whether to

condemn this as a lack of discipline, or to discern in it the multiple interwoven strands of women's lives as opposed to the linear pattern of male autobiography. Others wondered whether we should hope for finishedness or formal shaping in autobiography at all. Does its avowed closeness to 'fact' require us to judge it on different criteria, as a 'monument to truth'? (286).

Cavendish indeed claimed to write her *True relation*, as the title implied, 'not to please the fancy, but to tell the truth' (310). However, in an English Literature seminar it is the 'fancy' with which we generally concern ourselves; we needed to ask if, and how, we were 'pleased' by her autobiography, even against her stated intention. We agreed that we were enthralled by her breathless syntax, whose infrequency of sentence-breaks, unusual even by seventeenth-century standards of punctuation, added to the impression of impetuosity in her character. We were also intrigued by her peculiar stylistic zig-zag, giving the flow of writing an inbuilt dialectic, as demonstrated here:

as for my Disposition, it is more inclining to be melancholy than merry, but not crabbed or peevishly melancholy, but soft, melting, solitary, and contemplating melancholy; and I am apt to weep rather than to laugh, not that I do often either of them; . . . where I place a particular affection, I love extraordinary and constantly, yet not fondly, but soberly and observingly. (304)

Each statement is followed by a qualifying clause; the reader is presented with bold generality, checked by sensitive detail, and then launched into further expansive statements. Paradoxically, even as she defines herself, Cavendish rarely allows us to form a sustained or fixed impression of her character. Did she herself, in fact, have such a stable sense of her own nature? We began to realise that a woman's self-image can often be uncertain, shifting, found fleetingly in the shadow of oppressive stereotypes; and Cavendish, 'singular' though she may have been, was no exception.

Cavendish had a particularly distinctive sense of herself as a writer, as seen in the memorable account of her profuse mode of expression:

when I am writing . . . I am forc'd many times to express them with the tongue before I can write them with the pen, by reason those thoughts that are sad, serious, and melancholy, are apt to contract and to draw too much back, which oppression doth as it were overpower or smother the conception in the brain, but when some of those thoughts are sent out in words, they give the rest more liberty to place themselves in a more methodicall order, marching more regularly with my pen, on the ground of white paper, but my letters seem rather as a ragged rout, than a well armed body, for the brain being quicker in creating than the hand in writing, or the memory in retaining, many fancies are lost, by reason they ofttimes outrun the pen (297–8).

This is a splendid example of all that appealed to us in Cavendish's work: immediacy of voice, analytical impulse, tumbling style, vivid imagination, and a complexity typified in the exploration of female creativity in such martial terms. Yet just before this passage she described herself as one who merely passed her time 'rather with scribling than writing, with words than wit' (297), and the majority of her subsequent readers have been content to accept her self-condemnation. But were we?

Cavendish's contemporaries, including Pepys,[4] had condemned her not so much as an author but as a social oddity who wore bizarrely unfashionable clothes. In the *True relation* she mentions the fact that she 'invented' her own outfits and 'did dislike any should follow my Fashions, for I always took delight in a singularity, even in accoutrements of habits' (304). Autobiographies by their very nature celebrate uniqueness, but here was eccentricity being positively paraded. How were we to react? If we allowed ourselves to describe Cavendish as 'attractively eccentric' – for defiantly exercising some control over her 'fashions' – were we, disconcertingly, still upholding the norm against which she, and we, defined herself? This led us into two more fruitful areas of discussion: the impossibility of finding a genuinely private self, at least without reference to familial and public expectations, and the gendered foundations of our notions of formality.

Not surprisingly, issues of gender cropped up a great deal in our consideration of this text. Cavendish's generalised references to 'our Sex' (290) are, like many a seventeenth-century woman's, rarely favourable, coloured by inbred assumptions of inferiority. However, the dominant figure in the autobiography is her own mother, who

had such a Majestic Grandeur, as it were continually hung about her, that it would strike a kind of awe to the beholders . . . : her beauty was beyond the ruin of time, for she had a well favoured loveliness in her face, a pleasing sweetness in her countenance . . .; by her dying, one might think death was enamoured with her, for he embraced her in a sleep, and so gently, as if he were afraid to hurt her.
(282–3)

Among the other qualities of her mother noted affectionately by Cavendish was her loyalty to her husband even after his death: 'she never forgot my father so as to marry again' (292). This stands in ironic opposition to the marital history of her husband hinted at in the concluding words of the autobiography, where the author reminds us that she was 'second wife to the Lord Marquiss of Newcastle; for my Lord having had two Wives, I might easily have been mistaken, especially if I should dye and my Lord marry again' (310). There is a further irony contained in these closing lines, in which Cavendish identifies her genealogy for fear of her memory being obscured. She writes a memoir of her own female self which is framed by, and dependent upon, the males to whom she is related. This paradoxical circumstance underlies the entire autobiography. It opens, 'My father was a Gentleman' (265); she constructs her image in self-deprecating opposition to the model of her husband; the work concludes with a placing of herself as daughter of one man and wife of another. The patterns of women's history could not have been more clearly articulated.

As our seminar drew to an end, we discussed what Cavendish's motives could have been, driving her to write an autobiography against these odds. She herself evidently feared criticism for writing her *True relation*:

I hope my readers will not think me vain for writing my life, since there have been many that have done the like, as Cesar, Ovid, and many more, both men and women, and I know no reason I may not do it as well as they: but I verily believe some censuring Readers will scornfully say, why hath this Lady writ her own Life? since none cares to know whose daughter she was, or whose wife she is, or how she was bred, or what fortunes she had, or how she lived, or what humour or disposition she was of? (309)

She responds with considerable self-assurance to the idea that others had 'done the like' and so why shouldn't she – though the parallels she chooses, Caesar and Ovid, are wonderfully grandiose! As she writes earlier in the *True relation*, she has 'an ambition . . . to live by remembrance in after-ages' (307), the autobiographer's desire to evade anonymity. But, as ever, she has a quality which tempers that ambition, the fear that she might 'incline to vain-glory' (307). From this emerges the confessional element in autobiography, the need to tell one's story to others so that they will accept and enjoy it: writing of her brothers and sisters, Cavendish admits that she was 'ambitious they should approve of my actions and behaviour' (278). Such an attitude across the work as a whole assumes that it will be read – indeed Cavendish addresses her readers at times, and hers is no introverted, readerless text – but once again she pulls back from permanent rapport with her readers, in asserting finally that she wrote for her 'own sake, not theirs' (310). Apart from Cavendish's evident personal pleasure in words, her desire to write autobiographically might be explained by her isolation; she wrote from a position of political exile after 'these unhappy Wars' (281) and presents herself as an outsider both physically and psychologically. She repeatedly describes herself as 'bashful' by nature (292), adding that she had, since childhood, been 'addicted to contemplation rather than conversation, to solitariness rather than society' (299). This solitary individual, it seemed to us, certainly did write for herself – for the pleasure of contemplation, of self-identification, of creativity – but part of that personal need was the approval of others and the reassurance that her individuality would not be totally forgotten.

There was, therefore, a satisfying sense that our seminar discussion, limited and perplexed though it was, had helped to set Margaret Cavendish on the way to equivalence with Caesar and Ovid, at least in respect of rescue from anonymity. We had, in addition, found that her text raised fundamental questions concerning individuality in terms of literary style, genre and purpose, and concerning matters of womanhood in both 1656 and 1983. But at the end of the seminar there were many unresolved paradoxes in our handling of the material. We had, it seemed to us, bravely ventured off the beaten track to look at an untried non-fictional female text – but were we then simply putting new subjects through old mills? Though we tried to hold back from over-hasty judgements (such as, 'Was she a "good" writer?'), in the end we were to go away and make literary comments in the same old critical essay format. Had we broken any moulds? We had certainly found it liberating to link written style with wider issues of gender, and we had felt some scope for including a more personal perspective in the discussion; but the frame-work of assessment and departmental restrictions would allow little room for such sociological or autobiographical tendencies in, for example, exam essays. Other paradoxes were less problematic; they included the fruitful intersection of a private mode of writing with a collaborative mode of learning, and the exciting new-found confidence to make comments in the absence of a received view or tradition, yet in response to a work uncertain of its own status or audience.

This essay, like *Rasselas* or *Winnie the pooh*, has no conclusion save that there is none. The course is now well established, accepted if not approved by staff colleagues, remaining popular with students, not all of them female. Our own autobiographical memoir, individual and communal, of the course and the seminar, asserts the value and potential of women writers courses, and particularly the liberating experience of reading early female autobiography. Ironically, though, much of the fervour which we recall from the discussion of Cavendish's *True relation* stemmed from the newness of our endeavour (its teaching context, its genre, its text) and the freedom from restricting literary tradition and practice. Though both the newness and the freedom may have been to some extent illusory, we were – like Margaret Cavendish – partially enjoying our exile, our marginality, even while resenting its imposition upon us. When women writers courses, and feminist critical approaches, and autobiography, are all accepted parts of English literary study – as they are rapidly becoming[5] – what then? We are sure that this account of our own experience is already tinged with nostalgia; but then it is right that a pioneering moment can never be recaptured. Feminist criticism and history, like Cavendish's sentences, never stand still!

Notes

1 Margaret Cavendish, Duchess of Newcastle, *The lives of William Cavendish, Duke of Newcastle, and of his wife*, Library of old authors (London, 1872) p. 299. All page references are to this edition.

2 *The memoirs of Anne, Lady Halkett and Ann, Lady Fanshawe*, ed. John Loftis (Oxford, 1979).

3 Margaret Cavendish, Duchess of Newcastle, *Nature's pictures* (London, 1656), pp. 368–91.

4 Samuel Pepys, *Diary*, ed. R. C. Latham and W. Matthews (London, 1970–83), XI vols., VIII, p. 163.

5 We are currently assisting in this process by preparing an anthology of seventeenth-century women's autobiographical writing (edited by Elspeth Graham, Hilary Hinds, Elaine Hobby and Helen Wilcox) to be published by Routledge. It will include substantial extracts from Cavendish's *True relation*.

A course of our own

Introduction to
Part Three

For many feminist teachers of English the first priority is to establish a course of our own, a course on women's writing and/or on feminist criticism where we have the space to rediscover lost texts and reread familiar ones from a feminist perspective. The relation of such a course to the department and to the institution in which it operates as well as to the students is likely to be a matter of complex and continuing negotiation. We all feel we have achieved something when we have set up such a course, but that is not the end of the story. In contrast to the situation in North America, where entire degree programmes in women's studies are not uncommon, most of us working in the British system must live with a minority position where our course will remain an oddity. We are fascinated and encouraged by books on the American experience with titles like *Learning our way* (Bunch and Pollack, 1983), *Theories of women's studies* (Bowles and Duelli Klein, eds., 1983) and *Gendered subjects: the dynamics of feminist teaching* (Culley and Portuges, eds., 1985), but feel that our own more modest contributions are more likely to be reflected accurately in *Men's studies modified* (Spender, ed., 1981).

Feminist studies, like feminism itself, remains very much an 'option' within departments and institutions which may be openly hostile or cautiously tolerant. Even when such courses are freely chosen, students will often resist the 'feminist' label, or if they endorse it will encounter problems when they apply feminist approaches in other courses they are taking. The name of the course turns out to be surprisingly important: in their essay in the previous section Louise Stewart and Helen Wilcox recount how 'British and American women writers' was an acceptable course title when 'Women and writing' was not, while the Leeds women's group here remark on the way in which the political identity of their 'Feminist approaches to literature' course is defused when staff and students invariably refer to it as 'the women's course'.

The authority of the teacher, thrown into question throughout this book, is particularly problematic here. Isobel Armstrong, who is in the unusual and perhaps enviable position of teaching such a course with the status of being a professor, is dismayed at the degree of coercion experienced by some of the students and by her own position as 'phallocentric mentor'. The Leeds group, who began by allowing students to initiate discussion as much as possible, felt the need to reassert pedagogic authority and to claim 'an academic rigour and respectability for feminism which would be seen by some feminists as hopelessly reactionary'. The teachers on the 'Women and literature' MA course at Hull felt threatened by a male student's knowledge of French critical and psychoanalytical theory and felt obliged to compete with him and privilege his discourse at the expense of their female students.

The extent of teachers' honesty about difficulties and failures is particularly impressive in this section, especially when it is related to a general context in which academics rarely talk, let alone write, about such things. Alongside a high degree of commitment, energy and attention to students' needs and responses, there is an awareness and an analysis, quite painful at times, of teaching strategies which did not work and students who were not satisfied. Those who think that feminist teachers are concerned only with indoctrinating their students will find something very different here.

Equally, feminist teachers must be aware that women students are not all identical simply because they are not men. Students taking courses on women's writing or feminist criticism are not necessarily feminists any more than they are necessarily heterosexual. Women from ethnic minorities may feel alienated by a predominantly white European or American perspective; working-class women may feel that the theoretical approach is irrelevant to the issues confronting them in real life. We cannot afford to be complacent about any of these problems or to ignore any of these differences.

As for the nature of the syllabuses that are described, it is notable that all these courses are essentially interdisciplinary ones, despite the fact that they originate within university English departments whose main function is still the teaching of traditional one-subject or 'single honours' degrees. As Patsy Stoneman indicates, even when 'Women and literature' is deliberately and officially set up as a non-interdisciplinary course taught entirely within one department, the wider poststructuralist theoretical approach is itself a hybrid of linguistics, anthropology and psychoanalysis and obliges students and teachers to transcend traditional academic disciplines. None of these courses is exclusively a 'women's course': all of them include male authors, critics and theorists as well as, on occasion, male colleagues and male students. Juxtaposition is a shared technique: canonical texts are taught alongside non-canonical texts, the literary alongside the non-literary, medieval alongside modern. The results are often exciting and illuminating, though it seems at times as if we are demanding more from these courses than they can possibly provide: at the end of the day we agree that feminist criticism is not just another, optional, way of looking at literature but an instrument for personal, institutional and social change.

7

Painting the lion: feminist options

Lesley Jeffries, Lesley Johnson, Lynette Hunter, Vivien Jones, Margaret Reynolds

'Who peyntede the leon, tel me who?'[1]

Like this article, the third-year option course 'Feminist approaches to literature' is a product of the Women's Group in the School of English at Leeds University. Both the course and the article are collaborative ventures, attempts to use our experience of meeting regularly as feminists within a particular institution, initially in a teaching context and now as the basis of a piece of (academic) writing. The option is team-taught, with two members of staff present in each seminar and at least three teaching on the course as a whole; the article has been written by five members of the Women's Group, of whom only two have taught regularly on the option. We have based the article on a series of lunchtime discussions which were written up by members of the group in turn. Drafts were then redistributed for revision. These were new experiences of collaborative teaching and writing for all of us, and this change from our usual academic practice, often solitary and implicitly defensive, and from the principles of author, period or genre on which courses are normally organised has been exciting and liberating, but also problematic. In this article, we describe briefly the evolution of the 'Feminist perspectives' course and the course itself, then focus on Christine de Pizan's *The book of the city of ladies*, Chaucer's *Wife of Bath's prologue and tale* and Freud's 'Dora', texts which are juxtaposed to form one five-week section of the course. Our aim is to explore some of the interrelated issues raised by these particular texts, by the form and teaching method of the course, and by the Women's Group itself.

Feminist approaches to literature

For the past four years the Women's Group in the Leeds School of

English has been meeting regularly during term for a weekly lunch-time discussion. Because of the size of the English department (thirty-five full-time members of staff, of whom eleven, including one professor, are women; seven part-time or fixed-term contract staff, of whom five are women – a telling proportional difference) there are enough women who identify themselves as feminists to make a women's group viable and significant within the School. All women who teach in the department are invited, though there is a small nucleus of regular attenders and some members of the department have never been. Topics range from discussion of literary and critical texts and films to teaching practice, institutional experiences and (often) immediate personal concerns.

The option course grew out of the group. In both the second and third years, students taking Single Honours English at Leeds take two optional courses alongside compulsory period courses and language courses. Three years ago we offered 'Women in language and literature' as a third-year option, taught by a total of six women whose interests – language, medieval literature, and nineteenth and twentieth century fiction – were reflected in the format of the course. An initial section on women and language was followed by a study of a selection of medieval texts about women and by women, and then by various nineteenth- and twentieth-century novels, in some cases juxtaposed with different kinds of feminist readings. The course was popular and the student response was very positive for the most part – largely, perhaps, because it was at that time the only course on offer with any kind of theoretical identity. However, we were unhappy with the course for various reasons. We felt that the mixture of topics, as we had presented them, was confusing rather than helpful; possibly discouraged by the title, no men took the course; and the lack of an introductory and theoretical section tended to perpetuate rather than address the tensions the students themselves felt between those members of the course who identified themselves as feminists (and had a background in feminist theory and practice) and those who were using the course to discover and test out what 'feminism' might mean. In fact, the immediate effect of our dissatisfactions with the course in its initial form was that we ourselves had to define what feminism meant for us in terms of teaching practice.

This resulted in various changes. We now offer the course under the title 'Feminist approaches to literature'. The new title both announces the course's political identity and avoids the ghettoising effect of 'Women in language and literature' with its implicit reproduction of the patriarchal view of female identity as an undifferentiated object of knowledge.

Similarly, changes in format have given the course much greater coherence and direction. During the first year, theoretical issues had arisen haphazardly in the process of looking at particular texts. The course now begins with a section looking at the work of various representative feminist theorists of the 'Anglo-American' and French schools and opening with Virginia Woolf's *A room of one's own*. Our collaborative teaching and variety of interests can now be seen in the context of feminism's critique of academic hierarchies, canons and traditional notions of historical periods and, indeed, of the varieties of approach within 'feminism' itself. The rest of the course is arranged so that texts are paired in various ways to introduce some of the issues and focuses of feminist criticism and women's writing: Christine de Pizan's *The book of the city of ladies*, the newly recovered, non-canonical text with the canonical *Wife of Bath's prologue and tale*; *The Wife of Bath's tale* with Freud's case history of Dora – male readings of women, purporting to answer the question 'what do women want?'; *Jane Eyre*, with its twentieth-century re-writing, *Wide Sargasso Sea*; Woolf's *Orlando* and Piercy's *Woman on the edge of time* as examples of female fantasy and sharing a concern with androgyny; Margaret Llewellyn Davies's anthology of working-class women's autobiography, *Life as we have known it* and Maya Angelou's *I know why the caged bird sings*. So far, assessment has been by two long essays; in future, students will be given a choice between essays and a three-hour examination. The course continues to be popular (this year fifteen women and five men took the option), and it continues to evolve as we try to respond to student reactions and to the interests of particular groups. Space is left for additional, collectively chosen texts and an informal retrospective session at the end of the year provides a forum for responses to the course.

'. . . let us go to the Field of Letters. There the City of Ladies will be founded on a flat and fertile plain, where all fruits and freshwater rivers are found and where the earth abounds in all good things'.[2]

Most members of the course have read Geoffrey Chaucer's *Wife of Bath's prologue and tale* before they take the option; few have read Christine de Pizan's *Book of the city of ladies* or Freud's 'Dora': these texts are discussed as a follow-up to the introductory section on feminist critical theory. The combination of familiar/unfamiliar texts by female and male writers provides a useful testing ground for considering feminist approaches to criticism in practice and for assessing the way in which our reading preconceptions may be influenced by the sex of a writer. The theoretical section of the option concentrates on introducing students to the politics of the text, raising questions about who is writing, who is reading, what constitutes a literary tradition, how we recreate a context for a work. All these issues are brought to the fore in discussions of this juxtaposition of medieval/modern, canonical/non-canonical texts. Discussing medieval works in a feminist critical context is still a relatively uncommon activity and goes against the prevailing trend of much modern feminist criticism with its emphasis on nineteenth- and twentieth-century novels written by women. It also goes against the grain of much criticism of medieval literature which, if it addresses the subject of gender representation and sexual politics at all, tends to get caught up in discussing images of women in medieval literature in terms of Eve/Mary stereotypes, as if these images could just be culled from texts and are not the product of any reading activity. Rereading medieval texts in this context is double-edged. But this is an area of literary study which is changing fast. Much more primary and secondary material on medieval women writers, the sexual politics of medieval texts, the construction of women's place in medieval society, is available now than three years ago so the marginal status of feminist work on medieval texts is changing too.[3]

In five weeks we can draw attention to the problem of how to contextualise all three works, but recognise how much skimping we have to do on getting to grips with the very different cultural contexts in which the work of Christine de Pizan, Geoffrey Chaucer and Sigmund Freud was produced and received. The book of the city of ladies offers one possible starting point for a feminist view of literary history in so far as it promotes Christine de Pizan herself as a pioneering woman writer, the first in the field to offer a positive representation of women, their qualities and activities (BCL, pp. 10–11). Our approach to her work is to consider the claim made by some twentieth-century readers that she is the first modern feminist writer, and we discuss the narrative in conjunction with Joan Kelly's own pioneering article on 'Early feminist theory and the "Querelle des femmes" 1400–1789'.[4]

'One day as I was sitting alone in my study surrounded by books on all kinds of subjects . . .' (BCL, p. 3)

The opening scenes of The book of the city of ladies focus on the relationship between gender and the reading and writing of texts as Christine, the narrator, reflects on the literary images of women that surround her in her study and, as a result, comes to despair of her sex. The production of her book, this city for ladies which she constructs with the help of Reason, Rectitude, and Justice, offers a remedy for her despair. In constructing the city, Christine de Pizan takes a leaf out of previous male, clerical, compilations about women and produces a book of narratives about women, predominantly from the Classical and Christian past, which are written from, and reflect a different view. The result is a biographical collection which challenges some conventional readings of the activities of celebrities and throws the spotlight on some previously 'unknown' shapers of history.[5] Many of the textual strategies employed by Christine de Pizan in constructing her city have parallels with those employed by Virginia Woolf in making *A room of one's own* (1929), our opening text. Both writers play on the subjective/objective stance of their narrator and on the corresponding fictional/historical status of their narrative; both offer a difference of view based on their access to female experience; both challenge the distinction between theory and practice, between analysis and action by literally activating the process of reading and writing – writer and readers together construct cities and rooms of their own, but not separatist states.

In seminar discussions we have found that it is Christine de Pizan's revisionary stance and her comments on the sexual politics of literacy and education that have most fired the enthusiasm of our students for the work. These perhaps are the kind of 'potent observations for our times' which Marina Warner suggests fill the Book of the city of ladies (Foreword, p. xiii). But we have also found that reading this medieval narrative sharply focuses the differences between the kind of 'feminist' theory and practice possible in fifteenth-century France and that of our time.

'if Nature did not give great strength of limb to women's bodies, she has made up for it by placing there the most virtuous inclination to love one's God and to fear sinning against His commandments. Women who act otherwise go against their own nature.' (BCL, p. 37)

Christine de Pizan's collection of citizens is made up from a mixture of *exceptional* and *exemplary* women. The exceptional women are those who have challenged the prevailing stereotyped views of women's capacities. The Amazons, for example (pp. 40–51), are exceptional women because of their physical strength and courage; Novella (p. 154) is exceptional because she has been educated and has proved herself to be a first-class lecturer in law (although her lectures have to be delivered from behind a curtain so her female identity will not be seen). It seems from such examples that women are made and not born and that Christine de Pizan is indicating that gender identity is culturally formed, and is not an essential, biological given. However other aspects of the city's construction challenge that view.[6] The exemplary women of the city, those who provide models of conduct for all time, are those who embody the traditional, 'natural' virtues of the 'weaker' sex. Griselda, for example, is presented as a woman strong in natural virtue who can endure the ordeals inflicted on her by a husband who wishes to test both her patience and her constancy (pp. 170–6). In its context in the Book of the city of ladies Griselda's story appears to function as a straightforward example of wifely behaviour and a model for those wives, addressed at the end of the book, who have husbands who are 'cruel, mean, and savage' (p. 255).[7]

The most difficult problems for modern readers of Christine de Pizan's compilation come at the end of the book when the categories of exceptional and exemplary women are integrated as the elite of the city of ladies appear on the scene. A company of female saints and martyrs, headed by the Blessed Virgin Mary, is introduced by Justice as the crowning glory of the city. These are exemplary, Christian Amazons but how do we read their histories? Are they pornographic narratives of 'masochistic martyrs of sadospiritual religions'?[8] Should they be read in the context of medieval hagiographic conventions as a kind of narrative in which women as well as men are empowered to triumph over earthly power structures and be a witness of transcendent spiritual power? May the histories of these women and the kinds of physical, sexual torments they suffer be read as an analysis of the nature of earthly, if not spiritual, patriarchial designs and power structures? Confronting these areas of the city has generated serious debates in our seminars about the sexual politics of Christianity and about the kind of historical context in which the book as a whole should be placed. At the very least, reading Christine de Pizan's book demonstrates how the perception and representation of female experience is itself a historical variable.

'I grante thee lyf, if thou kanst tellen me / What thing it is that wommen moost desiren.' (*Wife of Bath's tale*, ll. 904–5)

Almost all the members of the option course have read Chaucer's work before and some have studied *The Wife of Bath's prologue and tale* as an A level set text too. From our point of view as teachers, Chaucer's text raises questions about possible differences in approach when we teach it as part of a general medieval literature course and on a feminist option.

And those questions about the politics of who reads, writes and categorises texts, introduced in the initial theory section and developed by juxtaposing Christine de Pizan with Chaucer and Freud, are exactly the questions raised in the voice of the Wife of Bath in her Prologue.[9]

The disruption of historical and literary traditions in the Wife of Bath's Prologue again rests on a claim to have access to authentic female experience, as in *The book of the city of ladies*. The autobiographical monologue from the Wife of Bath challenges man made theories and representations of the experience of a married woman. Or does it? Reading this text too generates radically divergent interpretations amongst members of the option which are often split initially over whether the representation of a sexual stereotype is subverted or confirmed by the voice of the Wife of Bath in her Prologue and the construction of her Tale. Does her monologue titillate the desires of a male audience by exposing female secrets (her 'pryvetee') to public view? Does the Prologue highlight a difference of view in revealing the economic constraints on female expression of desire? Does the Wife's Tale articulate an archetypal male fantasy (that women's desire is a riddle and yet there is a key to their desire) or expose that very fantasy for what it is – a male construction?

Clearly, a range of such possible interpretations ought to be examined in every context in which the work is discussed. Those who teach on the feminist option and on general medieval courses felt that students taking the option were much readier than those on other courses to comment on the economic determination of the Wife's career and on the power politics of literacy, that they had a vocabulary and a context which allowed them to challenge readings of the Wife as a normative comic character. The juxtaposition with Christine de Pizan's work makes the analysis of the prevailing representation of women in the Wife's performance seem less of a historical aberration – though it also reveals the way in which reading preconceptions are partly determined by the sex of the author. This last point, that the position of the viewer already determines the perspective of the view, is one made throughout the Wife's performance itself through the attention given to the sources of representations of married women and through the allusion to the Aesopian fable about lion-painting. Women-painting, she suggests, has largely been the prerogative of male clerks.[10]

'By God if wommen hadde writen stories / As clerkes han . . .' (*Wife of Bath's prologue*, ll. 693–4)

On the feminist option we explore *The Wife of Bath's prologue and tale* by considering some of the other texts which overtly and covertly are used in the making of the Wife's performance. We do not attempt anything like a thorough source and analogue study but confine our attention mainly to the function of the Wife's allusions to Aesop and Ovid; to the Christian views of marriage, widowhood and virginity based on St Paul 'th'apostel'; to analogues to the Wife's tale (the version the Wife tells is unique in being triggered by a rape); and to the representation of a Widow in the thirteenth-century narrative of *La veuve*, by Gautier Le Leu, in which a male voice is used to present a female biography similar in some respects to that of the Wife of Bath.[11] The politics of book writing and book learning is the anchor for our discussions as we consider how power structures affect communication and how textual dynamics affect interpretation. Our aim is to raise awareness of the construction of the voice of the addresser and the roles of the addressee; of the way in which a cultural tradition may determine not only the nature of the representation of a women's voice but also any attempt to disrupt that practice of representation, limiting the forms such disruptions can take. The Wife's token revolt takes the form of ripping out part of a clerical compilation about wicked wives: in confronting her sources in literary tradition, the Wife literally takes a leaf out of that book. What we don't have time to do on the course is hear how the Clerk on the pilgrimage uses the tale of patient Griselda to answer the Wife's challenge that 'it is an impossible / That any clerk wol speke good of wyves, / But if it be of hooly seintes lyves' (pp. 689–90) – a further contextualisation which is open to students of the text on medieval courses. Instead, on the feminist course we turn to a rather different representation of a woman's desire in Sigmund Freud's case history of Dora.

' "I knew you would say that."
"That is to say, you knew that it was so." '[12]

The juxtaposition of 'Dora' with the *Wife of Bath's prologue and tale* is calculated to shock students used to chronologically arranged courses into a re-assessment of ways in which texts might be linked. The danger of course is that the axis of a feminist perspective implies an essential continuity or transhistorical sameness in the experience of female repression, whereas one of our aims in disrupting chronology is to highlight the specificity of historical conditions. To ask ostensibly the same question – 'What do women want?' – within discourses as different as medieval romance and nineteenth-century psychoanalysis is in effect to ask different questions, though those differences might be mutually illuminating. Just as the Wife is ultimately restricted to speaking from within the discourses of male literary representations of women, Dora's words and her sexuality are always already interpreted by Freud's theory. The Wife's rebellion was voiced by her tearing of the book; Dora's (as interpreted and appropriated for feminism) by the eloquent silence of her withdrawal from analysis. The politics of speaking and being heard are central to each.

'Dora' is the most consistently successful text on the feminist course. The feminist context gives the students the confidence to contradict and explode Freud's authority and to offer their own rival interpretations – a latter-day version of the Wife's bold questioning of the inevitability of clerical authority. But what also happens is that the students' excitement at the more recent text overshadows Christine de Pizan and Chaucer, and our intentions to explore the implications of the juxtaposition. Though disrupting established assumptions by unexpected juxtapositions looks good in theory, very few students follow it up in their essays. And in this case, as with Christine de Pizan and Chaucer, the different arrangement of the feminist course means that other kinds of contextualisation are skimped: it is almost impossible to offer an assessment of Freud's achievements to balance the student's sense of having seen through his sexist strategies. But with Freud as with all the other topics on the course we can do little more than suggest starting-points, possible feminist *approaches*. It is up to the students to explore further and to define their own version of feminist criticism. Our hope is that at the very least, they will develop the conviction that familiar arrangements and modes of interpreting texts are not natural, but open to constant question and disruption.

Feminist options?

Our aim when the Women's Group was established was to have a gradual feminist impact on the degree course as a whole; a collaboratively-taught option course seemed the best way of immediately highlighting feminist concerns in the meantime. Since then, we have become very much aware of the problems and compromises which mark both areas of our experience as feminists and practising teachers. We still face problems within the option course itself: the new mixture of men and women has sometimes created difficulties in the balance of contributions and participation in seminars; different degrees of political commitment among members can cause tensions; some texts have been more stimulating than others (though not always the same ones from group to group and year to year). Perhaps more seriously, we recognise that the choices of principle that have governed revisions of the course – as well as the rationale imposed on it retrospectively in the process of writing this article – have led us into political minefields. We have, for example, consciously rejected a course on 'Women's writing' which is identified solely by the sex of the writers included, and which leaves links and issues open to the directions seminar discussions take. On the contrary, bad experiences at the beginning of the course when we left the initiation of discussion up to the students as much as possible meant that the gradual revision of both content and teaching method has tended towards greater direction of the students' attention, implicitly reasserting pedagogic authority and claiming an academic rigour and respectability for feminism which would be seen by some feminists as hopelessly reactionary. Nevertheless, we still team-teach the option, with two of us present at each seminar, in a conscious attempt to suggest that one aspect of feminism might be to subvert the teacher/student hierarchy established by the single authority of the teacher/lecturer which students are used to. But we are aware of our need to think through the effects and success of this different teaching practice: does it simply multiply authorities or does it actually achieve its intended effect (as some students have said)? And the residual competitive tensions between us as teachers have never been properly addressed.

Outside the option, the course causes other difficulties which we have not resolved. The very fact of offering feminist *options* reinforces the idea held by some students (and colleagues) that, whatever feminist perspectives may be, they are of marginal interest and status, and probably associated with an aggressive, trendy and ephemeral kind of political activity. Some students' attempts to extend the methodologies discovered on the option to their compulsory course work have met with a hostile response – and in this way the apparent marginality of feminist concerns is reinforced as the student loses the confidence to extend the challenge to established critical methods outside the safety of the option. Alternatively, tolerant and even sympathetic members of the department find it all too easy to assume that the presence of feminist options within the degree course (there is also a feminist option for second-years on eighteenth-century fiction) means that 'women's' topics are adequately catered for. Significantly, the feminist options are invariably referred to by staff and students as the 'women's courses', a formulation which tends to contain and defuse their political identity and bite.

Such institutionalised containment makes it all the more important that we continue to try to make feminist reappraisal familiar and everyday – outside the designated context of the options. On the simplest level, we can highlight gender prejudices by questioning the conventional exclusion of women from the acts of writing and reading (when presented with an unfamiliar text, a large number of students will assume the author to be male); we can discourage the use of the masculine pronoun (albeit in defiance of linguistic convention) which tacitly excludes the majority of the lecturer's audience in most English departments; and it is always possible in studying any text to raise questions about attitudes to and representations of women. But outside the feminist option course, we have often found it difficult to help students to move beyond 'images of women' criticism to consider the historical and textual construction of gender. A large conceptual leap is needed to move from culling images of women to asking how those images are produced and interpreted; and compulsory courses generally, based on traditional and untheorised notions of historical period and literary value, fail to address theories of literary production and reception. Many students have never been encouraged to think about the reading process – 'I just read' – and without a theoretical platform, it is hard to persuade them that the construction of the writer's/reader's 'self' will exert its influence at both ends of the literary act. Feminism thus raises fundamental questions about the construction of courses and the role of theory.

Even visible feminist interventions can have undesirable results. We apparently collude in the stereotyping we would wish to avoid when, say, the one woman teaching on a compulsory course in Romantic literature gives the lecture on Jane Austen using feminist theory, or agrees to provide the token 'woman' question for the exam paper (which is not to say that we can yet do without either). Similarly, we may ourselves be partly responsible for the view that the 'women's courses' are for the minority. We have, after all, a 'Women's' Group, fiercely separatist and ridiculed for being so, and yet we run 'Feminist' options which we encourage men to take. We are strategically essentialist when it comes to creating a space for ourselves as women within the department but explicitly critical of forms of essentialism (such as any simple idea of 'women's writing') when we teach the option. The inconsistency may be strategically understandable, but it can be difficult to explain to those (mainly male) colleagues whose reactions to the options and particularly to the Women's Group range from puzzled indulgence to covert hostility. Within the options and the Women's Group, where feminism is accepted as inevitable and right – students taking the options have expressed 'the relief of not always having to explain why one's interest is woman-centred' – it is also recognised as plural, fraught with internal debates. Outside the options that constant need for explanation, self-justification, can make it difficult to explain feminisms or the role of strategic 'inconsistencies' and to avoid a defensive and simplifying position.

But the defensiveness is not simply a response to external challenges. Throughout the development of the course we have been aware of a tension between our appropriation for feminism of the 'scholarly', 'rigorous – but also hierarchical and individualist – methods in which we have been trained, and our sense of more fluid and experimental alternatives; and the same debates over how to put feminist theory into practice have recurred within the Women's Group and in the process of writing this article. What we are aware of now is how we have tended to give the course retrospectively a consistent rationale and underplayed the haphazard process of its development. We have suppressed problems within the Women's Group and recognition of the variety and inconsistency of our viewpoints and writing practices in the interests of producing a smooth narrative, failing to escape the simplifying coherence imposed by the form of the academic article, in spite of multiple authorship. But whatever the result, the value of the exercise has been in the support and challenge which collaboration in this context has produced, demanding from us the constant self-assessment and the political and critical self-consciousness which, as individual feminist teachers, we hope to encourage in our students both inside and outside the feminist option course.

With thanks to Jill Le Bihan, Sally Shuttleworth.

Notes

1 'The Wife of Bath's prologue and tale', in *The complete works of Geoffrey Chaucer*, edited by F. N. Robinson (2nd ed., Oxford, 1957), l.692. All subsequent references are to this edition and will hereafter be included in the text.
2 *The book of the city of ladies*, translated by Earl Jeffrey Richards (London, 1983), p. 16. All subsequent references are to this edition (BCL) and will hereafter be included in the text.
3 In fact in choosing to include *The book of the city of ladies* on the course, we no longer have to

venture too far into the wild zone of non-canonical texts. The work is available in a good modern translation, published by a major company (Picador) at a relatively accessible price. The book is packaged to meet a modern feminist market, as the cover quote from Judy Chicago indicates ('That this book has been unknown for so long is nothing less than a tragedy for women'). The growth of interest in the life and work of Christine de Pizan is confirmed by the recent appearance of *Christine de Pizan: a bibliographical guide*, by Angus J. Kennedy (London, 1984). Since the *Book of the city of ladies* comes with a modern frame we also discuss the commercial and academic context that has been created for this work.

4 *Signs* 8 (1982), pp. 4–28; rpt. in Kelly, 1984.

5 See the introduction to Richards's translation for a good account of Christine de Pizan's transformation of her sources. Most notably, she turns many of the infamous women of Boccaccio's *De claris mulieribus* into illustrious citizens of her city (Introduction, pp. xxxii–xli).

6 The difficulty in reconciling the analysis of gender construction with assertions of natural identity in *The book of the city of ladies* can be illustrated from Reason's comments on the intellectual capacities of women and their activities. She declares that women know less than men 'because they are not involved in many different things, but stay at home', but they stay at home 'because . . . it is enough for women to perform the usual duties to which they are ordained' (pp. 63–4).

7 In contrast, the exemplary value of Griselda's story is explicitly challenged in other versions such as that found in the conduct book of *Le menagier de Paris* and in Chaucer's *Clerk's tale*.

8 Daly, 1979, p. 14.

9 Of the many studies of this text, we have found the following articles particularly useful: Mary Carruthers, 'The Wife of Bath and the painting of lions', *PMLA* 94 (1979), pp. 209–22; Lee W. Patterson, ' "for the Wyves love of Bathe": feminine rhetoric and poetic resolution in the *Roman de la rose* and *The Canterbury tales*', *Speculum* 58 (1983), pp. 656–95.

10 The allusion in l. 692 of the Prologue is to a fable in which a lion questions whether the picture of a man killing a lion represents proof of the superior power men have over lions. If a lion had painted the picture, he suggests, it would present a different view. See Mary Carruthers (cited above, note 9).

11 Gautier, *Le Leu, La veuve* in *Le jongleur Gautier Le Leu*, edited by Charles H. Livingstone (Cambridge, 1951), pp. 165–83. A translation (*The Widow*) is available in *Fabliaux: ribald tales from the Old French*, translated by Robert Hellman and Richard O'Gorman (London, 1965), pp. 145–58.

12 *The Pelican Freud Library* vol. 8, *Case histories 1. Dora and Little Hans*, edited by Angela Richards, p. 105. And see Bernheimer and Keohane, 1985.

8

Teaching women's writing
and feminist theory:
diary of a two-term seminar
Isobel Armstrong

'I applied to the course not knowing what exactly to expect but because I wanted "space" in my last year to concentrate on this area' (third-year student). 'I didn't know exactly what to expect when I signed up for Feminist Theory and Criticism – but decided to do it so as to decide once and for all what my opinions are on the subject . . . I think I expected a slightly more basic, militant approach, as opposed to the theoretical and historical aspects we've studied' (second-year student). 'It was with some surprise that I learned in the first few weeks of the course that it was assumed that all members of the group were feminists; I always resented the fact that we had to read all texts with an anti-patriarchal attitude. I thought that the course would deal with the current application of feminist theories in society today' (second-year student). 'Studying feminism has forced me to reconsider my reactions to literary texts and made me far more aware of the way women are treated. However, I have also found this a very depressing course to study. It would appear that many of the issues which the feminist critics are challenging are ones which the ordinary person in the street would consider irrelevant. To spend time reassessing the Oedipus complex may well be interesting but most women who are struggling, bored and dissatisfied with their lot could well see it as a debate doing nothing to help them . . . there is a lot more practical work in changing laws and conditions which may be more vital' (second-year student).

These comments – I have chosen the most critical – were made by a mixed group of second- and third-year students in response to a relatively new special option, taught by seminar, on women's writing and feminist criticism. They were made about two-thirds of the way through the course. Up to the point when the option began the students had received some first-hand teaching on feminist criticism and a number of my colleagues teach mainstream courses with a very great awareness of gender. But three themes emerge strikingly from the students' comments. First, great uncertainty about what to expect from a course on feminist criticism. Secondly, real concern about the practical relevance of their experience. Thirdly, the perception that there was an element of resistance in themselves encountering some coercion in me: 'forced to', 'we had to read'. Though I had no predetermined notions about the direction in which our explorations would go – I hoped that each student would end up with her own conceptions of feminist studies and her own way of doing them – I was certain that what we were doing was close to our lives and would shape our experience and choices. It had certainly shaped mine. Many of the seminars turned into a debate about this. Because I wanted the seminars to become a collaborative and open exploration, we read a number of very different theories and texts (perhaps, in retrospect, too many). But I did and do believe that to arrive at a gender-conscious reading, and above all to understand that gender is constructed in texts, is a liberating experience in itself. It is an analytical and imaginative venture which carries the shock of delight and freedom with it. Deborah Cameron puts this beautifully elsewhere in this book in relation to language when she speaks of releasing people into language. To understand the power of language when it works both for and against one is to begin to make a critique of cultural forms. In the same way, to free people into an understanding of the structure of cultural forms is a political act: not only because one gains possession of one's choices, but also just to understand that the process is a political one is important in itself. However, perhaps because I was dealing with a number of often abstruse and abstract theories, and because I was inevitably more familiar with them than the students, they often perceived me as a coercive figure. Even to want someone to be free to think is to put yourself dangerously into a position of power. Oddly, because I wanted so intensely to persuade the students that critique is imaginatively and intellectually enabling I found myself often placed structurally in the position of phallocentric mentor by the group.

In order to circumvent this problem I tried to formulate the course in terms of the kinds of question we might ask rather than a body of knowledge we might learn. Foremost was the question, what is a gender-conscious reading? And bound up with this, how is gender constructed in literary and non-literary texts? These two questions dominated the year.

The course I evolved in order to be able to ask these questions was heterogeneous. We looked at literary texts by women from the nineteenth and twentieth centuries – Mary Shelley's *Frankenstein*, George Eliot's *The mill on the floss*, Christina Rossetti's *Goblin market*, Doris Lessing's *The golden notebook* and poetry by Sylvia Plath. These pretty obvious texts were studied in historical order. Interspersed with these were theoretical and polemical texts by men and women, not by any means in historical order. Freud followed upon Mary Wollstonecraft and Mary Shelley. Marxist feminism and the Freud/Lacan debate among feminists, Kristeva, Cixous, and Deborah Cameron's book, *Feminism and linguistic theory* (1985), were juxtaposed with both nineteenth- and twentieth-century texts. The aim was to see how the construction of gender could be illuminated by non-literary texts even when they were not written at the same time as the literary texts. I hoped this would free the students by suggesting that feminist criticism is not a homogenised enterprise, and that as a consequence they had choices to make. The non-historical ordering of the theory was not intended to be a-historical. I hoped that it would register difference in a dramatic way – in fact, the course was arranged as a drama of different readings. The risk of this, of course, was eclecticism and confusion.

Some sessions went well, some badly. The literary texts tended to lead to agreements, the theoretical texts led to disagreement and sometimes to resentment. I describe two sessions which went well, Mary Shelley's *Frankenstein* and Freud's 'Dora', and two sessions which went badly, Rossetti's *Goblin market* and Kristeva's 'Women's time', and then sum up the experience of the seminar by returning to students' comments.

Mary Shelley's *Frankenstein* came early in the course. We all felt exhilarated after the session. People were immediately struck by the narrative structure of stories within stories. Walton's letters to his sister, whose answers do not appear in the text, were immediately seen as a circumventing of a woman's voice, just as the production of the monster bypasses female biology, constructed as it is technologically, from dismembered bits and pieces. (This theme of dismemberment turned up again and again in discussions of other texts: it fascinated the group and they returned to it in Sylvia Plath's 'The applicant'.) The most striking discovery was the indeterminacy of the monster's gender. Frankenstein does not attribute gender to the monster until its horrible foetal life stirs as it comes alive. It is a 'creature' and a 'wretch' until with life it becomes 'his', the genitive almost denoting that the creature takes possession of 'his' gender. And yet the monster does not seem to discover its gender until well on into the narrative, even when it achieves self-consciousness through understanding opposition and difference and sees its reflection in the water (Chapter 11). It attributes maleness to itself when it is 'civilised' through the episode when it watches the de Lacey family in the cottage. It learns language, discovering the single name given to the old man, 'father', and understanding the place that sons and daughters find in the family structure. The absence of the mother and of the word 'mother' seemed striking. The patriarchal structure of the adopted family was very clear.

We saw that a further indeterminacy comes into play when the monster's gender seems to be established. As soon as it wishes for a female mate (learned, it seems from *Paradise lost*), its status as a *species* is questioned by Frankenstein. The monster may be a male but it is not 'human'. Frankenstein imagines the earth overrun through the obscene Malthusian reproduction of an alien species. The 'woman' who might be responsible for this is aborted. But the strategy for constructing the 'other' as aberrant and 'outside' human categories seemed almost more important than this and reminded one girl of the treatment of Caliban in *The tempest*. The overdetermined presence of the law in the novel, which puzzled everyone at first, came to seem important here. For the Law is society's way of legitimatising categories.

Finally, the violence of the last power struggle between Frankenstein and the monster (we noticed, incidentally, that we were using the term 'monster', given by subsequent films rather than the text), who seem to need each other so badly, was difficult to interpret. Some people thought that the struggle was a conflict between men (as Eve Sedgwick, 1985, thinks of it). Some people noticed that the roles of pursuer and pursued were continually reversed, though the *structure* of master and slave was the same. They wondered if Frankenstein and his monster became male and female to one another, or parent and child, or tyrant and revolutionary, or colonial power and alien race. Were these analogies of like with like? Was the paradigm of self-perpetuating violence between two parties locked in conflict the final image of the novel? We seemed to have got to grips with power relations and the cultural constructions of gender.[1]

We finished in a mood of high confidence which collapsed as soon as we reached Freud's 'Three essays on the theory of sexuality', with which we prefaced a reading of the 'Dora' case history. The 'Three essays' are so condensed that they seem to shift on every reading.[2] Because I did not want to offer a formula for reading anything, Freud included, we were all at sea. Whereas some Marxist approaches seemed to offer an intractably closed formula to the group which they could do nothing with at first, Freud made them angry, confused and worried by the openness of his questions.

They could not see the point of starting with the aberrant to question norms, and when we had tried to clarify the Freudian model, the oedipal structure and the problematic nature of feminine sexuality outraged them. The thought of being construed as the objects of phallic loss was infuriating, even when the symbolic nature of the phallus as against the literalising of the penis was established. It became me against the group: I found myself defending Freud instead of exploring him. My argument that this was a *structural* way of thinking about women's oppression looked weaker and weaker as they attacked its determinism. I said that to triangulate a relationship, as the oepidal situation does, was to think of ways of releasing a relationship from the binary conflict such as we find in *Frankenstein*, but they argued that the father is so powerful in Freud's model that this freedom could not occur. There must be some other model. But what? I tended to use my knowledge of the difficulties of other models unfairly, shooting them down too quickly because I wanted the possibilities of Freud's drama at least to be acknowledged. In the end I suggested that something they all had experience of, women's lack of confidence (the woman student's disease) could be brought to Freud's model of phallic loss. By showing that it belongs to a structure rather than being each individual's own psychic or moral responsibility Freud's paradigm at least releases one into an understanding of oppression which can be theorised rather than simply experienced as a mystified condition. This helped, but I felt as if I was arguing unscrupulously, ignoring problems and forgetting about some real difficulties, such as the ahistorical nature of the Freudian model. At that stage my group hadn't the confidence or experience to be as knowingly angry with Freud as Hélène Cixous, whose work they later liked (Cixous, 1981).

In spite of this session I did not count the response to Freud as a failure, for when they approached the Dora case history the students began to use Freud against himself. One woman student contrasted the certainty of Freud on Dora with the 'Three essays', where feminine sexuality was an unknown and difficult entity. She contrasted his attitude to Dora with a much more tentative response to Little Hans. Dora, said another, was the only sane person in the bunch. 'Dora can't say "no" because it means "yes", and if she says "yes" it also means "yes" ', said another. Without having read any of the voluminous writing on this case history, they saw

Freud himself as the victim of patriarchal structures, participating in the exchange of Dora between men. They proceeded to deconstruct Freud's reading of Dora's first dream by reading it in terms of her relationship to her mother, the housewife Freud deemed obsessive and relegates to a footnote.

The helpfulness of Freud became apparent when we read *The mill on the floss*. The students began by seeing that they could read the constructions of gender in the book in a way which did not necessarily coincide with the promptings of the authorial voice. Throughout Maggie is positioned in the text in a way which always makes her seem as if she *wants* too much, as if her need for love is an excess, a hysterical symptom. The punitiveness of the novel is always in excess of what she has done, as if the text is internalising the male symbolic order just as Maggie attempts to when she reads Thomas à Kempis. What she desires is seen as forbidden. Some people made an analogy between Maggie and Dora as property negotiated between males. Her refusal to return to Stephen Guest was seen as the re-assertion of patriarchal power rather than a moral choice. Maggie's economic dependence on Tom, who will 'look after' her if she minds 'what I say' is a critical element in her predicament. People began to see that questions of property and economics were embedded in the novel and bound up with its exploration of violence and masochism in a way the text does not always acknowledge overtly. They began to read Maggie's dream, after her transgression, as a critique of her position as well as in terms of anguish and desire.

'But why does it make you cry?' We considered the death in terms of the 'flood' of feminine desire which metaphorically overwhelms Maggie at the end of the novel. One girl suggested that the terror of Maggie's rebellion against what Kristeva calls the sacrificial oedipal contract, which leaves her with nothing to do but to die, is behind our intense response to the novel. But on the whole the session on Kristeva's essay, 'Women's time' (Kristeva, 1986(b)), was flat. Having embarked on their own critique of Freud, the group was not ready to assimilate another. 'Why is linear time masculine?' asked one student. They were worried, as I was, that they seemed to be carried further away from finding a way of understanding how to incorporate a social and economic analysis into their reading. This, by the end of the course, was our biggest problem.

Oddly enough, it emerged when we read Christina Rossetti's *Goblin market*. It was a dreary and difficult session, because the group tended to read Laura's taking of the fruit from the goblin men as a moral transgression rectified by Lizzie. Nothing we had read seemed to help us. I found myself isolated again, drumming home a reminder of the economic motifs of buying and selling in the poem. In the end we trudged through the poem's re-reading of Eve's situation in the biblical Fall and *Paradise lost* through Laura and the idea of payment. But it was not a success. I could only assume that the poem was too complex – and too scandalous – for us to assimilate it in one session. It became clear that we hadn't a sufficiently sophisticated understanding of reading in terms of cultural critique, and that we lacked sufficiently theorised accounts of language in the female text. We did not want to think of an essentialist 'feminine' language, but even those discussions (e.g. by Mary Jacobus) of language which refused essentialism seemed to fall into it.[3]

Most of the women who took the course agreed that it had altered their way of conceptualising gender – in texts and out of them. 'To look at authors from Mary Wollstonecraft to Freud has been a revelation in terms of changing attitudes to women and their role in society' (second-year student). 'Originally, I saw it [feminist criticism] as a limited movement with a single aim: gaining freedom of speech and equal rights for women. I was somewhat surprised to find the variety of aims and approaches ... many of which are more subtle (less polemical) than I imagined' (third-year student). One finalist felt that the importance of feminist criticism (or -isms) for her, was that 'they are not usually concerned with fitting things together'. There is no possibility of reaching a "harmonised state" '. The course 'completely altered my conception of the feminist argument – it now seems more a question of feminisms plural. I also feel I've made a constructive movement from anger to inquiry ... Feminist theories are the only ones which go any way towards tackling not only intellectual concerns with literature, but my personal position within society.'

My own response to the course is mixed. It has made me overwhelmingly aware of the responsibilities of teaching feminist criticism. Properly speaking, this diary should be matched by one from a student. I've always believed that analysis is a prerequisite for action and yet I have some sympathy with the students quoted at the start of this essay who registered the gap between thinking and action. Was I encouraging students to rest with enquiry? And what about the loss of 'anger'? Is it necessarily a good thing? Next I was aware of the immense power of the teacher – in choosing texts, in manipulating argument – however collaborative the enterprise is. Lastly, I was aware of the immense power of Freud. My own interests have been in Hegel and Marx, and yet Freud took us over. Perhaps because Marxist feminists have mostly been concerned more with sociological questions than literary texts, and because alternatives to Freud are difficult to come up with, he dominated us even when we used him against himself, as some French feminists do. But I began to wonder if Freud evades the political. Because gender is at the heart of his work he provides a way of deconstructing accounts of gender in texts. We are all post-Freudians, but I would like to find more ways in future of enabling students to think through alternatives. It was not quite the drama I'd hoped for. It seems fundamentally against the principles of teaching feminist criticism to accede too readily to a single model produced by a male writer. I worry about this coercive power. Invaluable though they have been, and profoundly influential, literary discusssion seems to be stuck in post-Lacanian accounts of gender.[4] Feminism in the next decade needs to think much more about class, culture and politics. It needs to return to the question of language and look further afield – perhaps to Melanie Klein – in psychoanalysis.

Notes

1 It is interesting, though, that feminist or gender conscious readings of *Frankenstein* seem to become completely dissociated from political and socio-economic readings of the novel. The two never come together. See, for instance, an interesting political essay by Paul O'Flinn, 'Production and reproduction: the case of Frankenstein' in *Popular fiction: essays in literature and history*, ed. Peter Humm, Paul Stigart, Peter Widdowson (London and New York, 1986).

2 Sigmund Freud, *The Pelican Freud library*, vols. 7 and 8 (Harmondsworth, 1977).

3 Mary Jacobus, 'The question of language: men of maxims and *The mill on the floss*', in Abel, 1982, pp. 37–52. This impressive essay contains a useful reference (p. 52) to Gillian Beer's account of desire in *The mill on the floss*. Cora Kaplan, whose account of the structure of 'feminine' language differs from that of Jacobus, offers another view in her original and innovative essay, 'Language and gender' (Kaplan, 1986, pp. 69–93). There is a further essay on Christina Rossetti and Emily Dickinson in the same volume, pp. 95–115.

4 No one, of course, would be without the work of Juliet Mitchell and Jacqueline Rose in editing and translating *Feminine sexuality; Jacques Lacan and the Ecole Freudienne* (London and Basingstoke, 1982).

9

Powerhouse or ivory tower?: feminism and postgraduate English
Patsy Stoneman

Ideals and realities

While preparing to write this paper I have repeatedly been drawn to paraphrase Marx's words: '[Women] make their own history, but they do not make it just as they please; they do not make it under circumstances chosen by themselves, but under circumstances directly found, given and transmitted from the past.'[1] Most of the theoretical writing on the teaching of Women's Studies (from America) takes interdisciplinarity as axiomatic; the debate focuses on whether Women's Studies should aim for continued autonomy or press for an integration so total that a 'withering away of Women's Studies' is the ultimate aim (Bowles and Duelli Klein, p. 7). This (British) volume, on the other hand, demonstrates that numbers of feminist teachers are working within a single discipline, and that our teaching practices are determined only partly by pedagogic ideals, and largely by the crannies of institutional space which we can infiltrate or commandeer.

Our five-year struggle to establish a Master's degree at Hull University, for instance, took place in a university which had never had an interdisciplinary course of any kind; experience proved that our only hope was to repeat exactly the structure of an existing course in Victorian literature; in this way opposition was forced to address itself to the one innovatory item – 'Women' – and could not disguise itself as an attack on interdisciplinarity, continuous assessment, part-time access, or any other desirable, but in this context diversionary, feature. The result is that while every other Women's Studies MA in England has a broad approach and a modular structure designed to facilitate part-time attendance, ours is unique in being taught wholly within the English Department and exclusively to full-time students.

We would, however, defend our course in terms of strategy as well as tactics. We feel that it is important to develop feminist thinking within as well as between disciplines, so that Women's Studies is not perceived as a force outside the citadel of academia. Our full-time format, also, was only partly dictated by institutional pressure, and more intrinsically by our own determination that the course should have a theoretical basis, which in turn dictated a cumulative structure which cannot easily be adapted to part-time access.

Although our MA started only in 1984, it grew out of our long-standing undergraduate option on 'Women in literature and society since 1837'. This was, we believe, the first such course when Marion Shaw began it in 1973, and it has naturally reflected all the changes in feminist criticism since that time. Like other such courses, it began with the twofold purpose of introducing 'forgotten' women's texts into the curriculum and reading 'standard' texts with due attention to the fact that they were written by, for or about women. Literature was seen as evidence or misrepresentation of women's experience and we intended to put the record straight. By the late 1970s, however, we were encountering in a feminist context the 'crisis in English studies' created by post-structuralist and psychoanalytic theory. While we as teachers were struggling into the perception that the speaking subject is constructed in language and that writing itself is a historically determined process, our students were proving endlessly that women are victims of patriarchy, and lamenting that individual women (either characters perceived as real and autonomous or writers perceived as in total control of their text) did not throw off their shackles by a heroic effort. Catherine Belsey has shown how difficult it is for students to escape the dominant liberal orthodoxy by means of common sense, and how difficult it is for teachers to introduce non-standard theories into 'options' or sections of courses. Not only does the mainstream demand most of the students' time (Belsey, 1982, p. 65), but it creates a real resistance to adopting a new and difficult concept of reading for only one-ninth of their degree (see de Wolfe, in Spender and Sarah, pp. 49–50). As Belsey puts it, 'a space in the syllabus is not enough' (p. 65). This is a problem which we have not yet solved, although the appearance of more examples of applied post-structuralist readings helps. In planning the MA, however, we were strongly influenced by this experience. The MA is not just 'a space in the syllabus' but an area where we have total curricular control, and we were determined that, without prescribing any particular dogma, we would give our

students the opportunity to read, discuss and apply some of these new
and difficult ideas at the beginning of their course.

The structure of the course

The course lasts for a calendar year from October. Roughly two terms are
occupied by twice-weekly two-hour seminars, most of which take the
student-paper-plus-discussion format; there are three written examinations in May, following which each student writes a dissertation of about
15,000 words. The taught part of the course is in three sections:

(a) *Criticism and texts.* This is the theoretical section, and in order to put
the focus on theory, we deal with only three literary texts, chosen from
different periods and genres, by female and male writers, which will
support a variety of critical readings. So far we have used *Wide Sargasso Sea,
The waste land* and *Sense and sensibility;* this year (1987) we shall use *The lyrical
ballads* (with Dorothy Wordsworth's *Journal*), *Wuthering Heights* and *Mrs
Dalloway.* Since the first year of the course we have increased the amount
of 'teacher input' at this stage; some direct teaching helps the students to
produce a 'map' of how different theories relate to each other and also
helps to stabilise volatile groups by giving them a common body of
information. This year we began with substantial papers from each of us
at which all three of us were present: a general survey, and discussions of
psychoanalytic theory and discourse theory. Students then present
papers in two sessions for each text, co-ordinated by a single tutor, on
topics suggested by us to focus groups of critical readings. For *Wide
Sargasso Sea* the themes are 'gynocritics or the woman writer in a male/
female tradition' and 'Lacan, madness and the social construction of the
subject'. There is, even on an MA, not really time for students to read
monumental works like *Ecrits;* they are directed to read Rose and Mitchell
(1982) on Lacan and the 'Ecole Freudienne', Anika Lemaire's *Jacques
Lacan,* Althusser on Ideology and Shoshana Felman on madness as well
as more familiar works like Showalter (1978) and Gilbert and Gubar. A
large number of specific readings of the text are also suggested. The
presence of *The waste land* as a focal text highlights the fact that ours is
emphatically not a 'Women's Writing' course; we believe that feminist
criticism must engage with the whole of literature, just as feminism itself
is a total world-view. This does not mean that dealing with the 'canon'
has no problems; for *The waste land,* therefore, the topics are 'confronting
the male text' and 'feminism, modernism and the male literary tradition'. Theoretical texts include Harold Bloom's *Anxiety of influence,* Jona-

than Culler's *Structuralist poetics*, and essays on feminist approaches to the 'canon' such as Myra Jehlen and Adrienne Munich. Tony Pinckney's *Women in the poetry of* T. S. Eliot, Hilary Simpson's book on D. H. Lawrence and Penny Boumelha on Hardy are also suggested as examples of approaching a male text. For *Sense and sensibility* sociological/ideological readings are compared with readings prompted by new French feminist perspectives. Recommended reading includes Marks and de Courtivron's anthology (1981) and Toril Moi's *Sexual/textual politics* and *Kristeva reader*, while Margaret Kirkham and Janet Todd provide specific readings of Jane Austen which contrast with more conventional criticism.

(b) The second section is entitled *Writing and history* and deals with the short period 1848–61 (the 1890s and inter-war period are possibilities for the future). The aim here is to consider the relationship between literary and non-literary texts by reading canonical works (*The scarlet letter*, 'Maud', *Aurora Leigh*) in the context of 'minor' works such as 'Lizzie Leigh', *Lady Audley's secret* and *The germ*, and ideological works such as those by Acton, Coventry Patmore and Darwin. Modern theories such as Foucault's *History of sexuality*, various theories of masculinity, and the concept of *écriture féminine* are used to discuss these relationships.

(c) The third section, entitled *A female tradition*, is more fluid and open to student choice, but it attempts a survey of women's writing in the nineteenth and twentieth centuries based on a small number of characteristic 'metaphors of creativity', for instance 'birth' (*Frankenstein; The birth machine*), 'water' (*The voyage out; Surfacing*), 'screams and cries' (poetry of Adrienne Rich; *The Bloodaxe book of contemporary women poets*) and the different tradition of Black women writers, such as Maya Angelou, Alice Walker, and Toni Morrison. The students are free here to suggest texts and take their own critical approach. The course thus proceeds from a highly structured learning situation to a more informal one.

Students and teachers

The three of us – Angela Leighton, Marion Shaw and Patsy Stoneman – control admission, curriculum and examinations and also teach all the theoretical and 'Female tradition' sections of the course.[2] To reduce the vulnerability of the course to illness, study leave and so on, we have also invited help from two or three male colleagues, who teach part of the 1850s section and sometimes act as supervisors and internal examiners for dissertations. Although Duelli Klein identifies 'the problem of men' as 'the one issue which invariably seemed to come up' when Women's

Studies teachers discussed their experiences,[3] this small input from male teachers has, for us, been trouble-free. No student has reported difficulties, and our chosen (feminist) external examiner has agreed with male internal examiners' judgements. This consensus is presumably explained by the fact that, like us, our students, who need a 2 i to qualify, are already geared to perform to establishment criteria such as logic, balance and appropriateness, which in other circumstances (see Maggie Humm's chapter in this volume) discriminate against women. Another factor, however, is that by controlling examination questions and dissertation topics, we ourselves can set the standard of, say, 'relevance' with reference to women's experience and priorities.

Because of our full-time format and consequently high fees, student entry is limited both in absolute numbers (4, 4, 7 and 11 in the four years so far) and in the type of student. Students are either high-fliers with DES grants, overseas students supported by governments, middle-class students supported by parents or spouses, or pertinacious individuals who beg, borrow, take on part-time work and generally mortgage their existence. The high fees, though rarely mentioned, contribute to raise the emotional temperature; if the course doesn't satisfy, it is not only time, effort and trust thrown away, but hard cash. We believe that our course is a good one; the students are eager, able and highly motivated; they have chosen the single-discipline course with theoretical content. Yet none of the first three years were trouble-free. As teachers we have found this disheartening and were encouraged to read Valerie Hey's suggestion that both students and teachers on Women's Studies courses bring to the classroom their experiences 'of having been socialised as members of the "second sex" . . . WS practitioners are survivors but . . . it is not surprising that their coming together in a university classroom with its inbuilt structural problematics has all the characteristics of a volcano' (in Klein, 1987, p. 197). Duelli Klein comments that 'such "rumours from the cauldron" are to be expected' but that, 'surprisingly, they are rarely acknowledged or discussed in depth in the existing WS-material'. She cites Mary Evans's 'Teacher's tale' as an exception, and laments, particularly, that students have not come forward with their version even when given space;[4] none of our most vocal critics has actually returned the questionnaire we circulated! Nevertheless we have thought it useful to discuss three instances of 'rumblings and eruptions'.

The first is an example with which many feminists reading this chapter will have little sympathy, because it focuses on the presence of a male student.[5] Our course is open to men not only because we cannot legally avoid it but also because we hope that 'men, too, can learn to think and learn "like women" ' (Maher, in Culley and Portuges, p. 46). The problem occurred when the male student in that year proved to have an expertise in French critical and psychoanalytic theory which far surpassed our patchy knowledge. We experienced an automatic survivalist impulse to prove our competence; jargon and learned citations sprang to our lips. The women students, meanwhile, who knew no theory at all, felt excluded – and said so. This course was supposed to be for them, they said, so why were they sitting silent while we talked to a man who knew it all already? I think that what happened would have happened if the expert student had been a woman (see Culley et al., in Culley and Portuges, p. 17); the effect was to highlight and accentuate the authority conferred by knowledge, which a feminist teacher will normally try to minimise, aiming to make her students feel equal as people, even if not equal in professional competence. Ulricke Buchner (quoted in Klein, 1987, p. 194) suggests that we negotiate this difficult demarcation by perceiving the professional competence of the teacher as 'a source of "empowerment" rather than "power over" '. In the case under discussion, the teachers' knowledge was not being made available to the women students and hence functioned as 'power over' them, to keep them silent. It is a particularly crass example of what feminist teachers ought not to do. On the other hand, how were we to maintain the authority we claimed, the competence to 'empower' the expert student, without attempting to match his knowledge? The answer, as I see it now, was to refuse to perform this function; to explain the effect of exclusion which was developing and instead to exclude the expert until the other students were in a position to engage in dialogue; it is partly for this reason that we now begin the course with some direct teaching from the tutors. But teachers as well as students are vulnerable, and sometimes act in self-defence rather than in the common good. Although these tensions later eased in ways which I shall describe, the coincidence of maleness and expertness continued to alarm and anger all of us in different ways despite the personal charm and gentleness of the student in question, and the women in this year had the least satisfying experience of any so far.

The second example is more of a rumbling than an eruption, and happened when a group of students divided very markedly according to their critical stance – empirical versus post-structuralist, Marxist versus psychoanalytic and so on. Although this group was on the whole very lively, there was a tendency to talk 'across' rather than 'to' each other, and in particular to allow no space for more conventional thinkers. The atmosphere was not obviously antagonistic but there was some hidden tension and unhappiness. Oddly enough, this division was to some extent resolved by what was at the time a more spectacular problem.

Almost every member of this group experienced extreme examination nerves, an outbreak which highlights the contradiction of academic feminist teaching, since feminism is co-operative and non-hierarchical, yet academic institutions are based on competitive assessment. During assessment, when teachers change from enablers to evaluators, this contradiction becomes visible (see de Wolfe, in Spender and Sarah, pp. 50–1), and the eruption of protest registers a sense of betrayal. It was, however, this shared grievance which, according to one of its members, helped to unite the group. In this context, as Culley *et al.* put it, 'students see teachers as old-fashioned mothers – powerful enough to command children, but necessarily rejected by all who would call themselves adults' (p. 15). Although the process is painful, examinations may be useful if they perform the role of forcing women students to accept responsibility for their judgements. One of this group afterwards admitted that it was good for her to be forced to state conclusions briefly and clearly instead of remaining within the flux of process and debate. The danger is that women may simply refuse to jump hurdles not of their choosing. The reality of the situation, nevertheless, is 'almost total agreement' among WS teachers 'that assessment and final grades are a necessity in WS courses in higher education' if only to 'confirm [their] legitimacy within the academy' (Klein, 1987, p. 196).

Other women's experiences with WS courses suggest that we cannot guard against the problems I have described by making structural alterations; almost any form of assessment, for example, is going to cause trouble for someone. What could make a real difference, however, is to put classroom relations on the curriculum (see de Wolfe, in Spender and Sarah, p. 43; Hey, p. 301). Thus, instead of meeting tensions with embarrassment, private interviews or dramatic scenes, we may hope to discuss them as part of what feminism is about, what literary criticism as a *political* activity is about. If individual feelings of vulnerability, exclusion, exasperation and outrage can be shown to relate not just to other individuals but to an ongoing struggle for the meaning of the text, about who has the right and power to speak about the text, then the division between the personal and the political will be challenged in the context of the classroom and of literary criticism, and one of the aims of feminism furthered.

Next year, therefore, we shall begin the course by describing our own education in literature and feminism, and inviting the students to do the same. Since two of us graduated more than twenty-five years ago, and have struggled out of New Criticism and Leavisim through Marxism into feminism and post-structualism, this should demonstrate that teachers do not leap from the head of Athene ready armed with Foucault and Kristeva but have many layers of half-discarded attitudes and half-achieved priorities which make us fallible and vulnerable. We shall also describe the history of the course itself, distinguishing features we positively chose from those accepted as a condition of validation. We, the teachers, will then be revealed not as personally responsible for every feature but as making our history, like the students themselves, in circumstances not of our choosing.

What the students do with the texts

In concentrating on problems I have been responding to Renate Duelli Klein's appeal (1987, p. 197) for honesty and information, but I am also aware, like her, that such willingness to be open may result in feminist teachers over-exposing problems and 'writing our history "lop-sided" ' (p. 194 footnote 15). I am glad, therefore, to be ending this chapter with some real achievements. Since our aim has been 'empowerment' rather than indoctrination, we are especially pleased with the wide variety of work done by students in the context of the same, fairly structured, learning situation, and what follows is an account of student responses to the same course material in three consecutive years. I have chosen one of the first texts to be dealt with, *Wide Sargasso Sea* (see p. 98, above, for the structural context).

The first group was unusual in that only one had a wholly literary first degree; they were content, therefore, to devote the 'gynocritics' session to a straightforward exposition of Showalter and Gilbert and Gubar. Because of their inexperience, I was apprehensive about the second, Lacanian, session, but the student who led the discussion appointed herself 'teacher' of the others and produced a simple but remarkably lucid account of the Imaginary and the Symbolic, the mirror-phase and so on. She read Section 45 of *In memoriam* to prove that Lacan did not invent these ideas, and used a classic demonstration of Lacanian misre-cognition – she presented a mirror to a fellow student who, when asked, 'Who's that?', obligingly replied, 'That's me!' The explanation took up the whole session, and we never got to Jean Rhys, but the group went away reassured that theory was accessible, even without teacher's help (I did almost nothing). The mature student who led this session went on to use Freud and Lacan to give stability to some original but unfocused ideas on repetition as haunting in *Wuthering Heights*, and has recently read a paper on the same topic to The Brontë Society amid considerable acclaim. This lifelong enthusiast for the Brontës, who might well have been perceived as a middle-aged housewife with a bee in her bonnet, has thus gained academic prestige and enhanced self-esteem.

The following year was quite different; the session on 'gynocritics' was completely taken over by the group's common enthusiasm for Jean Rhys's newly-published *Letters*. The paper for the session was forgotten as we swapped examples of Rhys's marginalisation and silencing, her continued self-descriptions as 'mad', a 'harridan' or a 'witch'. Since the session came immediately after the crisis with the expert student, it was extremely valuable in re-establishing equality of access to a text, while as the unstructured discussion proceeded we all became aware that what we 'just happened to notice' in the letters had in fact been suggested by the prescribed texts, Showalter, Gilbert and Gubar, and *Wide Sargasso Sea* itself; a good demonstration of the fact that 'spontaneous' and 'subjective' responses to a text are in fact determined by previous reading experiences.

The second session, on Lacan, was inevitably assigned to the expert student, but without warning he ignored his brief and instead produced a very detailed syntactical reading of Section II (Rochester's narrative) of *Wide Sargasso Sea*, demonstrating how the male speaker endeavours to maintain control of the narrative by means of 'objectifying' placing and distancing devices which are then threatened by experience which forces him to adopt intersubjective positions (Antoinette becomes 'you' instead of 'she') and open-ended (present-tense) narrative which denies him the authority of closure. The session was fascinating because it presented a mode of reading which was not difficult, but new to most of us, and which could easily be adapted to other texts. In the pedagogic context the presenter also showed remarkable tact, since by aligning himself with the male speaker he showed his consciousness of the power politics of speech, while by deconstructing one of the mechanisms by which such power is maintained, he showed his willingness to be 'dethroned' and to share his expertise with others. The crucial distinction between him and the women, however, was his ultimate scepticism about social change. His drive towards knowledge 'for its own sake' emphasised the esoteric and exclusive aspects of theory and deflected the rest of us from the more pragmatic amalgam of theory-with-practice which feminism demands.

The following year's students were quite clear that however elegant and exciting feminist theory might be, they needed it to be an instrument of change, not just of explanation. In the first session a student who had already been working on feminist theory used *Wide Sargasso Sea* as a focus to analyse the main points of difference between Anglo-American and French feminist criticism, positing the familiar dilemma between Anglo-Americans who use the language of patriarchy at the risk of incorporation, and the French who while seeking a female voice in madness and the female body, risk remaining 'in a sulk in the face of history'. She was especially suspicious of the idea of a female 'wild zone' free from ideological construction, arguing that to negate a construction is not to escape from it. In a later session, on Angela Carter and Elizabeth Baines, another student argued similarly, and elegantly, that the 'widdershins logic of smashing what is fixed and fixing what is smashed' leaves women trapped in the infinite regressions of a pair of opposing mirrors. In the discussion of *Wide Sargasso Sea* it was assumed that Anglo-American critics, with their greater emphasis on social process, would see Antoinette's death as a final victimisation, while 'triumphant' readings of her madness and dream of revenge would be supported by the French school, with its emphasis on the body and the unconscious. A discussion of various critical articles read by the group revealed, however, that the situation was less simple, and that readings are clearly produced by political priorities as much as intellectual allegiances. Selma James, for instance, is writing about social and economic change, yet produces a 'triumphant' reading of Antoinette's leap to join Tia because she needs the novel to perform an enthusing function in linking the struggles of black and white American women. Elizabeth Abel, on the other hand, while focusing on sexuality and the unconscious, reads madness as a sign of defeat because her priority is the Laingian reform of the family.

In the second session the presenter produced a neat Lacanian reading of *Wide Sargasso Sea* based on Antoinette's entrapment in the Imaginary, but the general feeling both of the speaker and the group as a whole was, 'So what?' It was felt that the novel itself is so explicit about the function of mirrors and names in constructing the self that a Lacanian reading simply said the same thing in a different way and certainly didn't suggest what we should do in response to the text.

Subsequent sessions with this group were informed by the consciousness acquired in the early meetings that we must not accept either/or
options – flesh or spirit, passion or reason. A student speaking on
Frankenstein began her paper with the questions, 'what are the political
implications of the binary chain? how can they be challenged or
subverted?' and found her answer in dialectical materialism; although
the structure of opposition remains fixed, the opposed terms can be
shown to shift with ideological changes deriving from material history.
Thus, she argued, we should challenge Mary Shelley's reluctance to
present her writing as 'work', in order to subvert the ideological chain,
male/female, work/birth. 'Nature' is the enemy; 'if something is natural
. . . it cannot be challenged; if it is seen as political or cultural the notion of
change through revolution or action becomes possible'. This student is
now using a combination of Foucault and Gramsci to examine the diaries
of Hannah Cullwick as a locus of struggle in the construction of nineteenth-century female working-class sexuality. And although our
students all have different perspectives, they all seem motivated by the
idea that literary criticism is an active force effecting social change. One is
using conventional scholarly methods to 'make visible' a forgotten
Australian woman novelist. Another is using the more materialist psychology of Dinnerstein and the American object relations school in
combination with French feminist theories to investigate how female
autobiographers can exploit the (marginalised) voice of the mother to
produce texts which are nevertheless within culture.

Some of the most productive sessions came in the historical Section II,
and some of the most enjoyable in Section III, where there was a good
deal of laughter and improvisation as well as hard thinking.[6] The sessions
on Black women writers particularly, where students felt themselves to
be in uncharted territory, produced speculative and inventive readings
in which the politics of culture were necessarily prominent. I hope,
however, that my examples from early sessions have shown that a
formal, single-discipline course with a highly-selected intake can
respond to a remarkable variety of student needs and talents not by
imposing any particular 'line' but by offering a range of possibilities.

Our students have gone into jobs ranging from managing an old
people's home to being a union administrator, but many will go into
teaching and research, and the basic group in each year has also been
augmented by MPhil and PhD students who find the initial sections of
the MA invaluable in offering, within an overall feminist perspective, a
flexible and usable range of critical approaches. These students are now

working on topics as diverse as Elizabeth Gaskell and Ruth Prawer Jhabvala, and will teach as far apart as Canada and Malaysia. We feel, therefore, that our course is contributing powerfully to a new Kuhnian paradigm by helping to create not just arguments of 'compelling intellectual power',[7] but also a body of practising thinkers linked by a shared feminist perspective. Institutionally small and constrained, our course might seem an ivory tower; but in terms of people and ideas, even a small course can be an empowering-house.

Course texts mentioned

Abel, Elizabeth, 'Women and schizophrenia: the fiction of Jean Rhys, Contemporary literature, 20, no. 2, pp. 154–77.
Althusser, Louis, Essays on ideology (London, 1984 [first published 1971]).
Bloom, Harold, The anxiety of influence: a theory of poetry (Oxford, 1973).
Boumelha, Penny, Thomas Hardy and women: sexual ideology and narrative form (Brighton, 1982).
Chodorow, 1978.
Couzyn, Jeni, ed., The Bloodaxe book of contemporary women poets (Newcastle, 1985).
Culler, Jonathan, Structuralist poetics: structural linguistics and the study of literature (London and Henley, 1975).
Felman, Shoshana, 'Women and madness: the critical phallacy', Diacritics, 5 (1975), pp. 2–10.
Foucault, Michel, The history of sexuality vol. I (Harmondsworth, 1981 [first published 1976]).
Gilbert and Gubar, 1979.
James, Selma, The ladies and the mammies: Jane Austen and Jean Rhys (Bristol, 1983).
Jehlen, Myra, 'Archimedes and the paradox of feminist criticism', Signs, 6, no. 4 (1981), pp. 567–601.
Kirkham, Margaret, Jane Austen: feminism and fiction (Brighton, 1982).
Lemaire, Anika, Jacques Lacan, trans. David Macey (London and Boston, 1977 [first published 1970]).
Marks and de Courtivron, 1981.
Mitchell and Rose, 1982.
Moi, 1985 and 1986.
Munich, Adrienne, 'Notorious signs, feminist criticism and literary tradition' in Greene and Kahn, 1985.
Pinckney, Tony, Women in the poetry of T. S. Eliot: a psychoanalytic approach (London, 1984).
Showalter, 1978.
Simpson, Hilary, D. H. Lawrence and feminism (London, 1982).
Todd, Janet, Jane Austen: new perspectives (New York, 1983).

Notes

1 Karl Marx, Selected works, ed. V. Adoratsky, 2 vols, (London, 1942), 2, p. 315. It is ironic, but appropriate in this context, that though Marx says just what I want to say about history, I cannot use his formulation without altering the key word.

2 Although I (Patsy Stoneman) have actually written this essay, I could not have done it, of course, without Angela Leighton and Marion Shaw, since we devised the course together and are constantly conferring about its teaching and administration.

3 Renate Duelli Klein, 'A brief overview of the development of women's studies in the UK', *WSIF*, 6, no. 3 (1983), p. 258; see also Duelli Klein on 'The "men problem" in women's studies', *WSIF*, 6, no. 4 (1983), pp. 413–21.

4 See Roisin Battel, Renate Duelli Klein, Catherine Moorhouse and Christine Zmroczek, 'Editorial', *WSIF*, 6, no. 3 (1983), pp. 251–4.

5 See Duelli Klein, 1983 (as above, n. 3), and Pat Mahoney, 'Boys will be boys: teaching women's studies in mixed-sex groups', *WSIF*, 6, no. 3 (1983), pp. 331–4.

6 I am reminded of Sue Wise's saying that 'the sound of women laughing is the sound of revolution' (in Klein, *WSIF*, 6, no. 4 (1983), p. 421).

7 See Sandra Conyers, 'Women's studies as an academic discipline: why and how to do it', in Bowles and Klein, pp. 46–71.

Women and the male canon

Introduction to Part Four

Whether or not we can as feminists establish a 'cranny in the syllabus' for a course of our own, most of us are still obliged (and may in fact choose) to spend much of our time teaching the traditional male canon and coming to terms with traditional texts as well as with traditional methods of teaching and examing.

Does this mean that we lead a schizophrenic existence, teaching one set of texts in one way on 'our own' courses and teaching another set in a different way on courses which are more likely to be in effect compulsory, for us as well as the students? What happens when the same text appears in two places, on a feminist course and on a non-feminist course (as *The Wife of Bath's prologue and tale* does at Leeds and Charlotte Perkins Gilman's 'The yellow wallpaper' does at Lancaster)? What happens when students find themselves confronted with radically different approaches to literature on different courses, taught sometimes by the same people?

Feminist teachers of English cannot afford to turn their backs on the male canon and retreat into a cosy 'women only' ghetto on the edges of the discipline. We do not have either the political power or, necessarily, the will to censor or ban those patriarchal authors whom we find most offensive. Instead we must find different ways of teaching them that allow us to overcome our negative responses and address the issues positively. We may have already found gender-conscious reading to be liberating on our women writers and feminist criticism course, but we now need to raise questions about the ways in which all texts are 'gendered'. Knowing that all female authors do not write feminist texts, we can consider whether all male authors write masculinist texts. As we move beyond the relatively primitive stage of deploring some of the 'images of women' that we find in canonical texts we can learn how to approach texts which apparently denigrate, marginalise or totally exclude women.

Su Reid begins from the idea that 'female' reading is irrelevant: 'novels are about *people*, for heaven's sake'. But she goes on to delineate some of the problems that arise from ignoring gender when reading classic male texts, her thoughts prompted by a sympathetic male colleague as well as by a male theorist and a male critic. She experiments with the technique of rewriting passages from classic texts, substituting female pronouns for male ones in order to expose the familiar assumptions about gender which underlie the poetry or prose. The next stage is to rewrite or reinvent female characters, at which point, as in the essays in Part II of this book, the personal memories and experiences of the readers suddenly become important, and the debate shifts to questions of the difference between feminine and masculine discourse. Both male and female students find Hélène Cixous' work valuable in allowing them to see femininity and masculinity as aspects of human experience available to both sexes.

Elspeth Graham and Ann Hancock bravely confront the problems of teaching some of the more overtly masculinist or patriarchal writers in the canon: Milton, Orwell and Lawrence. Curiously, all three were in their own time 'oppositional' figures who were by no means content with the world as they found it, but they are by now enshrined in the canons of secondary and tertiary education in such a way that anything short of panegyric from the teacher causes students to feel anxious and uncertain. This is perhaps a more acute problem at A level where, as Ann Hancock says, the predominant assumption is 'that literary study is about reading great books . . . and that a positive approach will be taken to them'. How can a feminist take a positive approach to novels like 1984 and *Lady Chatterley's lover*, and what responsibility does she have to suppress her own abhorrence of the attitudes to women they reinforce if any discussion of such matters will be seen as irrelevant by her students' examiners?

Elspeth Graham finds herself teaching in a more liberal atmosphere at Manchester Polytechnic where she and Margaret Beetham (whose essay appears in Part V) have done much to develop the teaching of gender issues, not just on specialist, optional courses but on compulsory 'core' courses with large numbers of students. Here, she takes on the apparently impossible task of producing a feminist reading, not only of the arch-patriarch Milton but of *Paradise regained*, a text which seems at first sight to exclude any reference whatsoever to women or femininity. Convincingly, she argues that the poem can be read precisely as being 'about' that lack or absence. Using the feminist psychoanalytical work of Melanie Klein and Julia Kristeva, Graham rereads the poem's concerns with personal growth, desire, food, and language in such a way as to offer an alternative and perhaps more interesting poem than the one we thought we knew.

Despite the difficulties we all share in trying to change traditional teaching structures and the worries we have about the appropriateness of assessment procedures, despite the risks we sometimes take of exposing students to uncertainty and insecurity, as feminist critics we must pursue this strategy of putting women and the feminine back into texts and classrooms from which they have too long been excluded. In fact, a gender-conscious approach to male-authored texts can be a crucial educational experience in itself, not just an accessible starting-point for the 'real' work of reading female-authored texts. We do continue to exist within the dominant culture, and before we can change it we must learn to (re)read it without succumbing to its assumptions.

10

Learning to 'read as a woman'
Su Reid

'Feminist writing and reading' is a course-unit of the BA in Humanities at Teesside Polytechnic. It ran for the first time in 1986–7, with twenty-two undergraduates, of whom eighteen were women and most were mature students. Most were specialising in English Literature. They met, in two groups, for two-hour seminars every week for twenty-four weeks. As well as informal papers, they wrote two 3,000-word essays, counting for fifty per cent of the final assessment, and a three-hour examination which included constructing a feminist reading of an unseen passage. This is the story of the course.

I once taught a seminar on Conrad's *Lord Jim* with a male colleague and mostly female students. We were happily discussing the novel's representation of the mismatch of expectation and event, and of the problem of self-definition, and Marlow's limited narrative point of view: my colleague asked us why we were reading a novel in which the only female characters were in entirely subordinate roles, and why we were ignoring this issue. At the time we denied the importance of his question, angrily, and proclaimed that the novel was about *people*, for heaven's sake. Later I decided that his question was valid.

It still remained clear to me that one did not *have* to read anything with an awareness of one's gender, but I saw that to refuse ever to do so was to deny the importance of specifically female experience. It also seemed clear to me that I had been reading with myself cast as honorary man, and that I had been teaching women students to do this too; and that if we had learned to read 'as men', men could also learn to read 'as women'. I designed 'Feminist writing and reading' as a collective attempt to evolve techniques of approaching a text which would involve our defining ourselves, and our hypothetical other readers, as women. Obviously, the theory of reading underlying this is one that denies a fixed connection between 'life-experience' and the text, and posits instead the concept of reading as a learned intellectual activity. I found support for these views and my aims in two works of critical theory by male authors. One was the essay 'Reading as a woman' in Jonathan Culler's *On deconstruction* (1982), which is offered as part of an argument about the construction of reader roles. The other was K. K. Ruthven's book *Feminist literary studies: an introduction*. Ruthven writes: 'Men who get into arguments with women about feminist criticism are often given the impression that they are disqualified from doing so simply because they are men. I find the objection puzzling, given the fact that feminists have put a great deal of effort into explaining the differences between sex and gender . . .' and '. . . it seems to me that whatever else feminism might be, and whatever ends it might think of itself as serving, by the time it enters literary studies as critical discourse it is just one more way of talking about books' (Ruthven, 1984, p. 8).

On this basis, I planned the course to lead up to a practical exploration of 'one more way of talking about books'; we would start by reading a variety of existing feminist criticism and theory, and would then look again at texts from the 'canon of great literature', chosen by the students, and try to read them with the assumption that we were female. What happened was that as we read the feminist theory we began at once to apply it to everything else we read; and we all realised this was not, after all, a mechanical exercise. Instead it seems desperately important, for both women and men.

As soon as we began, we realised the exclusion of women from books. Tillie Olsen's *Silences* gave us the image, both in its catalogues of inhibited or forbidden writing and in its own fragmented form. So of course did Virginia Woolf's *A room of one's own*, with its Milton manuscript inaccessible to a woman, its British Museum catalogue, its imagined Judith Shakespeare. From there on we saw ourselves as trying to recover something hidden or denied.

Other texts gave us more precise examples, and began to teach us that to 'read as a woman' meant that we had to confront and oppose much that we usually do as readers, in order to articulate things otherwise suppressed. The students often found that they dare not transfer our reading techniques into their other courses. The readers of this essay may well at first reject some of its observations as absurd; but we found ourselves bound to make them.

At first we thought Dale Spender's *Man made language* too essentialist in its accusations of male conspiracy, but when we read her account of trying to make a mixed class of teenagers rewrite sentences so as to remove one sex or the other entirely from them (Spender, 1985, p. 159), and tried, heretically, to rewrite familiar passages ourselves, we discovered something. We took part of Wordsworth's 'Preface' to *Lyrical ballads*[1] and, just to see what would happen, put it into the female:

What is a poet? To whom does she address herself? And what language is to be expected from her? She is a woman speaking to women: a woman, it is true, endued with more lively sensibility, more enthusiasm and tenderness, who has a greater knowledge of human nature, and a more comprehensive soul, than are supposed to be common among womankind; a woman pleased with her own passions and volitions, and who rejoices more than other women in the spirit of life that is in her; delighting to contemplate similar volitions and passions as manifested in the goings-on of the Universe, and habitually impelled to create them where she does not find them.

We discovered that 'he' and 'mankind' really do not include 'she' and 'women', because when these words are substituted the passage's meaning is dramatically different: and that this is so because the values and expectations we habitually attach to the female words are different from those we attach to the male. A 'woman speaking to women' is much less respectable than a 'man speaking to men'; a woman who creates 'volitions and passions' where she does not find them is a hysteric where her male equivalent is an artist.

We did the same thing with passages from a novel, from *Lord Jim* indeed. We found that this drew our attention immediately to ways in which familiar assumptions about the genders were essential to the construction of the prose, and of the novel's recurrent theme of the failure of ideals to match or describe experience. As it stands, this sentence, from a passage in Chapter 1 about Jim's childhood, is obviously ironic about his parson father's authoritarian beliefs:

Jim's father possessed such certain knowledge of the Unknowable as made for the righteousness of people in cottages without disturbing the ease of mind of those whom an unerring Providence enables to live in mansions.[2]

But if the word 'mother' were to be substituted, the implication of authority would weaken, and much of the ironic opposition between ideas and events would be lost. The mother would merely be foolish. In a sentence from Chapter 12 the familiar use of female pronouns for a ship is utilised so that the failure of the ship to sink as expected is embodied as Marlow's male exasperation at the stubbornness of the female:

But she turned her back on them as if in disdain of their fate: she had swung round, burdened, to glare stubbornly at the new danger of the open sea which she so strangely survived to end her days in a breaking-up yard, as if it had been her recorded fate to die obscurely under the blows of many hammers. (p. 106)

If the pronouns were male, the ship would be heroic.

This exercise made us realise that in learning to 'read as women' we were not concerned with the author's possible intentions. It simply did not matter to us whether Wordsworth realised or not that his definition of a poet in effect excluded women, or whether Conrad consciously built Lord Jim's mismatches of ideas and events around gender stereotypes. These questions are, of course, legitimate aspects of feminist history; but what we were trying to do was to observe what happens to us when we construct ourselves as female while we read. With these passages we found we had to choose either to acknowledge ourselves as marginal or to ignore the possibility of being female. For the male students this represented a clear injustice; for the women it threatened annihilation.

We did not, of course, proceed to 'translate' all we read in this way. But we decided that our first step approaching any text must be to observe the presence in it of any gender-suggestive words, whether male or female, and to observe the implications of the values that those words carried.

We also began to observe the representation of female characters in narratives. Some of us were reading feminist discussions of the representation of female characters in familiar myth and legend, and especially those in Mary Daly's Beyond God the father and Marilyn French's Beyond power. We all read Joanna Russ's discussion, in the chapter called 'Aesthetics' in How to suppress women's writing, of the distorted representation of women's lives in male-authored narratives: as an example she cites Dickens's Bella Wilfer in Our mutual friend flirting with her mirror, and observes that real women look in their mirrors in anxiety, not in flirtatiousness. Dickens, Russ writes, cannot portray women as women know themselves, but must use his female characters for his own purposes. The woman reader, however, must observe this process and draw her own conclusions about the values of the text. We also read Christa Wolf's Cassandra, in which a brief novel and four essays brilliantly reconstruct the Trojan woman. Starting from Aeschylus's representation of Cassandra in Agamemnon, Wolf observes the values of that patriarchal text, and also reinvents the obscured prophetess, employing her own know-ledge as a German socialist feminist confronting the arms race in the 1980s. She seizes that right.

We decided that in order to demonstrate a perception that women were being misrepresented in any particular text, we had to try to 'rewrite', to reinvent, the female character concerned. This exercise is as contrary to the familiar explicatory techniques of criticism as the rewriting of the Wordsworth and Conrad passages in the opposite gender was; but we found support for it in various feminist works. In particular, Adrienne Munich's essay 'Notorious signs, feminist criticism and literary tradition' (in Greene and Kahn, 1985) proclaims the recoverable exist-ence behind a male-authored text of the female it appears to be written to obscure; Rosemary Radford Ruether in *Sexism and god-talk* rewrites the story of Christ's resurrection so as to recover the experience of the women and demonstrate the values of a male-dominated church.

So we began also to seize the right to reinvent female characters. We found this had two results: it made the women students articulate aspects of their lives; and it made us all define the values of the narrative voice describing the woman. Our discussion of Wordsworth's 'The solitary reaper'[3] shows all this.

We began by making the obvious points about the thinking and observing man and the toiling, observed woman. Then we tried to reinvent her. We considered her song, whose words are incomprehen-sible to the poet but which provides the source of his words. Suddenly the female students produced memories and tales of women singing as they worked, in factories or at the ironing board or cleaning the oven; they were recapturing part of women's history. Then they wondered why her song is 'melancholy', 'plaintive'. The poet suggests it might be about '. . . old, unhappy, far-off things, / 'And battles long ago', which they chose to doubt, or that it might be about personal suffering:

> Or is it some more humble lay,
> Familiar matter of today?
> Some natural sorrow, loss, or pain,
> That has been, and may be again?

The discussion returned to the poet now, and observed that he regarded the domestic suffering as 'humble', less important than battles, and that her song's theme was actually unimportant to him anyway: 'Whate'er the theme, the Maiden sang / As if her song could have no ending . . .'

At this point we considered the second stanza's comparison of her

song to those of the nightingale and the cuckoo, and this led us into a
significant issue in establishing the values of the narrative. We found that
references within a text to legendary figures and to images traditionally
associated with them could, if followed, yield meanings which the
author might well not have been consciously aware of, but which nevertheless exist and are perpetuated in the culture.

Both cuckoo and nightingale have acquired possible sexual connotations in English poetry. The cuckoo connotes betrayal and the
nightingale sometimes happiness, as in Milton's Sonnet I. But the
nightingale is also associated with the legend of the rape of Philomel, and
is evoked as a combined figure of ecstasy and female suffering, as in
Lyly's song from *Alexander and Campaspe*:

> What bird so sings, yet so does wail?
> Oh, 'tis the ravished nightingale.
> Jug, jug, jug, jug, tereu! she cries,
> And still her woes at midnight rise.[4]

Coleridge's 'To the nightingale', written in 1795, invokes the conglomer-
ate image of nightingale, Philomel, sad singing, and his poetic muse. His
later 'The nightingale, a conversation poem, April 1798' dismisses this
image and insists instead that the nightingale be written of as 'merry': but
the later poem makes the nightingale male. 'The solitary reaper' does not
overtly name any of these connotations of either cuckoo or nightingale,
but it does name the birds in the context of a man listening to the
'melancholy' 'plaintive' apparently wordless, but beautiful, song of a
woman. Reading it does invoke a tradition in which a woman's pain is
perhaps somehow vindicated, for a male listener, by the beauty of her
subsequent song – a tradition whose malevolence is perhaps exposed in
Eliot's references to it in *The waste land*.

But then we asked why we had assumed the listener is male. The
answer lay in our assumptions, not in any specific statement in the text.
We had assumed the poem's persona to be male because we knew the
poet to be male, and because we habitually cast the role we had
observed as male.

We had to abandon any remaining assumptions about the self-contained nature of a text and about the unique importance of its author in
its creation. Author and readers were seen all to be part of a process in
which meanings are created: and assumptions about gender roles are
commonly significant in that process.

Our final experiments were with passages presented without the author being identified. In one group, we each brought an anonymous passage and the rest tried to identify the author's sex: the results were only randomly correct. In another group I presented a passage and told the students the author was male: they constructed a convincing reading on that basis. I then told them the author of the same passage was female, and they constructed a convincing but different reading on that basis.

Few of us were actually willing to assert that women's writing is not different from men's; but we had to agree that men and women are articulating themselves, as readers and as writers, with the same gendered cultural artefacts, within a discourse that subordinates the female.

This brought us to a point of debate that remained unresolved at the end of the course, and that was reflected in the students' essays. They wrote these on subjects of their own devising, and I can perhaps best demonstrate the debate by describing and quoting some of them, with their authors' permission.

We began to discuss discourse in terms of some French feminist theory, and especially the readings of Kristeva and Cixous in Toril Moi's *Sexual/textual politics*. It became familiar talk among us in class to label ordered rational discouse, even examination paper rubrics or the Introduction to Culler's *On deconstruction*, 'masculine', and to call disruptive or subversive discourse 'feminine'. Interesting essays were produced demonstrating the relevance of this to various texts, including *Northanger Abbey*, of which Mark Rutter wrote:

What interests me is the way in which the equation between the masculine [Tilney, the narrator!] and the linear, rational, and conscious, and the feminine and the non-linear, non-rational, imaginative, marginal, and repressed unconscious, is made so closely on the lines of those of French feminists, especially Hélène Cixous . . .

When we came to try to 'read' *King Lear* and *Hamlet* in this way we found Marilyn French there before us, and accepted her *Shakespeare's division of experience* gratefully.

But ideas derived from psychoanalysis were most directly useful to three of the men. They used this material extensively in their essays and in seminar discussions through much of the course, and they used it in order to discuss femininity as an aspect of human experience common to both sexes, and therefore available to themselves. Here is Mark Rutter again: 'In positing a masculinity and femininity for both men and women, in making masculinity and femininity non-gender-specific, Cixous gives me a place in the future, a part in the creation of a better world.'

Most of the women, and the fourth man with them, seemed rather to think that this, and further study deriving from psychoanalytic theory, might offer *explanations* of the suppression of those members of society who are labelled with femininity, but that they themselves had more urgent empirical business: they had to recover the articulation, not of 'the feminine' but of women! For the women this was a matter of self-respect; for the man it was a more detached matter of achieving justice.

Many of the women students were therefore eager to seek out and write about women authors, or, in one case, painters, still in the belief that these would inevitably represent women in their work. They discussed Alice Walker, Virginia Woolf, Doris Lessing, Anita Brookner, Margaret Atwood, Charlotte Brontë. Sometimes they wrote with passion, as Juliet Sherwood did when discussing the confrontation with the college beadle in *A room of one's own*: 'The words elevated from the page. I understood. *A room of one's own* hit me in a way that a book has never affected me in my life before. I was so angry. . . . I became acutely aware of the injustice of being a woman. It was so simple that I wondered why I had never reflected upon it before.' But, competent as these essays often were, they were frequently conventional. They were descriptive. The only thing about them indicating that their authors were 'reading as women' was their partisanship.

Some of the women and the fourth man chose to criticise the portrayal of women in a variety of texts. Some tried to reinvent female figures in fairytales, especially in 'The frog prince' and 'The sleeping beauty'; several approached biblical texts, daring to take issue with the narrative voice in Luke's account of the resurrection, for example. Some discussed the representation of women in various novels by both women and men, and one wrote a convincing account of *Jude the obscure* demonstrating the masculinist stance that undercuts the portrayal of the 'new woman' in Sue. Diane Parker tried to 'reconstruct' Mrs Touchett in James's *The portrait of a lady*, and ultimately found it impossible, concluding: '. . . the whole structure begins to crumble, and the underlying theme of the novel is exposed: that is, a male assertion that not only are women powerless to help each other, but that they are the agents of their own destruction.'

Partly, perhaps, because all the men were in the same group, the preoccupations of the two seminars frequently diverged. The all-women group looked for ways of articulating women's experience, and tended to blame men for the difficulties of achieving this; the mixed group was far more interested in considering the role of gender in a more abstract way.

At the end of the course, however, we could all relate these two preoccupations to each other when reading texts, fictional or otherwise, in which overt use is made of gender words. We returned to Conrad, and the question of how to read him. One student, Linda Bruce, attempted a feminist reading of *Heart of darkness* by seeing Marlow as a parallel figure to the feminist trying to articulate her identity in a hostile world that has no language for her. I prefer to see Marlow in both *Heart of darkness* and *Lord Jim* as a male figure failing in an attempt to impose reason on inchoate experience, often represented with female images. Marlow attempts to explain Kurz and Jim, and their adventures are often given female connotations: this is so not only with the Patna but also with Patusan and with Kurz's station in *Heart of darkness*, both reached by a journey up a river, and both associated with women. Jim and Kurz both become sexually active lovers in their private kingdoms. Both are destroyed. At the end of each novel Marlow has withdrawn, almost speechless, and can describe to us only a woman deprived of sexuality. These novels portray Marlow's fear of the disorderly in terms of his fear of the feminine. They make it easy for us to observe this association; they also give the feminine, in the sense of the inchoate *and* in the sense of women, a considerable power. They do not present a heroic male defeating that which he is afraid of.

Our relationship to non-narrative writing without specific reference to either gender remains more problematic, however. If we accept the ideas of Lacan, or of his feminist followers, at all, we perceive rational discourse as 'masculine', and as alienating to those of us who construct ourselves as 'feminine', as being formed in terms of that which the symbolic order denies. But if a text does not provide an overt image of this by using gendered words, metaphorically or otherwise, it is hard to argue empirically that women are still defined in negative terms. We are left with the knowledge that women are frequently excluded as writers, and are misrepresented as objects in texts of all kinds, but we may be unable to explain this except in terms of men's conspiracy.

Julia Dickinson, in her second essay, confronted the naming of women in terms of their fathers or husbands, and went on to contemplate the implications of this until:

the term 'she is a good mother' speaks of everything she is not. It is an opprobrium. It means she is a blocker of creativity, a blocker of light and freedom, someone from whom we must escape before we can become 'our own persons' and enter into the Symbolic Order . . .

So . . . now, I seem to have reached it – bottom line – male fear of women, a denial, a rejection of female power. Fear of reverting to the soft, wet, mewling, helpless object held firmly and securely in its mother's grasp. Separateness becoming a craving, superiority a necessity.

Notes

1 William Wordsworth, 1802 Preface, *Lyrical ballads of Wordsworth and Coleridge*, ed. R. L. Brett and A. R. Jones (London and New York, 1963), pp. 249–50.
2 Joseph Conrad, *Lord Jim* (Harmondsworth, 1957), p. 10.
3 We discussed this poem because of a suggestion by Judith Fetterley, quoted in Russ, 1983, p. 113.
4 *The Penguin book of Elizabethan verse*, ed. Edward Lucie-Smith (Harmondsworth, 1965), p. 174

Male texts and their place in the A level curriculum
Ann Hancock

Feminism has undoubtedly undermined cherished practices in English teaching; we have had to consider afresh the texts we offer students, our approaches to them and the individual responses of students themselves. Some texts which have been perennials no longer seem appropriate or interesting and many hitherto unfamiliar ones are replacing them. However there are limits to the changes that can be made especially if teaching to an A level syllabus or if a course requires CNAA validation. Even without these constraints hazards exist. In a job where male teachers far outnumber female, male colleagues can adopt attitudes which, if not openly hostile, can be restricting. Students too are not always as receptive to change as one might expect. Conflicts within oneself can be debilitating. Having been brought up, as many have, on the practical cricitism of great works, I have found it difficult to establish coherent new strategies for the selection and teaching of texts now that many of the ideas I have long accepted have been challenged. I have only provisional answers to the questions feminism has encouraged me to ask, of which the most pressing concerns the inclusion or exclusion of 'male texts' from literature courses. By 'male texts' I mean those books, and there are many, which are so drenched in male activities and values, and exhibit such contempt for and disregard of women, that a female reader may feel that she simply does not want to study them. This problem is particularly relevant to A level teaching though I shall refer also to degree courses. In both cases the majority of the students I teach are women, often in a proportion of five or six to one, and it seems quite wrong that this fact should be ignored, as it often is, when texts are being chosen. Yet, however strongly I feel about male texts and the omission from courses of so many good women writers, I suffer also from the syndrome Elaine Showalter calls 'divided consciousness' (1979, p. 39), a tension between teaching what one has been taught, with lofty objectivity, and infusing one's teaching with the new awareness feminism promotes.

English A level is studied every year by many students, young and old, male and female, and the content of the courses they follow, although examination boards vary especially in methods of assessment, have much in common. When students I have interviewed talk about their A level books, they tend to be within a very recognisable range. I assume then that the AEB syllabuses which I have encountered, that is, English Literature and English Language and Literature (the latter taught as an evening class) are not untypical. In each case the syllabus comprises the usual list of books prescribed for each paper, from which seven or eight texts overall must be chosen.

Making a choice can be exasperating for a number of reasons. Anyone who decides to favour women writers will be disappointed since, despite the explosion of feminist criticism, the availability in cheap editions of much good writing by women and the growth of Women's Studies courses, on these syllabuses women hardly feature at all. In 1986 and 1987 out of twenty-three texts on the Language and Literature syllabus only two were by women – Vera Brittain's *Testament of youth* and Iris Murdoch's *The bell* – though in addition Christina Rossetti was one of five poets chosen from *Seven Victorian poets*. The opportunity to include Sylvia Plath and Stevie Smith was not taken up; both poets' work is included in *Poetry 1900–1975*, a set book, but neither is on the list of nine poets chosen by the examiners. The omission of Sylvia Plath is a particular loss. Not only does she rate for me as a more important poet than some whose work is required reading, but her poetry is received with great enthusiasm by students, especially women. The Literature syllabus contains nothing written by women in this century, but three well-established nineteenth-century favourites: *Wuthering Heights*, *Mansfield Park* and *Mill on the Floss* (dropped in 1987).

There are some striking ironies in the selection of texts, particularly in the juxtaposition of books by male and female writers. In 1986 Maggie Tulliver jostled with Scobie (Greene's *Heart of the matter*); in 1987 Fanny Price and Catherine Earnshaw sat alongside Marlow and Kurtz. Maggie and Fanny suffer a great deal, usually in silence, repress a great deal and are very good. Catherine Earnshaw is not so good, but of course Emily Brontë was herself an oddity. While these heroines are making themselves miserable and/or dying, their male counterparts are engaged in noble suffering which plumbs the depths of human understanding, getting to the very heart of darkness. While I should not say that any of these books was not worth reading, placed together they reinforce a curious view of the world.

More significant is the matching with *Testament of youth* of 1984 and Thomas Keneally's *Schindler's ark*. These books are readily comparable, especially *Testament of youth* and *Schindler's ark*. They are all about cruelty, injustice, prejudice, about rebellion and risk and war. In this context *Testament of youth* might seem a good choice given Vera Brittain's feminism; her relentless pursuit of education and independence, her determination to participate in the re-making of Britain and Europe after the First World War are admirable. In the past the book has been an inspiration to many women readers but it may be read rather differently today. Students with whom I have read it, and I share their views, find the writing poor and the book rather boring, its effect not helped by the author's portrayal of herself as tediously self-centred, entirely without humour, obsessed with every trivial detail of her admittedly remarkable life.

By the standards of Coombes, whose textbook on practical criticism[1] was for a number of years an A level set text, *Testament of youth* would fare badly in comparison with the other two in terms of the quality of the writing. Coombes's stern Leavisite warnings against the horrors of sentimentality would make it difficult for an A level student trying to apply his critical methods to see as anything but contrived and cliché-ridden Vera's account of the day she learned of Roland's death. In content, too, there are notable differences. The heroism of Oskar Schindler is different in kind and scale from Vera Brittain's; he saved thousands of Jews, she had to cope with the loss of the man she loved (and we're never allowed to forget it). We are encouraged by the writers to admire Winston Smith and Oskar Schindler; although their flaws are evident, their heroic individuality is highlighted throughout. Most students do not in the end feel much admiration for Vera Brittain.

What might be concluded by the proverbial Martian, on studying these syllabuses, is that women don't write much and what they do write is either sentimental and self-indulgent or confirms that it is woman's fate to be frustrated, unhappy and misunderstood. Many men are noble, strong and deep. Others fantasise about having two wives, or better still no wife, and being constantly drunk (*Under Milk Wood*). They pick their mates by way of a speedy and unilateral courtship ritual, marking out strangers who walk innocently down the street (' "That's her", he said':

The rainbow). When they are not doing these things, men write a great deal of poetry and a lot of plays.

If the syllabus is not all that a woman teacher would want, especially if her students are predominantly female, many mature, what can be done with it? In the long term some careful re-thinking of A level English is needed, not only in relation to texts; but in the meantime courses have to be taught. A different syllabus might be the answer, with a wider choice of texts, but these tend to require coursework folders and extended essays which cannot easily be prepared during a one-year evening class.[2] When one teaches an evening class, the temptation is to select those books which can be read with comparative ease and studied in a reasonably short time. Thus Chaucer and Milton are usually avoided and the stress is often on novels. With these thoughts in mind, 1984 stands out as an obvious choice: most students know something of it, there is a film to confuse them completely, study notes abound, it is an accepted modern classic. If the novel is approached disinterestedly, topics for discussion are easily found and it is quite straightforward to guide students towards the questions asked on exam papers. (Is this really what disinterest amounts to?) 'Was Orwell right?' 'How important is Newspeak?' 'Discuss Winston's role in the novel' etc. The same is true of other popular A level texts which I particularly dislike, for instance Lawrence's *Three novellas*, though to prepare seventeen-year-olds, as I have had to, for some questions is daunting. For example, on one paper a quotation from Leavis was presented for discussion in which he wrote of Lawrence's insight and wisdom as being what our civilisation desperately needs. In 1987 it is hard to perceive Lawrence as anybody's saviour. Nevertheless it is not a problem to teach towards the A level exams; the problem comes when such teaching begins to seem inadequate and empty.

I experience this problem quite strongly with 1984. My view is that male and female readers are likely to respond to it in different ways which have to be acknowledged. As a woman I find myself reading it against the grain but this reading does not accord with the accepted wisdom upon which exam questions are based. I shall not attempt a detailed study of the novel here; I should like merely to make a few points about the female characters and Winston's perceptions of them. I am well aware that argument of the kind I wish to pursue is vulnerable to attack. 1984 is a dystopia and so we might expect it to contain events, characters, beliefs which we would see as unacceptable; indeed it is important that we do see them as unacceptable. If Orwell intends that the book serve as a warning of a possible future, we must feel the horror of life in Oceania. The treatment of women might be just one symptom of a dystopian world. Another defence which has been put to me is that the novel is about more important issues than the position of women; woman's plight is not significant in a world where life itself is under constant threat. One could say too that Winston's attitudes are not necessarily to be taken as desirable ones – he too has been contaminated by the Party – or in any way representative of his creator's. No doubt there is still more to be said.

Having heard these sensible points being made, I remain unconvinced. There runs through the novel such an unpleasant undercurrent of contempt for women in all aspects of their lives that I think it important to highlight what is not usually treated to much, or any, discussion – the representation of women. I have suggested that Winston is depicted as a slightly pitiful man (thus an exam question which asked how much the novel gains from Orwell's depiction of Winston as a fallible hero), not altogether admirable, but he demands our sympathy because of the nature of his rebellion. In an appalling world he stands for the last traces, desperately clung to, of a humanity which is finally destroyed when Winston succumbs to Big Brother. However, while Winston fights for the old human values, for love and individual freedom, his attitude to women dehumanises them, viewed as they are through sentiment and fantasy. Whether or not Winston's thoughts accord with Orwell's is not really the point; what Orwell actually thought of women matters little to me. The point is that a female reader, offered such images, may lose all sympathy with both the character and the book.

The most significant female character in 1984 is obviously Julia. The desire which we are to believe develops into love brings Winston hope of a return some time to a world where such relationships are commonplace. I assume that their liaison is supposed to pass for romantic love though the impression one is left with is very different. It's a nice fantasy. Winston has violent thoughts of raping and murdering a girl to whom he is attracted and suddenly she drops him a note announcing 'I love you'. She offers him sexual gratification – 'she was utterly unresisting, he could do what he liked with her' (Part Two, 2) – in a way which reminds us of his earlier greedy longing for chocolate. At the high point of their relationship she dresses up in a 'real woman's frock' and paints her face, an act which atones for the horror inspired by another of her sex, the prostitute whose womanly charms turned out to be fake, very old mutton dressed as lamb. Julia seems to offer everything but apart from being a 'rebel from the waist downwards', as Winston calls her, much to her but not our delight, she is in no way a companion in Winston's fight against the Party. It is pointed out on many occasions that she doesn't think, but merely seeks a good time, and she even falls asleep when Winston reads to her from 'the book'. When they visit O'Brien the latter ignores Julia completely, 'seeming to take it for granted that Winston could speak for her' (Part Two, 8) and does not even notice when she leaves; in this context she is an irrelevance. As a sexual fantasy come to life, Julia has a role but beyond that she is nothing. Winston says of his estranged wife that she had 'without exception the most stupid, vulgar, empty mind that he had ever encountered' (Part One, 6); the only difference between Katherine and Julia is that Julia rejected the indoctrination of the Party against sex. Winston's feelings about these two women seem largely to include only intense desire or violent loathing.

Other women in the novel are viewed from a greater distance. Worthy of attention are Winston's mother, whom he often recalls, and the prole he watches from the room over Mr Charrington's shop; both of them are seen through a haze of sentiment. The mother is a typical martyr figure whose sufferings Winston attempts to ennoble. As he remembers the dreary and painful life of his mother, so he imagines that of the prole 'laundering, scrubbing, darning, cooking, sweeping, polishing, mending, scrubbing, laundering, first for children, then for grandchildren, over thirty unbroken years' (Part Two, 9). He sees her on several occasions, singing a 'drivelling' song, 'tirelessly' hanging out nappies, and despite a superficial understanding of what the woman's life may have been like, he sentimentalises it with his 'mystical reverence'. His view is patronising and for female readers intolerable. 'One has the feeling that she would have been perfectly content, if the June evening had been endless and the supply of clothes inexhaustible, to remain there for a thousand years, pegging out diapers and singing rubbish' (Part Two, 4).

Winston's thoughts about his mother and the prole seem intended to reveal his finer feelings – sensitivity, remorse, compassion, respect. Likewise his fascination with the paperweight in which he sees his life and Julia's 'fixed in a sort of eternity at the heart of the crystal' shows his romantic longing for peace and happiness. However the validity of these feelings is constantly undermined, in ways I have already suggested. Where women are concerned, there are no finer feelings in 1984.

The views I hold on 1984 make me read it sceptically and focus on issues which are not 'obviously' of importance. If I choose to teach it, what responsibility do I have to present to a class, or elicit from them, lines of argument which will prepare them for the exam ordeal? I should not want to suggest that A level examiners expect a York Notes answer or a glib reproduction of notes given by a teacher; examiners' reports stress that they are pleased by fresh responses from students who have not been too rigorously drilled. But relevance is all. Candidates must answer the question and if questions do not invite discussion of aspects of the novel I have concentrated on, they cannot include such material.

There are other problems which quickly become apparent when expressing unorthodox opinions on an A level text. Many A level and degree students arrive at their first class lacking in confidence and with a limited literary background. They expect certain things, firstly, that if a book is on a syllabus, and the teacher has told them to read it, it must be worth reading. What constitutes worth is not something they are at that stage ready to investigate though they seem instinctively to assume that enjoyment is not necessarily a mark of worth, often the reverse in fact. They do not expect that a book will be criticised in such a way as to challenge its status. Having heard my opinions on *Lady Chatterley's Lover*, one third-year degree student asked me: 'If it's as bad as you say, why did you make us read it?' My only answer was to say that I was giving my opinion not definitive truth and there was nothing stopping her reaching a judgement very different from mine. It seems to run deep that literary study is about reading great books, or at least good ones, and that a postive approach will be taken to them.

A second problem concerns the nature of the understanding to which students aspire. On reading 1984 many of them find difficulty with the extracts from 'the book' given to Winston by O'Brien and with the explanation of Newspeak. They need to go through these sections of the novel quite carefully and become involved in lengthy discussions of the meaning of 'doublethink' for instance. Focusing on the representation of women in the novel may seem to them a level of reading beyond what they require.

Finally one returns to the thorny problem of objectivity. If one does not claim to be giving an objective view of a book but presents an informed personal response which may not accord with what the students read or hear elsewhere, is a dive into total chaotic subjectivity inevitable? I often find myself telling a student who is making a simplistic connection between literature and life, or has an intuitive response that seems to me wrong, based on misunderstanding, that he or she will have to think again. How do I make a distinction between my individual appraisal and theirs? It makes what is always difficult in teaching literature, drawing boundaries around 'right' responses, that much more difficult.

There is though a very much more positive side to the problems I have outlined above. Adopting a critical or hostile attitude arouses students to think for themselves and question ideas in a way which they might not otherwise. It is common for some A level students to go through an entire course simply absorbing everything that is said to them without any engagement with the texts they are studying. I have found that my statements about 1984 and other male texts, for instance Russell Hoban's *Riddley Walker*, in which two marginal women exist in a world of men as objects of fear, have provoked extremely profitable discussion. More generally, this approach shows students that there are many ways for books to be 'good' or 'bad' and forces them to examine the easy assumptions they rely on concerning the evaluation of set texts. Degree-level students can gain the confidence to make their own assessments and to realise what criteria they are bringing to bear in making them. A level students, as the year progresses, often find it easier to express their views if the teacher reveals a preference. For those students going on from A level to a degree course an awareness, however undeveloped, of the state of literary criticism in the 1980s can be important.

Perhaps it is possible to integrate male texts into courses without denying the wide range of reactions students and teachers may have to them. The alternative would be to avoid teaching 1984 and others like it altogether. I said once to a male colleague in a moment of exasperation that I thought 1984 should not be the standard O and A level text it has become. He accused me of censorship. However the exclusion from literary courses of scores of women writers seems to be perceived as censorship only by students who have, as they see it, been deprived of the opportunity to study texts written by women which they have discovered for themselves. When does exclusion become censorship? For myself I should be happy to see a number of standard works by male writers quietly disappear; and indeed some of them have already been removed from the degree course on which I teach. Leavis thought life too short to read J. B. Priestley; I certainly haven't the time to read any more D. H. Lawrence. On the other hand there are a great many women writers I would bring in to courses or give more prominence to, especially contemporary ones. Might I then be merely replacing Leavis's quaint idiosyncrasies with my own? When does personal choice become good judgement, or is 'judgement' a word no one uses any more?

The limitations of a syllabus save one from confronting the full implications of the problem of choice. When devising a degree course, the problem cannot be evaded. I have often thought that many books are selected for courses because (a) the teacher likes them and (b) the teacher has plenty to say about them, that is, a favoured critical approach can be successfully applied to them. Remaining books tend to be there because they always have been. When contemplating change, feminists can obviously take several directions. First, one can make strenuous efforts to achieve a better balance of male/female literary works on courses and make one's views known on offensive male texts. Alternatively one can opt for women's literature courses taught by and almost always for women. The old arguments recur. Up to now, I have preferred the former strategy in the belief that all students should be exposed to the broadest possible range of texts and opinions. Thus we have no courses specifically on women's writing. I have always feared that, especially in a small college with small groups of undergraduates, the existence of such a course would allow everyone to sit back comfortably and conclude that nothing further need be done. My mind is not closed on the matter however; the greatest contribution feminism has made to teaching, for any teacher who is not a completely lost cause, is its attack on complacency.

Notes

1 H. Coombes, *Literature and criticism* (London, 1953).
2 We have on occasions considered the alternative AEB syllabus, which allows greater flexibility in choice of texts, but because more and more of our students opt for part-time A level courses, it has not seemed practicable. However, it remains a possibility.

12

Feminist teaching and masculine modes:
Paradise regained as an instance
Elspeth Graham

The thoughts and questions I want to set down here mainly come out of my experience in teaching in a polytechnic English department, where a great deal of my work has been concerned with developing the teaching of gender issues – not on women's writing courses, not even on optional courses, but on compulsory core courses, both in literature and culture studies. But I teach, too, for the Open University where I have no influence on syllabuses or material and on a university part-time degree course, where I have little influence in syllabus planning. So, in this essay, rather than describing a single set of circumstances, I conflate ideas stimulated by teaching in all these institutions. Teaching as a feminist, much preoccupied with the centrality of gender issues to all thought, on courses that are not, either in their mode or content, exclusively informed by feminist literary thinking, has raised issues for me that variously seem crucial, stimulating, agonising, fruitful and unanswerable . . . And it is in this general context that I should like to speculate on one strand of feminist English teaching: on the implications of taking feminist ideas into mainstream core-course teaching.

Perhaps it is useful to say something here about the make-up of the sort of courses I refer to. Some are taught in relatively intimate groups of twelve to fifteen. More typically, courses are large (from thirty up to 120 students). They are taken by both women and men and they are taught by both women and men, working closely together in teams, sitting in on one another's lectures, sometimes co-leading seminars. And as these are also, sometimes, interdisciplinary courses, matters of sexual difference are compounded with differences of discipline and the intellectual modes, academic and pedagogic approaches and expectations that arise out of them. I think particularly, here, of our 'common courses' at the

Polytechnic, taken jointly by students on English Studies and Historical Studies degrees, which aim to challenge discipline boundaries and query assumptions about the nature of English and History as disciplines. These assumptions often, initially, take the form of conscious or unconscious perceptions of history (identified with concern over political structure, institutional and constitutional change, with 'factual' truth) as a 'hard' discipline; of English (concerned with the imaginative, the wacky, the artistic, the fictional) as a 'soft' discipline. The metaphors need no elaborate reading! Such distinctions may be reinforced by the differing ratios of men to women, as teachers and students, in the disciplines. The questions raised by teaching of this sort differ from those I would see as surrounding the teaching of women's writing courses, for, although the issues arising from teaching women's writing are complex, some concerns may be identified fairly definitely: such a course will, I assume, be taught by women and may set out to consider women's articulations of themselves, women's constructions of meaning, phantasies, strategies of representation, positions within the symbolic . . . in brief, will take women as its starting point. To this extent, perspective is clear.[1] On courses established with quite different objectives and with a more dispersed focus, other considerations may be dominant. Further than this, though, my own concern to establish feminist thought and practice as integral to such courses, difficult enough in many ways, has been intensified and brought into particularly sharp light by my teaching (and research background) in seventeenth-century writing.

In this area, there is clearly and initially, the difficulty of the lack of women's texts. Restoring the feminine is especially problematic in the seventeenth century and earlier. So, the retrieval of women's writing from this period is a crucial project. Then, this acknowledged, we may turn to the question of how women are represented (by men) as the next area of scrutiny. But the larger question of the relation of the feminine and feminist to the masculine/masculinist is only touched on here. And central problems remain about how we read seventeenth-century texts produced by men. How do notions of masculine and feminine texts relate to the sexual status of an author? Is a text produced by a man necessarily masculine? (And if we shift into discussion of masculine and feminine discourses, do we so alter the grounds of debate that we lose the political aim of feminism?) Are neutral readings possible? *Are* there ungendered issues? To what extent is it desirable or legitimate to bypass issues of gender in the interests of exploring ideas in other ways? These are familiar enough theoretical questions but they take

on new colourings when we face them as questions about course planning and teaching method. In so far as the seventeenth century is concerned, the extent of women's exclusion presents these matters in peculiar ways. For example, although women's and men's roles and identities
were heatedly and often anxiously debated and women did, indeed,
make public interventions, it is probably true enough to argue, as Catherine Belsey does, that 'from the discourses defining power relations in the
State, women were simply absent'.[2] Do we collude in this exclusion by
taking texts that explore or define sovereignty on their own terms and
talk of seventeenth-century notions of power without stressing the lack
of reference to women? Do we simply (and with constant repetition,
this easily becomes reductive) point to the absence of women, and no
more? Or do we, in turn, exclude such texts from our courses,
redefining what is of interest in the period? In doing this might we lose
much that is important? And if we retain many conventionally valued
texts do we present these as masculinist texts, integrating a concern with
gender and other ideological factors, showing how all ideological factors
intersect and mesh even with the aesthetic and affective? In short, do
we privilege gender, allow for non-gendered issues or try to do it all at
once?

This last – which is for me, in this context, the most intellectually and
ideologically tempting (but also demanding) option – carries with it any
number of potential dangers. There is the possibility of it all turning out
as a hotch-potch, a pluralist accumulation of bits and pieces, a literature-
history brew with a dash of feminism thrown in. Or if, by premissing the
course on a set of post-structuralist theories, we consider 'the politics of
the sign' as a conjuncture of the historical, social, experiential, gendered
and aesthetic, we run the danger of collapsing the course into theory-for-
its-own-sake. Then the very weight of this theory can bear so heavily that
primary texts are squeezed into position merely as illustrative material.
We may all be de-pressed into frightened despair at the thought of
another few runs-through of Althusser, Lacan, Kristeva, Foucault and Co.
And we may end up more concerned with twentieth-century metatexts
than with the seventeenth century. All of this has been much and
elegantly debated elsewhere and full discussion of such issues is beyond
my scope here.[3] But I point, if no more, in their direction, since they
become very real, daily anxieties when struggling with the attempt to
accommodate feminist thought and revisions of what is meant by 'literature' within the constraints of fairly traditional teaching structures still
demanded in many contexts.

But I mention them, too, because they relate to my own research interests in the seventeenth century, with which (for me, at least) all of this began. All the queries I have about *teaching* in this field are intensified and coloured by my own self-pondering in relation to my preoccupation with seventeenth-century writing. During the whole period I have been teaching and struggling with the issues I outline here, I have also been involved in what I have come to refer to (not so jokingly) as my 'affair with Milton'. It is because of this that I want to turn from these questions in the abstract and to use *Paradise regained* as an instance and symbol of these problems.

Paradise regained, like *Paradise lost*, seems interesting on several counts. Firstly it presents a pedagogic challenge: teaching Milton is never easy. Many students find his poetry inaccessible, alien, representative of both a lost and an elitist culture. Questions about why we should teach Milton at all, secure in the canon as the father of subsequent mainstream poets, are present from the start. How to teach his poetry is another problem. Such matters are then compounded with feminist considerations. The 'anxiety of influence' engendered by Milton for men writing after him has often been seen as doubly inhibiting and disabling for women writers.[4] In general, Milton's place in cultural tradition, his poetic status, his overtly patriarchal cosmological myth, biographical snippets (his apparently misogynistic relationships with his three daughters, his troubled first marriage) add together to suggest that Milton is indeed the great patriarch and defender of patriarchy (however noble some of his concessions to the companionship of marriage as evidenced by the Divorce pamphlet and his depiction of Adam falling for love of Eve may be). Milton's apparent immersion in patriarchal and masculinist structures might easily suggest that his works can provide an archetype for any attempt to ask questions about what a feminist does with masculine texts. At the very least Milton might be used to show what we are up against. But I think looking at Milton can do more than that. His writing raises more interesting questions than simply those concerned with identifying the *power* of patriarchy – whether Milton is seen as a source of literary anxiety, or as the great depictor of the secondary place of women in the human dimension of the cosmos, or as defender of an all-powerful-God-the-Father.

But my teaching strategies must start with reactions of this sort, for it seems to me that *Paradise regained* is interesting precisely because it marginalises women characters literally: Mary indeed, only appears at the beginning and the very end, at the edges of the poem. There is no other feminine figure or reference to any in the poem. It is a poem concerned with the relationship of the Son to the Father (and hence all sons to all fathers). Centred in this relationship, the poem can be read not as a defence of patriarchy but as an analysis of that central relationship. The very exclusion of the feminine becomes a crucial lack and one that ultimately seems to me to be the poem's subject. Predicated on shifts of relationship between Father, Son and failed son (Satan) the poem psychologises theoretical and political issues, revealing their interconnections and the implications of a lack of a full feminine principle in patriarchal structures: personal, mythic, doctrinal, political. *Paradise regained* brings together various interests, then. It serves as a paradigm of many of my concerns with the seventeenth century. Because of the intensity of the Father/Son relationship it focuses religious, ontological, political, psychological and gender issues extraordinarily sharply and opens up possibilities of discussion about gendered identity, gendered writing, in both general and in historically specific contexts. And it is at this point that speculation (sometimes private, but kept in mind; sometimes public and confessional) about my own interest in Milton can be useful. For, in spite of all the difficulties presented by Milton, his work never ceases to absorb and fascinate me. Why is this? What attraction does his work hold for a twentieth-century feminist? My own engagements with the texts interest me: I identify, have sensuous pleasure in the verse, feel an erotic attraction for Miltonic heroes. What is going on here? Attempts to share attractions with (and disengagements from) Milton's writing with students, and to relate those to constructions of gendered identity pose useful questions of then and now (that is, of history), of consciousness, unconsciousness, cultural institution and literary process. By problematising his writing as simultaneously alien and attractive, historically close and distant, the difficulties of Milton are legitimated but, I hope, transformed into a matter of interest, open to scrutiny.

Paradise regained, in its very choice of Christ, a 'greater man', as hero, seems to announce itself as trans-historically psychological – hence, perhaps, its allure – but it also bears witness, quite clearly, to a precise historical moment. It has strong generic connections. It contains many ingredients of conversion narrative, depicting spiritual crisis as a key moment in a life that proceeds towards truth and right relationship with God. 'Truth', in it, is revealed as self-knowledge: *being* the right thing rather than doing it is all-important. As such, it relates to other Renaissance writings on the 'self', to the growth of individualism, to questions about post-Restoration quietism (for instance, whether this is political retreat, waiting, or a more complex articulation of the relationship of the personal and political?) The poem, however, does not entirely follow conventional patterns of either spiritual biography or meditation: neither the causally ordered, linear-structure of Puritan spiritual autobiography nor the metaphoric structure and sense of stasis of traditional meditation. Yet it has something of both of those. Famously, there is no event in the poem: it is largely dialogic. The debates between the Son and Satan, which make up the body of the text, in fact take place in the interstices of event, geographically symbolised (as well as psychologically and spiritually) by location in the wilderness. (The choice to focus on and explore this particular biblical episode, rather than any other in Christ's life, is fundamentally significant, of course.) Yet the psychic and spiritual manoeuvrings formulated in the Son/Satan dialogues are bracketed by event. The initial six-times narrated Baptism, or naming of the Son and statement of his role and his relationship to God the Father, presents the complex of issues that are to be disentangled. The almost incantational repetition of accounts of the Baptism of the Son, by different voices, in Books I and II, establishes this event as symbolic, something to be interpreted. It is the Son's task to understand the meaning of the words pronounced from heaven, 'beloved son' (PR I, 285) and the prophecies and foretellings of the coming of the Son of God, to internalise and integrate their meanings. Explicitly, he states:

> O what a multitude of thoughts at once
> Awakened in me swarm, while I consider
> What from within I feel myself, and hear
> What from without comes often to my ears,
> Ill sorting with my present state compared. (PR I, 196–200)[5]

Inner/outer dualisms, which later slide into being/doing oppositions, in the discussions of political role in Books III and IV, are set up. Since the Son, referred to by the Father as 'This perfect man' (PR I, 167), also has the ultimate in ego ideals, this inevitably takes the form of a struggle for psychic integration. The poem charts this process, culminating in the moment when the Son can vanquish Satan by naming him: 'Get thee behind me; plain thou now appear'st / That Evil One, Satan for ever damned' (PR IV, 193-4). The Son's attainment of absolute masculine poise is then (rather obviously) further symbolised in his balancing on the pinnacle, in the course of the final temptation, while Satan falls from it. The Son's ambiguous, 'Tempt not the Lord thy God' (PR IV, 561),

referring to both himself and the Father as God, enacts his arrival at a
position of shared authority with the Father. So, for the Son, the process
embodied in *Paradise regained* has involved the interpretation of a naming
(the Baptism), episodes of psychic exploration, which are simultaneously verbal exploration, and arrival at a moment when he can name
both himself and Satan (what he, the Son, is not) and thereby master (I
use the word carefully) all that Satan represents. Satan, whose self-given
task, he tells the Son, has been to:

> learn
> In what degree or meaning thou art called
> The Son of God, which bears no single sense;
> The Son of God I also am, or was (PR IV, 515–18).

fails to progress in hermeneutic skill. The meaning of 'Son of God' and
the nature of the Son's kingdom remain baffling: 'Real or allegoric, I
discern not' (PR IV, 390) he agonises to the end. The sense he has of the
indeterminacy of his own and the Son's relationships to the Father, his
inability to accept, variously, authority, possibilities of change,
movement or to fully distinguish self from other (he has a curiously
mutable, protean appearance, he lacks substance and boundary and is
constantly associated, here, as in *Paradise lost*, with the illusory, delusory,
hallucinatory), are revealed as failure to relate, to negotiate signifying or
hermeneutic processes.

At the back of my mind, while I give this sketch, is the aphoristic
summary Lucan gives of the psychoanalytic process: 'The subject begins
the analysis by talking about himself without talking to you, or by talking
to you without talking about himself. When he can talk to you about
himself, the analysis will be over.'[6] If we apply this concept here, Satan
never becomes either the signified of his own discourse, nor is he able to
make sense of whom he speaks to. Phatic, affective and addresser/
addressee relationships elude him, too. But the Son, in attaining right
relationship with the/his Father and by identifying Satan, takes up a
position within the symbolic – and this is where the peculiar intensity of
issues in *Paradise regained* is so interesting – that identifies him AS the *logos*.
His personal utterance becomes biblical quotation (in the response to
Satan given above: PR IV, 193–4; 515–18), he becomes the word of God,
the rational plan of the universe, the psychological blueprint for mankind, the creative medium of the Father, the expressed Truth, or as
Milton puts it, the 'living oracle' (PR I, 460), all in one go. Milton's
phallocentric analysis of the construction of phallogocentrism is not too

distant, maybe, from Lacan's, in our own century. But as we know, and as Milton knows, too, language and relationship are not simply predicated on negotiations of father/son relationships. There are maternal and feminine principles to be negotiated, as well.

Notoriously, obviously and crucially, Christianity, especially orthodox seventeenth-century Puritanism (with which Milton partially aligns himself) presents this problematically. The event which finally closes *Paradise regained*, the briefly mentioned return of the Son to 'his mother's house' (PR IV, 639) appears especially significant in this light. So, too, does the first set of temptations by Satan: temptations of desire, not directly sexual (that would be too crass, Satan has argued to Belial) but to appetite, symbolised by food. In his holding fast against both temptation to turn stones to bread and to partake in the Satanically conjured Banquet, the Son's resistance is articulated in his association of oral functions, linking food with words. He accuses Satan:

> The other service was thy chosen task,
> To be a liar in four hundred mouths;
> For lying is thy sustenance, thy food (PR I, 427–9)

and then defends himself: 'Man lives not by bread only, but each word / Proceeding from the mouth of God' (PR I, 349–50). Good food becomes truth, spoken and lived; bad food is equated with sin and distortions of the verbal, both lying and a tendency to understand things too functionally or too literally and so failing to recognise metaphoric truths. We find that amongst the foods presented by Satan, in the Banquet temptation, there are some forbidden by Mosaic Law, although Satan denies this, perhaps with intent to trick the Son. What is interesting, here, is that the Son refuses to enter into discussion of whether the foods are legal or not, to enter into debate on legalistic terms. Instead, he extends the meaning of the word 'right' beyond legalism and rejects the food on the grounds of the giver, so refusing the relationship implied in the giving of a gift, and since the gift is food, in the offer of nurture or 'sustenance'. Such a method of refusal is important in various ways. It establishes a method whereby the Son *never* offers an absolute statement of what is right or wrong in legalistic terms, never offers a manifesto. (The famously worrying denials of political power and of learning in Books III and IV make sense only if read as strategic or positional statements, part of a series of manoeuvres in relationship with Satan, not as dictats – we need to read the Son's pronouncements in terms of structural development, not simply at the level of content.) It enacts a shift from Judaic

codes of legal/illegal to a New Testament notion of internalised sin. But it
also introduces sticky problems of relationship and maternal/paternal
function. By turning from legalistic prohibition (the Law of the Father) to
good food/bad food, rightness of self/sin, good words/lying oppositions
– all in the context of a series of temptations that take place in the absence
from Mary, certain coalescences and displacements become evident.

The poem, here, shouts an invitation to psychoanalytic reading. And
John Broadbent, for instance, has, indeed, read *Paradise regained* as an
anxious expression of incestuous desire for the mother on Milton's
part.[7] This seems both a useful and a limited view. Broadbent bases his
reading partly on a sense that 'the temptations objectify sexual interests'
so 'their rejection allays the taboo anxiety'.[8] I am not at odds with this
recognition that the poem enacts a working-out of the relationship of the
Son to the mother (although I might not identify Christ with Milton quite
as easily as Broadbent does). But I would want to complicate his Freu-
dianism and stress the themes of absence and loss that inform *Paradise
regained* as well as *Paradise lost* and consider the use of food symbolism.[9]
Here, a feminine or feminist psychoanalytic theory yields particularly
interesting ideas. It might be particularly direct to turn to Melanie Klein's
depiction of the dyadic mother/child relationship which instigates feelings of good and bad objects, associated with the presence and absence
of the breast, which, introjected and projected in various patterns, in
conjunction with processes of splitting and identification come to
inform senses of self and other, structuring the depressive, paranoid-
schizoid phases and positions and so on.[10] Or, moving beyond object-
relations theory, we might consider *Paradise regained* in the light of Julia
Kristeva's theorising of the relationship of the semiotic to the symbolic
and her insistence that the structures of the symbolic are articulated
upon, intermixed with, modified and disrupted by the semiotic.[11] Here,
we might move from the articulation of relationship to the material in
terms of content or structure, to matters of language and to consider the
reputation of *Paradise regained* as the most 'plain' of Milton's long poems,
often displaying obsessional, sometimes tautologous, features. Stylisti-
cally, there is an apparent assertion of the symbolic as rational, non-sen-
suous, fixing and linear. This is at odds with other features of the poem,
particularly those features which can be linked with Quaker belief. The
practice and doctrine of seventeenth-century Quakers emphasised a
notion of reaching inwards towards a core of spirituality that could be
experienced and communicated non-verbally, or through disruptions of
the verbal (through 'quaking' or silence). This all suggests a 'poetic'

attunement to the workings and disruptions of the semiotic.

I do no more than sketch these ideas here, since my aim is not to present a 'finished' reading of *Paradise regained*. Rather I hope to suggest ways I may think and talk about the text that can lead into questions of femininity and masculinity and the reformulations of patriarchal power that emerge in the seventeenth century. It seems to me that Milton's writing, however consciously or unconsciously, however anxiously, evidences a sensitivity to the implications of a masculinist mythology, theology, social and political structure that is worthy of our attention – even of our sympathetic attention. The absence of the feminine in dominant ideological formulations needs to be analysed in terms of damage done to constitutions of masculinity as well as femininity and to make evident the confusions of gendered identity which patriarchy offers us all. It is not just a matter of crudely suggesting that God-the-Father, nurturing through word-food-truth, becomes awfully like God-the-Mother in *Paradise regained*, or that there is no way round the absence of the feminine in seventeenth-century Protestant thinking, or that *Paradise regained* is one of any number of conventionally highly valued texts which deal with this absence by confirming it. This text is, I believe, more complex in its articulation of masculine/feminine structures. In part, it does seem to define achievement of masculine maturity as arrival at a point of completeness, self-sufficiency beyond desire, absolute presence. But it is equally clear that this cannot be entirely so and that the masculine, too, is a function of desire. (Milton is good on the loneliness of God, even He feels loss and desire in this way . . .) Reading the confusions, recognising the absences of *Paradise regained*, maybe even accepting it as a poem that mourns the feminine as much as *Paradise lost* can be seen to, allows us to ask questions about the seventeenth-century, particularly about radical dissent which is often seen as a feminisation of orthodox Calvinist Puritanism.[12] And it enables us to consider, too, our own immersions in patriarchal traditions – psychological, literary and cultural. Our own gendered, cross-gendered, non-gendered identifications with and attractions to aspects of the text can be scrutinised.

If this provides a sense of the sort of issues that underlie my desire to include such texts on mainstream courses, and gives some sense of what I hope to get out of them, it also must be said that ways I have of reading Milton also come out of my experience of teaching in the sort of context I have described. *Paradise regained*, on a course like this, is read alongside texts which present concepts of gender quite differently. We read conduct manuals, autobiography, political theory, ballads and jest-books and popular narratives, theological treatises and medical textbooks. And these are read in the context of discussion arising from twentieth-century historical theories of gender, the construction of the family, women's legal positions. Here, different methodologies (using 'literary' texts or demographic techniques, for instance) are assessed. In this way we hope to complicate and historicise concepts of gender.

In all of this I have gained immensely from working with historians. Most of all, though, working in mixed groups has been stimulating, although occasionally alarming and difficult. I am encouraged by recognising that many students, young women and mature women students, arrive with a much greater assurance in talking in seminars about gender positions and sexuality than I used to have. Centralising gender as a challenge to traditional ways of reading literature, through reconsiderations of revered masculinist texts and as a way of confronting discipline expectations, serves to make visible and authoritative in a wider arena, what women have been learning. This is vitally important. But there is still a long way to go. In teaching texts of this sort, in this context, different sensitivities are needed from those appropriate to teaching in a women-centred context. I remember blunders and errors of judgement where I have failed to recognise uneasiness and resistance surrounding the discussion of gender and sexuality in formal contexts. Sometimes people have simply absented themselves. Sometimes there has been uneasy silence. But just as tellingly, I recall too, one occasion when, while I was lecturing on the body and notions of femininity and sexuality in the seventeenth-century, in a hot stuffy lecture theatre, I paused to take off my jumper. The glazed expressions and silent note-taking which I had attributed to the boringness of my lecture (not one of my liveliest performances) suddenly gave way to a roar of giggles, whistles and shouts. Embarrassment has its aggressive and defensive forms, of course, but I was astonished. In spite of the sophistication of much theoretical discusssion in seminars, such an episode reminds me that these are still delicate but urgent issues that need confronting.

Times are hard for those of us who would like to refashion teaching structures in fundamental ways. Current economic and political constraints inhibit or deny many possibilities of revolutionising conventional structures of teaching, academic authority, assessment. For many years I exclusively favoured development away from traditional course structures and lecture-plus-seminar formats. And I still remain anxious about whether and how work on issues such as notions of gender should be assessed. At times, it seems the political ambitions of feminist teaching are quite lost through its incorporation in mainstream core-course teaching. Feminism, concepts of gender and sexualities have simply been recuperated into a mesh of new orthodoxies – schemes of ideas to be learned well to achieve good marks, to please. But more often advantages gained by such a legitimation of feminist thinking outweigh this, I think. A formal course that raises questions about the very nature of what we are doing and our inheritances often leaves teachers and students alike with uncertainties and insecurities, but it reminds us, too, of the seriousness and the centrality of those insecurities to our habits of thinking and feeling. It is more than revisionism. One day it will be unthinkable for people in a lecture hall to resort to whistles to express themselves. And, at a moment when all the changes we have fought for in teaching practice, as well as in understanding and legitimising a diversity of sexualities and gendered identities, seem under strong attack, teaching a text such as *Paradise regained*, also written at a moment of apparent defeat, may have its impact.

Notes

This paper touches on questions that have arisen out of work I have shared with many others and I should like to thank all of them. In particular, my thanks go to all whom I have worked with on culture studies courses in the Department of English and History at Manchester Polytechnic. Above all, thanks to my good friends and colleagues Margaret Beetham and Pam Watts. Thanks, as well to members of Northern Network who heard a rather different version of this paper and whose stimulating responses are still with me.

1 For an account of the sorts of questions concerning teaching women's writing that I have in mind here, see Margaret Beetham, 'Between the Polytechnic and the Station or "Oh! The difference to me" ', *Literature and History*, 13, no. 1, (spring 1987), pp. 95–103. This paper, like both the papers Margaret Beetham and I are contributing to *Teaching women*, arises out of work undertaken in our department. In my paper here, I concentrate on course content and general issues. This is intended to complement Margaret Beetham's contribution which focuses to a greater extent on actual seminar teaching strategies.
2 Catherine Belsey, *The subject of tragedy: identity and difference in Renaissance drama* (London and New York, 1985), p. 149.
3 Discussion of such issues is dispersed through much recent writing on teaching English and on teaching feminism or Women's Studies. The journals of 'Literature, teaching, politics' recurrently address such questions and the special Education Issue of *Literature and History*, 13, no. 1 (spring 1987) is devoted to these considerations. Peter Widdowson, ed. *Re-reading English* (London, 1982) is also useful, as is Dawn Currie and Hamida Zazi, 'Academic feminism and the process of de-radicalisation: re-examining the issues' in *Feminist Review* No. 25 (spring 1987), pp. 77–98, which summarises some recent, related debates in Women's Studies.
4 The phrase is Harold Bloom's: *The anxiety of influence* (New York, 1973). In their chapter on

Milton, 'Milton's bogey: patriarchal poetry and women readers', Gilbert and Gubar, *The madwoman in the attic* (New Haven and London, 1979) extend Bloom's argument and apply it to women writers. It is views, such as theirs, of Milton as the great masculinist that I want to think round.

5 All references to *Paradise regained* (referred to in the text as PR) are from John Carey, ed., *Milton: complete shorter poems* (London, 1968).

6 Jacques Lacan, *Ecrits* (Paris, 1966 edn), p. 373. Trans. and quoted by Anthony Wilden, *System and structure: essays in communication and exchange* (London, 1972), p. 21.

7 John Broadbent, 'The private mythology of *Paradise regained*' in J. A. Wittreich, ed., *Calm of mind: tercentenary essays on 'Paradise regained' and 'Samson agonistes'* (Cleveland and London, 1971).

8 John Broadbent in *Calm of mind*, p. 83.

9 My favourite analysis of symbolism related to food and part-taking in Milton's writing is Geoffrey Hartman's essay on *Paradise lost*, 'Adam on the grass with Balsamum' in *Beyond formalism* (New Haven and London, 1970). Herman Rapaport, *Milton and the postmodern* (Lincoln, Nebraska and London, 1983), considers all Milton's poetic writing to be a 'work of mourning'.

10 The most useful summary of Melanie Klein's ideas that I know is Juliet Mitchell's 'Introduction' to and selection of Melanie Klein's writings *The selected Melanie Klein* (Harmondsworth, 1986). For a discussion of relevant theories of food symbolism and identification derived from Freud, see Jacqueline Rose, *Sexuality in the field of vision* (London, 1986), pp. 181–2. Most importantly, I would read *Paradise regained* in the light of Julia Kristeva's *Powers of horror: an essay on abjection* (1980), trans. Leon S. Roudiez (New York, 1982), especially Ch. 5, '. . . qui tollis peccata mundi', on abjection, dietary taboos, sin and Christianity.

11 Julia Kristeva, *Desire in language: a semiotic approach to literature and art* (1977), ed. Leon S. Roudiez, trans. Thomas Gora, Alice Jardine and Leon S. Roudiez (London, 1981). Useful summaries of Julia Kristeva's ideas, I find, are: Allon White, ' "L'éclatement du sujet": the theoretical work of Julia Kristeva' (University of Birmingham Centre for Contemporary Cultural Studies, 1977) and the essays of Alice Jardine and Donna C. Stanton in Miller, *The poetics of gender* (New York, 1986).

12 See, for instance, Richard Bauman, *Let your words be few: symbolism of speaking and silence among seventeenth century Quakers* (Cambridge, 1983). Assumptions about masculine and feminine theology colour much writing on seventeenth-century religion. Christopher Hill, for example, notes: 'Milton's theology was as masculine as Crashaw's was feminine. He thought of God as 'a most indulgent Father governing his church as a family of sons" ', *Milton and the English revolution* (London, 1977), p. 269.

Beyond the boundaries of 'English'

Introduction to
Part Five

The interdisciplinary nature of feminist teaching has been apparent throughout this book (perhaps most obviously in Part III). Most of the courses described contain non-literary works and most, almost by definition, contain non-canonical works. Feminist teachers are not only proposing an alternative canon of lost or undervalued texts and rereading the traditional canon but also find themselves at times challenging the very idea of a canon and the conventional ways in which 'English' has been constructed as a subject.

This in itself is not new. 'English' is already very broadly defined in many institutions so as to include not just the study of English language and literature but linguistics, drama, the study of foreign literatures (notably American, Irish and Commonwealth) and even film, television and media studies. Progress in interdisciplinarity has however varied in different institutions. It has often been difficult and slow in the more traditional universities with their commitment to single-subject departments and single-subject degrees, but easier and faster in the more flexibly structured newer universities and polytechnics. We need also to re-train ourselves as teachers, since many of us are products of the single-subject degree system and must acquire a grounding in history, philosophy and sociology before we are competent to handle what now seem important aspects of the texts we teach. These issues are not exclusively feminist ones, but in this section all four essays are concerned in different ways with specifically feminist modes of extending and developing the canon.

To Alison Easton, and indeed to anyone who has taught American literature, it is apparent that the American canon is more problematic than the British canon: the myth of American-ness behind it, created at a specific time and place, is masculinist and exclusive in the extreme, ignoring the work of Black and working-class writers as well as that of most women. Compared with the relatively simple task of setting up a women writers' course, the business of reforming the American canon seems daunting, both in the energy required to overthrow current assumptions and in the practical frustrations of the non-availability of texts. Easton's account provides a very useful survey of work already done in this area as well as a description of the trials and errors of her own practice.

While we may not be surprised to be told that British students begin by knowing very little about either American history or American literature and are consequently unusually dependent on what their teachers tell them, it is perhaps more of a shock when Gabriele Griffin reveals in her essay that her British students are equally ignorant of what 'should' be in a course on Victorian literature. Offering them an alternative canon containing predominantly female authors, she finds that they do not even notice the gender bias and that they are much less conditioned by notions of the canon than she is as the teacher. Obviously this renders it much more difficult to involve them in making meaningful choices about the construction of the course. Focusing on the teaching of Harriet Martineau's *Deerbrook*, and on her own reasons for choosing that text, Griffin explores the contradictions of the father-identified woman and challenges traditional assumptions about the relationship between ideology and literature. While the actual text may not seem as far outside the standard canon as some discussed in this section, the line of argument pursued problematises the 'records of choices' represented by both canon and courses.

Susanne Greenhalgh notes the special problems for the feminist teacher of drama, given the widespread notion of the theatre as a 'public' space and hence inappropriate for women. The dismal record of women's absence from the theatre as writers, directors, or even equally valued performers is however at last beginning to change and women are beginning to occupy that empty space. In doing so, they are developing specifically feminine forms – 'work that employs the circular rhythms of myth and religious ritual rather than linear patterns of conflict and self-discovery'. There is a striking resemblance between the distinctions made here and those made between male and female autobiographies in the essays in Part II: in both areas women are not only requiring access to male forms of artistic expression but are changing and adapting those forms for themselves. Not surprisingly, when this is done in a pedagogic context, problems arise about examination and assessment and about the dominant role the teacher/director finds herself playing in relation to her students.

Throughout this book, specific teaching situations have frequently been evoked, but nowhere more vividly than in Margaret Beetham's 'realist fiction' about a particular seminar held in a particular oddly-shaped room of a particular nineteenth-century building in the 'decaying industrial centre of Lancashire' on a particular grey Monday afternoon in February 1987. While interdisciplinary study here has itself been institutionalised by becoming part of the compulsory course, students still experience uncertainty, both about the non-canonical texts they are faced with and about the ambiguous authority of their 'nutty' feminist teacher. The immediacy of the setting serves to emphasise the difficulty of discussing the construction of gender when it might involve the deconstruction of our familiar selves, and the whole enterprise of feminist teaching seems at once exciting and depressing, powerful and fragile.

13

With her in Ourland: a feminist teaches nineteenth-century American literature
Alison Easton

Like many a feminist critic before and after me, what I most wanted to do first was set up a Women Writers course. Such a course resembles Charlotte Perkins Gilman's utopian *Herland* – a feminist enclave at the edge of the patriarchal academic empire, a utopia probably without male colleagues and possibly even without male students, where only texts by women are discussed and by a kind of critical parthenogenesis women without the aid of men produce analyses of the writings of women.

But Gilman's novel had its sequel, *With her in Ourland*, and likewise the feminist critic has sooner or later to leave her entrancing academic Herland to confront all the other established mainstream courses which she and her non-feminist colleagues teach, and like Gilman's heroine asking those naive but devastating questions about the United States, she will find herself querying the version of literary history which these courses embody.

It is this encounter which I want to explore in relation to my experience of teaching pre-1900 American literature. It raises interesting questions about received conceptions of American literature, but I offer it also as a case study of the pedagogical implications of feminism on the traditional literary canon. It has also been striking how different my experience in this area has been from the simple business of setting up our Women Writers course, where there had been no canon or non-feminist colleagues to negotiate, and questions of critical theory were a conscious part of the course.

I blush to admit that I had been contentedly teaching the same American survey course for at least eleven years before it began to give way under pressure from my burgeoning feminism in the early 1980s. This particular course 'covers' (or so we liked to say) American literature in

English from its seventeenth-century New England beginnings to 1900. It has attracted forty to sixty students a year, and as a result it is taught by three lecturers (myself and two male colleagues), sharing out the lectures and teaching separate seminar groups. These colleagues would not call themselves feminist critics; they are generally supportive but basically their interests and methodologies lie elsewhere, and yet together we have to agree on a syllabus. It's a testimony to the fascination of these texts that they never went stale for me in all those years in which there was little change in what we taught or how we approached it.

This approach was a perfectly standard one, typical of those reared on 1960s critical versions of American literature, nurtured by such classics as *American renaissance* (F. O. Matthiessen, New York, 1941), *The American novel and its tradition* (Richard Chase, New York, 1957), *Symbolism and American literature* (Charles S. Feidelson, Chicago, 1953) and their many critical offspring. What the students got was cultural criticism in a rather vaguely defined sense: by close literary analysis of particular texts, we sought to show how a particular canon of texts reflected, explored and questioned what we, with a wonderfully all-encompassing generalisation, called 'The American experience'. This essentialist and totalising enterprise was achieved through an attention, for example, to themes, images, myths and certain cultural ideas as expressed in literature, backed up with a fairly rapidly sketched-in and highly selective version of history (most British students have practically no knowledge of American history or its earlier literature). This social, political and intellectual 'context' remained rather semi-detached from the texts.

There was nothing remarkable about all this. The course, like many other similar ones here and in the United States, simply and directly reflects the rationale behind the deliberate construction of the canon itself in the 1930s and 1940s. The literary history of the United States has been written comparatively recently, and unlike its British counterpart its choice of texts has not been validated by some supposed Arnoldian 'test of time' or Leavisite 'Great tradition' or Eliot-inspired revisionism – indeed a number of American 'classics' are notorious for being rejected by their contemporaries, neglected for years or going unpublished until this century. American critics could not turn to a supposedly longstanding tradition against which to assess the worthiness of a particular text for inclusion in the canon (a characteristic procedure for a time in Britain). Instead the American critic attempted to assess the 'Americanness' of a text and to judge it on its success in seizing on this assumed essence of the nation. Any resemblance to the Committee of Unamerican Activities is not purely coincidental, for although many of these 1940s and 1950s critics were far from right-wing, their enterprise was fed by postwar nationalism as well as influenced by the New Critical aesthetic. It was a criticism blind to its own and the texts' ideological bases because it assumed that the literature it admired transcended its original social and historical context and achieved some universal Americanness.[1]

As the authors of Rewriting English have remarked about such so-called liberal criticism, 'beneath the disinterested procedures of literary judgement and discrimination can be discerned the outlines of other, harsher words: exclusion, subordination, dispossession'.[2] The canonical texts for nineteenth-century America represent a political choice by a privileged group: those white male middle-class English-speaking critics chose authors almost entirely of their own race, sex, class and language, and called this 'American' literature. It is true that these authors undoubtedly felt an alienation from their culture, but even this reputed radicalism can be challenged: they still had access to some of the power which their class, colour and sex afforded them. The myth of America which their texts are seen to construct, reflects both their own specialised situation, needs and contradictions.[3]

Traditionally critics have described the myth as one of individual selfhood achieved in difficult negotiation with a mass democratic society, and hence often achieved only when alone (or nearly alone) in a natural unspoiled wilderness. As most critics have acknowledged, without fully pursuing its implications, women tend to enter the texts merely as representatives of the conformist oppressive forces of civilisation which the hero must separate himself from; it has been assumed about women that 'their gender made them part of the consensus in a way that prevented them from partaking in the criticism'.[4] Blacks and native Americans feature either as the good companion of the solitary hero, or as faceless victims, or as symbols of destructive forces at large in the nation. The working class of this rapidly industrialising nation (by 1860 one in every seven Americans worked in mines and mills) features not at all with the exception of fleeting references by Whitman and Thoreau and, far more substantially in a seldom-taught Melville tale, 'The Tartarus of maids'.

So, in comparison with British literature of the same period, I was confronted with a canon which is for the greater part exceptionally masculinist, which excludes women writers and, in some of its examples, is overtly misogynist let alone implicitly racist and class-ridden. One survey found that in fifty introductory courses in American literature offered at twenty-five colleges in the United States, only seven of the sixty-one most frequently taught authors were women, and of these only Dickinson appeared more than a mere handful of times and even she featured in only twenty of these courses. Black authors fared even worse – only five cited in all, none of them female.[5] Paul Lauter cites further valid examples in *Reconstructing American literature*: two courses at prestigious institutions, one on 'The American literary imagination' (thirty white male authors plus Dickinson and a poem by Moore), and the other 'Life and thought in American Literature' (twenty-three white male authors and Dickinson).[6] Anthologies and bibliographies are similarly culpable.[7]

There's nothing new, of course, in seeing this male bias in 'classic' American Literature; it was recognised in 1960 by Leslie Fiedler in *Love and death in the American novel*, though he was concerned with castigating the inadequate manhood of the heroes rather than deconstructing the images of the female.[8] Twain and Cooper are obvious cases, and Poe's disturbing use of women is part of the same complex. And yet, despite this recognition, most of these texts have gone on being offered as an expression of some essential experience of life deemed to have *universal* significance and positive value. These experiences were ones with which we were therefore all asked to identify in a Whitmanesque fashion ('And what I assume, you shall assume'). The female reader has a hard time of it: Judith Fetterley's *The resisting reader* has argued the case for female readers who are customarily asked to identify themselves with the male protagonist in his rejection of the female and the world she is supposed to represent.[9] There has undoubtedly been a tendency to argue that those classic locales of American fiction – the wilderness, ocean, battlefield, raft on the Mississippi or hut at Walden Pond – represent a more profound engagement with life on earth than the domestic scene which this canon so ignores or distorts.

So far this was familiar ground to me, but as a literary critic turned feminist I could hardly now just take note of it yet again and then carry on with the same old course. My first move was pure tokenism: one lecture on nineteenth-century women's history crammed with the names of women writers the students were not going to get to read on the course – at that time Dickinson and Bradstreet reigned alone with the very occasional appearance of *Uncle Tom's cabin*. Not surprisingly the frustrated students were not grateful for my efforts. I then saw two options which promised change, but which, as I'll discuss presently, were ultimately as problematic as the problem they sought to resolve. I began a re-visioning of the standard authors and conventional images of the culture they are purported to embody, and I also planned the introduction of new women authors into the canon. I proceeded in a piecemeal fashion, each successive year seeing a few more revisions and adjustments as I tried out, especially in lectures, the feminist New Look – it was evolution, not revolution.

The problem is, of course, that both these strategies left the idea of the canon itself untouched or merely modified. None the less the cumulative effect of all this has ultimately been to reveal to me the old order as a fiction undermined to the point of collapse by a new history. It appears that the writing had been on the wall for me right from the start, for long ago in 1979 I happened unsuspectingly on Rebecca Harding Davis's remarkable industrial novel Life in the iron mills (published in 1861). It cut a swathe through my received ideas about the history of the American novel: that social realism begins after the Civil War with people like Howells, and that earlier we had 'major' romance writers who were not able to deal directly with social reality (Lionel Trilling had magisterially declared, 'American writers of genius have not turned their minds to society').[10] Further bewilderment swiftly followed on learning that Harding Davis had been influenced in her desire to record the working-class lives she could see from her window by Hawthorne's supposedly 'sentimental', 'minor' sketches of ordinary life (my training had led me to dismiss such pieces as 'Little Annie's ramble'); furthermore, Hawthorne so admired Davis's novel that he came out of profound retirement to entertain her.[11]

My revisions to the content of the nineteenth-century course proceeded to confirm this initial unease. For example a reconsideration of the myth of the frontier has led me, under the influence of Annette Kolodny's two studies, The land before her and The lay of the land, to identify the gender bias in this traditional image, and hence to make a distinction between male and female myths of the frontier (I find this also illuminates twentieth-century texts such as Cather's My Antonia and its final garden images). A distinction can possibily be made between male and female responses to the natural world: to identify nature as female now seems a response with particular and peculiar consequences for the male writer and male characters whose images of nature as 'virgin' or 'mother' suggest power fantasies of rape or infantile gratification.[12] The American Adam, always problematic, is no longer such a seductive figure.

Notoriously, the domestic world is absent or to be escaped from in classic nineteenth-century texts, so much so that when for the first time I gave students two short stories by women writers dealing with this setting (Mary Wilkins Freeman's 'A New England nun' and Charlotte Perkins Gilman's 'The yellow wallpaper'), they initially did not know how to respond: these versions of female experience which suggested a celebration of housekeeping as artistry or the imprisonment of the woman within the patriarchal household, wouldn't fit into the patterns of interpretation the students had hitherto picked up from other texts.[13] On the other hand the students on our Women Writers course had no difficulty at all with the same texts (as an experiment I tried it on both courses). Nowadays my reading of The scarlet letter should prepare them for such ways of seeing these stories: Hester, and Hawthorne's analysis of her society and its power structures, became clearer for me when I considered Puritanism and its God as forms of patriarchy. I teach this novel now partly as the clash between woman and a deeply warped patriarchy whose fantasies of power originate in a fear of the body, especially the female. As Michael Colacurcio has argued, Hester, far from being the 'safe conserving force the seventeenth and nineteenth centuries decreed her to be', makes us recognise the 'anti-social meaning of self-conscious female sexuality'.[14]

I find that students will now question both Twain's particular construction of 'sivilisation' in Huckleberry Finn and the implications of Thoreau's view of 'housekeeping' (traditionally women's work) in the first chapter of Walden. Though I admire Thoreau's challenge to the economic order, I note how he writes women out of the text – it took the 1960s Canadian novel, Joan Barfoot's Gaining ground to rewrite his experiment in female terms – with such devastating effects on her heroine's family that the reader probably responds more ambivalently to her absorption with the wilderness than to Thoreau's. We see how Huck's flight from society is expressed as an escape from the manipulation of the women who are made to represent but surely do not constitute the real power in that world. I also savour Jane Tompkins's observation in Sensational designs that the reputedly sentimental and fantasist domestic fiction written by nineteenth-century women actually explored very accurately the painful realities of the female child who cannot run away; in contrast, Twain's reputedly realistic novel has a consistently improbable escape plot.[15]

As for Melville, I want to move beyond simply wondering at those who take the womanless Pequod as a paradigm of all human societies, though it may indeed symbolise his own contemporary world which feminist historians have shown to have been sharply divided into male and female 'spheres' of existence and where women were excluded from the public realm.[16] 'Warn all gentle fastidious people from so much as peeping into the book', wrote Melville humorously to a woman friend, yet qualities associated by the nineteenth century with the feminine are introduced into his all-male naval texts as a necessary opposing element to the 'masculine', most notably in the figure of Billy Budd. And can we see the form of Bartleby's refusal to participate in the rituals of patriarchal legal and economic structures – 'I prefer not to' – as typical of the female who cannot light out for the territory?

Whitman's verse ostensibly militates against these nineteenth-century gender divisions, and for that reason he had always had more to say to me about the ideal of the autonomous self than the male heroes of other standard novels of the period. It was therefore with regret that I came to question what I had defended in the past: his assumption, indeed presumption, that he speaks for both men and women. He expresses women's sexuality entirely in child-bearing terms – breasts and wombs (all too typical of the social constructions that Whitman so proudly saw himself rejecting) into which the male 'pours his meaning'.[17]

Dickinson is the only woman whom the canon had been able, by ignoring her sex, to assimilate into its structures of meaning. But here my efforts to privilege her gender made for problems as well as interpretative insights. I enthusiastically rehearsed Adrienne Rich's arguments in 'Vesuvius at home': that Dickinson remained unmarried and a recluse in order to foster her creativity and this is expressed in masculine terms in her poetry, the Master figure not being some actual male acquaintance but a male muse.[18] The students enthusiastically played these complex notions back to me in an over-simplified form in essays and exams and I grew wary of the reductiveness I had given birth to, even though the ideas had opened up the meanings of some poems as never before and directed my attention to others which Ted Hughes's Faber selection (the only available British edition with the correct text) had not found space to reprint. I encountered the same kind of feminist over-reading in students' accounts of the Freeman and Gilman tales mentioned above. Having argued too hard for the artistry of Louisa's celibate housekeeping, I began to long for a more ambiguous reading which might include my view of the text but also reflect the complexity of Freeman's picture; instead I had produced a simple set of new counter-culture heroines and a new orthodoxy.[19]

So I have found a feminist analysis a powerful tool in getting familiar things into sharper focus, without necessarily having to see them only from this perspective. At first I feared I'd come to dislike some much beloved texts (the involvement of the female critic in male texts is something to be explored positively rather than merely suspected or seen in oppositional terms). A certain resistance to these works has offered an even greater complexity and has brought me into a fuller relation to them. These feminist approaches form only part of a larger critical enterprise at present engaged in rethinking American literary history. This considers not only gender but race and class as integral to textual analysis and has moved away from the limited repertory of the classic canon. It argues for a more complex mediation between text and the social order, indeed redefines 'literature' and 'history' by simultaneously insisting on 'the historicity of the texts and the linguistic, expressive dimensions of historical experience', and it has come to focus on ideology as a key problem in this area.[20]

The other area of my reforms – the would-be introduction of non-standard figures – has also been helped by recent critical efforts. Given the work of reclamation which has gone on, rediscovering and republishing work by women, there is a wealth of material clamouring for consideration: essays by Margaret Fuller, novels by Harriet Beecher Stowe, Rebecca Harding Davis and a host of popular domestic fiction writers, tales by Sarah Orne Jewett, Mary Wilkins Freeman and many others, Kate Chopin's works, some Black writers (slave narratives such as Harriet Jacobs's 1861 *Incidents in the life of a slave girl* and the first Black women's novel, Harriet Wilson's *Our Nig*, published in 1859), and so on.

Much of this was of course previously known, but has required re-evaluation. For example, the demeaning term 'local colourist' which relegated Freeman, Jewett and Chopin to the 'Minor' league, needs to be discarded or positively reclaimed. Women were America's earliest realists. Freeman's stories reveal, as Marjorie Pryse points out, strong alternative paradigms for American experience in a New England world 'transformed into a quasimatriarchal one by Civil War casualties and emigration of its remaining young men',[21] Jewett's tales of the New England coast, *The country of the pointed firs*, also offer us revisionary versions of familiar themes. They focus on the lives of the women left behind at home by the whalers; whereas *Moby Dick* told us nothing of Ahab's wife and child left behind on 'the treacherous, slavish coast', here it is the men who disappear into the sea and silence, and the women who, even in post-Civil-War America, find a positive, pastoral vision.[22]

Cheryl Walker has argued about nineteenth-century women's poetry, that 'The problem is we don't know how to read their poems', because it is difficult to analyse 'the effect of patriarchal domination on the way women themselves describe their experience'.[23] Only Dickinson seems to have transcended the limiting stereotypes in which women poets expressed themselves, and it is important to know something of them to see the context and terms in which Dickinson would have been expected by her culture to conceive of herself.

More problematical is the possible inclusion of speeches and manifestoes (for instance, abolitionist and suffragist), autobiographies, letters, journals and diaries (for example Alice James's and Mary Chestnut's are both available in Britain), work songs, children's literature. To include these would at least acknowledge that these, along with popular domestic fiction, were the available forms of writing for women largely excluded from the production of the kind of literary works which would fit more easily into the traditional canon's definition of 'literature'. After all our courses on seventeenth- and eighteenth-century literature have always included this kind of material; and besides, the distinction between 'literature' and 'not literature' is one not recognised in most of this period. Judith Fetterley's excellent anthology of pre-1865 writing, *Provisions*, argues that, rather than the novel, these women writers produced their 'best work in other forms – the letter, the sketch, the personal essay, the newspaper column, short fiction'.[24]

Then again, how do we understand and evaluate texts which are so different from the canon as we have it and which do not necessarily meet its criteria of 'stylistic intricacy, psychological subtlety, epistemological complexity' (Tompkins, p. 126)? I have found that Uncle Tom's cabin makes a good representative of this kind of fiction (it also has the merit of being easily available in Britain). Tompkins argues that 'twentieth century critics have taught generations of students to equate popularity with debasement, emotionality with ineffectiveness, religiosity with fakery, domesticity with triviality, and all of these, implicitly, with womanly inferiority' (123). This however was a literary world which saw nothing wrong with didacticism and the sentimental in its serious novels, and it is important for students to take this on board. There is a female tradition in American literature, and Jane Tompkins's account of Uncle Tom's cabin (pp. 122–46) is a triumphant example of reading a text within this different sexual, literary, social and political context in order to appreciate its devastating critique of American society.

The teacher, however, faces a different problem from these critics: is there space on this course to include some of this unfamiliar material which so changes the way we look at the familiar? I don't now feel like Ellador in Ourland, but more like Alice in Wonderland at the Mad Hatter's Tea Party where three creatures (all male) are seated who say it is their table and shout 'no room, no room'. Unlike Alice, I don't see lots of empty seats at the curriculum table. I've tried cutting out Poe and Cooper and giving Emerson very short shrift, but it's hard to contemplate omitting many other classic male novels of the period. Furthermore, some of these books by women are either too expensive in a world where student grants have lost a fifth of their value in the past five years, or not easily obtainable in Britain. I can't even make my own photocopied selection of Dickinson's poetry which reflects her use of women's topics and images because her poems, published long after her death, are still in copyright. Much other material, rediscovered in the last decade and not easily available in its scarce nineteenth-century editions, is still under printers' copyright. I have talked in my classes about the works discussed above, but I'll need a special anthology before I can have my students read more than a tiny selection of this material.

Even if we could include everything, the problem of organising this material remains.[25] In this situation I commend *Reconstructing American literature: courses, syllabi, issues* (edited by Paul Lauter) which offers examples of sixty-seven actual courses in American colleges which have attempted to solve the problem of what and how one teaches American literature once one takes off the blinkers of the established canon. (Obviously the needs, experience and opportunities are different on this side of the Atlantic, but its suggestions are stimulating.) It makes it clear that all this is much more than a solely feminist revision of a traditional course. It has become an attempt to recast radically what we want to call American literature so as to represent the culture in *all* its multiple differences.

Notes

1 For a full discussion of these issues, see Sacvan Bercovitch, 'The problem of ideology in American literature' *Critical Inquiry*, No. 12 (1986), pp. 631–53; Russell Reising, *The unusable past: theory and the study of American literature* (New York and London, 1986); Myra Jehlen, 'Introduction: beyond transcendence', in *Ideology and classic American literature*, eds. Sacvan Bercovitch and Myra Jehlen (Cambridge, 1986), pp. 1–18; Nina Baym, 'Melodramas of beset manhood: how theories of American fiction exclude women authors', in Showalter, 1985(a), pp. 63–80; and William C. Spengemann, 'What is American literature', *Centennial Review*, No. 22 (1978), pp. 119–38. See also Lilian S. Robinson, 'Treason our text: feminist challenges to the literary canon' in Showalter, pp. 105–21.
2 Janet Batsleer, Tony Davies, Rebecca O'Rourke and Chris Weedon, *Rewriting English: cultural politics of gender and class* (London, 1985), p. 30.

3 See Robert Clark, History, ideology and myth in American fiction, 1823–52 (London, 1984), p. 3.
4 Baym, p. 69.
5 Paul Lauter, 'A small survey of introductory courses in American literature', Women's Studies Quarterly, No. 9 (winter 1981), p. 12.
6 Paul Lauter, ed., Reconstructing American literature: courses, syllabi, issues (Old Westbury, New York, 1983), p. xii.
7 There have been many recent attacks on the inadequacies of bibliographies and of anthologies on which most college teaching is based in the States. See for example Reising, pp. 18–31; and Deborah S. Rosenfelt, 'The politics of bibliography: women's studies and the literary canon' in Joan E. Hartman and Ellen Messer-Davidow, eds., Women in print I: opportunities for women's studies research in language and literature (New York, 1982), pp. 11–36.
8 Leslie Fiedler, Love and death in the American novel (New York, 1960).
9 Judith Fetterley, The resisting reader: a feminist approach to American fiction (Bloomington, Indiana, 1978).
10 Lionel Trilling, 'Manners, morals, and the novel' in The liberal imagination (London, 1961), p. 212.
11 Olsen, 1979, pp. 52 and 78.
12 Annette Kolodny, The lay of the land: metaphor as experience and history in American life and letters (Chapel Hill, N. Carolina, 1975), and The land before her: fantasy and experience of the American frontiers 1630–1860 (Chapel Hill, N. Carolina, 1984).
13 Interestingly, Gilman's contemporaries also had problems in understanding her tale. See Annette Kolodny, 'A map for rereading: gender and the interpretation of literary texts', in Showalter, 1985(a), p. 51. The entire essay concerns itself with this general problem.
14 Michael J. Colacurcio, 'Footsteps of Ann Hutchinson: the context of The scarlet letter', English literary history, No. 39 (1972), p. 472. See also Nina Baym, 'Thwarted nature: Hawthorne as feminist' in American novelists revisited: essays in feminist criticism (Boston, Massachusetts, 1982), pp. 58–77. David Leverenz, 'Mrs Hawthorne's headache: reading The scarlet letter', Nineteenth century fiction, No. 37 (1983), pp. 552–75 offers a more ambivalent reading along similar lines.
15 Jane Tompkins, Sensational designs: the cultural work of American fiction, 1790–1860 (New York and Oxford, 1985), pp. 174–5.
16 See, for example, Barbara Welter, Dimity convictions: the American woman in the nineteenth century (Athens, Ohio, 1976); Ann Douglas, The feminisation of American culture (New York, 1977); Nancy F. Cott, The bonds of womanhood: 'woman's sphere' in New England, 1780–1835 (New Haven, Connecticut, 1977).
17 For an analysis starting at a similar point see Sandra M. Gilbert, 'The American sexual poetics of Walt Whitman and Emily Dickinson', in Reconstructing American literary history, ed. Sacvan Bercovitch (Cambridge, Massachusetts, 1986), pp. 123–54.
18 Adrienne Rich, 'Vesuvius at home: the power of Emily Dickinson' in Rich, 1979, pp. 157–83.
19 See Helen McNeil, Emily Dickinson (London, 1986) for a feminist analysis which avoids these pitfalls.
20 Bercovitch, 'The problem of ideology', p. 640. For theoretical discussions of these new critical directions, see the whole of this essay and Reising, The unusable past. For examples, see Tompkins, Sensational designs; Bercovitch and Jehlen, eds., Ideology and classic American literature; Lauter, ed., Reconstructing American literature.
21 Majorie Pryse, 'Introduction' in Mary Wilkins Freeman, Selected stories of Mary E. Wilkins Freeman (New York, 1983), p. viii.

22 Majorie Pryse, 'Introduction', in Sarah Orne Jewett, *The country of the pointed firs' and other stories*, ed. Mary Ellen Chase (New York, 1981), p. xx.

23 Cheryl Walker, *The nightingale's burden: women poets and American culture before 1900* (Bloomington, Indiana, 1982), p. 1.

24 Judith Fetterley, *Provisions: a reader from 19th-century American Women* (Bloomington, Indiana, 1985), p. 14. For discussion of women's domestic fiction, see Nina Baym, *Women's fiction: a guide to novels by and about women in America, 1820–1870* (Ithaca, New York, 1978). Three collections of nineteenth-century women's stories available in Britain (unlike *Provisions*), and all edited by Susan Koppelman, are *Old maids: short stories by nineteenth century U.S. women writers* (Boston, Massachusetts, 1978); *Between mothers and daughters: stories across a generation* (New York, 1985); and *The other woman: stories of two women and a man* (Old Westbury, New York, 1984).

25 Michael J. Colacurcio, 'Does American literature have a history?', *Early American Literature*, No. 13 (spring 1978), pp. 110–12 points out the absurdities and lack of rationale in present teaching practices.

14

Beyond the canon:
Harriet Martineau's *Deerbrook*
Gabriele Griffin

The context

Harriet Martineau's Deerbrook is not part of the current canon of Victorian literature. This was just one reason why I chose it as the opening text for a one-year option course on 'Victorian literature' for third-year BA students. Published originally in 1839 it has its place, chronologically speaking, somewhere in 'the desert' between Jane Austen's novels and those of George Eliot and the Brontës where, so literary history would have it, nothing happened in terms of women's novel writing.[1] The text thus points out the ph(=f)allacious nature of a canon whose negative consists of assumed gaps, fissures, absences.

There were a number of other reasons for choosing Deerbrook. For one thing, as a feminist I feel committed to promoting women's writing on the courses I teach. A case of definite and considered discrimination in favour of . . . Introducing texts that have fallen outside the parameters of the canon of Eng. Lit. and syllabuses of educational institutions affords the opportunity to ask the question why this has been so, to look at cultural politics, issues concerning the marketplace (until Virago republished Deerbrook and Martineau's Autobiography in 1983 her work was simply not available in cheap editions that students can afford), and so on in relation to gender. It allows one to foreground marginalisation.

Choosing Deerbrook was also a function of what might be termed a feminist paedagogy, more specifically, a desire to begin the course in such a way as to maximise student participation at the stage of course construction. One of the failings of higher education courses that I have become increasingly aware of is the lack of control students on them have over the structure and content of what they are supposed to take in.

One result of this is that students on undergraduate courses (lacking interest in what they are doing because they have no investment in it, no control over it) appear to develop in the main a learning strategy centred on exam success. Attendance and reading become selective, a function of how useful for passing exams any particular aspect of their course is. Worse than this, however, in my eyes, is the fact that by not involving students in the construction of the courses they take they are kept in a state of dependence on their teacher, existent authority structures are maintained with all that that implies about the distribution of power in the classroom, students are prevented from learning about democratic processes, responsibility, self- and other-assessment, negotiation, and so on, all the things, in fact, that provide practical and transferable knowledge for interactions outside the classroom. At the same time, student satisfaction remains minimal.[2]

It is, of course, not possible to choose in a vacuum,[3] and certain parameters were set by the course being on *Victorian* literature, and by the time available (one two-and-a-half hour slot per week over a whole academic year). Within these constraints, however, students were to have the choice of what topics we would pursue and which texts we would read. Other ways of increasing student participation in terms of course construction might include presenting students with alternative 'menus' to choose among, giving them the option of doing projects either individually or in groups (a more self-directed form of learning), giving them choices concerning learning strategies, asking them to construct essay titles and exam questions. One danger, of course, with giving students as much choice as possible is that they may well choose topics/texts, learning strategies, etc. that one oneself for some reason does not want to deal with. It is a risk I feel one has to take; after all, the lecturer, too, has a voice in the classroom and can argue her case. If she cannot 'get through' to students she ought to ask herself why this is so, and might want to offer this question up for discussion in the classroom.

The text. In order to facilitate the initial choice about topics/texts we started the course by reading *Deerbrook*, which is both a relatively early Victorian text, and very *Victorian* in terms of its style and subject matter. A number of concerns which are central to much of Victorian writing are surfaced within it: its central characters are middle-class (the reason, why, apparently, John Murray refused to publish the novel);[4] its male protagonist is a doctor, the prototype for many subsequent medical heroes such as Lydgate in George Eliot's *Middlemarch* and Fitzpiers in

Thomas Hardy's The woodlanders.[5] Among the issues explored in the text (which does not necessarily mean that a critical analysis is offered) are the relationship and relative merit of town and country, the clash between a democratised voting system and a hierarchical, quasi-feudal, rural community in which the individual is expected to vote according to the political persuasion of the biggest landowner, the social role of religion, the relationship between poverty, ignorance, and superstition, the social and political power of the middle classes as well as their potential for moral leadership, and the problematic of middle-class women's economic dependence on men.

As far as gender is concerned Deerbrook is of interest for three interconnected reasons: Martineau's treatment of women, her views on women writing, and the text's central moral concern of redemptive suffering.

Martineau's treatment of women. Martineau portrays women in a range of social roles and functions, all of them conventional, and defined primarily through their relationships (economic, sexual) with men. If the women are single (always involuntarily; their lives determined by their need to support themselves) they run schools, shops, or are governesses. If they are married they are characterised by their (in)ability to make good wives and mothers. Generally speaking, men are portrayed as rational creatures (compare, for instance, Mr Grey's and Mr Rowland's behaviour relative to that of their wives) who manage to resolve conflict and rivalry in a non-confrontational manner (witness the resolution of the sexual rivalry between Hope and Philip over Margaret, or the professional rivalry between the two doctors Hope and Walcot) whereas women, especially Mrs Rowland and Hester, are presented as emotive and irrational. At one point, Martineau unleashes a quite astonishing diatribe against those whom she calls, 'the unamiable', referring, as is clear from the context, to women (a fact not obliterated by her use of the masculine pronoun), '. . . of all mortals, none perhaps are so awfully self-deluded as the unamiable . . . the unamiable – the domestic torturer – has heaped wrong upon wrong, and woe upon woe, through the whole portion of time which was given into his power, till it would be rash to say any others are more guilty than he' (pp. 210–11).

One has to agree with Valerie Kossew Pichanick 'that Martineau failed to create a new image of woman in literature',[6] and this despite the fact that Martineau's own life – as a single woman and celebrated writer who, according to her own description, was 'lionised' by London society – was atypical for a woman living in Victorian times. One has to ask why this is so.

Martineau's views on women writing. In *Deerbrook* the figure of Maria Young is used to reveal the plight of the impoverished single middle-class woman, seeking to make a living. In conversation with another woman in a similar position, Margaret Ibbotson, Maria vividly describes the limited possibilities an educated woman has to earn her keep (pp. 448–9). One of the few options open, to write (Martineau, of course, herself chose that option after her father's bankruptcy and death) is dismissed by Maria suggesting that to write for pecuniary ends is doomed to failure:

. . . there are departments of art and literature from which it is impossible to shut women out.[7] These are not, however, to be regarded as resources for bread. Besides the number who succeed in art and literature being necessarily extremely small, it seems pretty certain that no great achievements, in the domains of art and imagination, can be looked for from either men or women who labour there to supply their lower wants, or for any other reason than the pure love of their work. While they toil in any one of the arts of expression, if they are not engrossed by some loftier meaning, the highest which they will end with expressing will be, the need of bread. (pp. 448–9)

Clearly, the above contradicts Martineau's own experiences, and, again, one has to ask oneself why she chooses to advance this viewpoint.

Martineau's central moral concern in *Deerbrook*. In her *Autobiography* Martineau commented, 'I believe it [*Deerbrook*] to have been useful, not only in overcoming a prejudice against the use of middle-class life in fiction, but in a more special application to the *discipline of temper*; . . .' (vol. 2, p. 116; emphasis added). The text's central moral concern is thus with the management of one's temper which, so Martineau suggests, is achieved through self-discipline (amounting in *Deerbrook* to self-denial) and adhering to one's sense of duty. Self-discipline and doing one's duty will carry one through periods of suffering, so the text would have us believe. Thus Hope, when he decides to marry Hester against his emotional inclinations, does so because 'He had pledged himself to act strictly according to his sense of duty. His consolation, his refuge in every former trial of life . . . had been in resolving to abide faithfully by the decisions of duty. In this he had found freedom; in this he had met strength and repose, so that no evil had been intolerable to him' (p. 116).

The trials to which the characters in *Deerbrook* are subject are invariably associated with denying one's desires in love, with repressing emotions and coping with thwarted love. This is of interest because love is at one point described as 'the chief experience, and almost the only object of a woman's life' (p. 222; emphasis added), yet, within the text, love is seen as the source of suffering for women and men in equal measure. In the course of the novel, which contrasts a woman and a man who are able to manage their tempers with a woman and a man who suffer as a result of a failure of self-discipline, the two latter characters are reformed through adversity. They suffer for the purposes of self-improvement. But those who are able to manage themselves do not escape suffering either; only in their case it serves to improve others through the example set. An analogy to Christ's suffering in the New Testament clearly exists.

It is in relation to the issue of moral improvement and the exercise of a conscious morality that Martineau differs from nineteenth-century women writers such as Jane Austen and Charlotte Brontë. In the latters' novels only the female characters get educated and are presented as in need of moral improvement while the male characters are either essentially good or irredeemable rakes. In Deerbrook both women and men are made to realise the importance of self-discipline and doing one's duty. Proceeding from the notion that 'happiness lies in the temper' (p. 21) Martineau de facto advocates a universal education (=of women and men) towards personal qualities 'normally' associated with women rather than men, i.e. the general adoption of the 'suffer-and-be-still'-syndrome.[8] The question arises why Martineau does not challenge either conventional notions of women's roles or the 'suffer-and-be-still'-mentality, here elevated to the level of an across-gender-applicable 'moral lesson'.

The subtext

In order to answer these questions it is necessary to look, briefly, at Martineau's Autobiography. There one gets the strong sense that she felt she could be what she was only at the expense of those aspects of herself which she associated with the feminine, such as emotionality. Thus from being an intensely emotional child she moved to a position of complete denial of emotional attachment in adulthood: 'I have never since [1826, aged twenty-four] been tempted, nor have suffered any thing at all in relation to that matter which is held to be all-important to woman, – love and marriage' (Autobiography, vol. 1, p. 131). Considering herself 'the happiest single woman in England' she asserted that 'My strong will, combined with anxiety of conscience, makes me fit only to live alone;

and my taste and liking are for living alone' (*Autobiography*, vol. 1, p. 133).

Martineau rejected feeling not only as the centre of her personal life, she also condemned it as a motivating force for the advancement of women's rights. Her judgment of Wollstonecraft (*Autobiography*, vol. 1, p. 400) reads very like Virginia Woolf's of Charlotte Brontë (*A room of one's own*, p. 67). Both advocate 'the rational and dispassionate', the suppression of the personal and emotive, in effect pleading for 'a mannish way of talking'.[9]

How is this to be explained? Martineau's rejection of the feminine and embrace of a masculine role in life can be analysed in terms of some of the ideas put forward by Julia Kristeva in *About Chinese women*. There language as a system of signs is defined as *the symbolic order*, 'the order of verbal communication, the order of paternal descent.' (Kristeva, 1986(a), p. 34). In the process of learning this order, i.e. with the acquisition of language, a child has the possibility of identifying either with the father or the mother (p. 28). It is only through an identification with the father, however, that the child can gain access to the public sphere, political debates, the literary scene (p. 37). Such identification, because it entails the rejection of the maternal, takes place, for the female child, at the expense of the 'the vagina and the possibility of finding an "opposite" partner' (p. 29). Hence Martineau's repression of her emotional self, and her life on her own, i.e. without a man. Given that this denial had gained Martineau access to the public sphere and self-fulfilment as a writer her advocacy of self-denial in *Deerbrook* is not surprising; to her it must have seemed the secret of her own success. It was a way of validating her own choices and existence.

Kristeva's suggestion that the father-identified woman (and Martineau can be described as that) as artist or intellectual 'wages war against her pre-Oedipal dependence on her mother' (p. 29) explains not only why men come off better than women in *Deerbrook* but also says something about Martineau's style of writing. According to Kristeva the pre-Oedipal phase of identification with the mother coincides, as regards speech, with 'an intense echolalia, first in rhythm and then in intonation' (p. 29). The symbolic order, in contrast, is characterised as 'a system of verbal communication that is increasingly logical, simple, positive, and stripped of stylistic, rhythmic, "poetic" ambiguities' (p. 31). As Valerie Sanders (1986, chap. 1) demonstrates, Martineau opted for an embrace of the symbolic order as the basis for her literary expression.

If one accepts that Martineau was a father-identified woman then it follows that one way of validating those choices she had made which had

– within the conventions of the Victorian age – to be regarded as feminine (as, for instance, operating on the basis of self-denial) was to create an ideal, in the case of Deerbrook a moral position, which demands of women and men alike to act in accordance with the supposedly feminine. Martineau could not, after all, advance a moral position based on activities ascribed essentially to women without undermining her own choice to identify with the father.

Both Martineau's conservatism and her radicalism can thus be explained in terms of Kristeva's theory; on the one hand, the father-identified woman who because of this identification 'has nothing to laugh about when the paternal order falls' (p. 30) finds herself having to support this order; where she is subject to the maternal, on the other hand, she has to find a way of reducing conflict as Martineau does, for instance, through the moral position she posits in Deerbrook.

The supertext

Once one looks at Martineau and Deerbrook in terms of Kristeva's theory and begins to examine the ways in which, simply because she was writing as a woman in a particular historical period, Martineau both serves and subverts the dominant culture in which she finds herself, one is engaged in a process which seeks to expose the relationship between ideology and literature and thus challenges traditional methods of literary criticism as exercised in much of tertiary education. This, in turn and by analogy, can lead to a questioning of notions of 'the canon'.

In discussion with my students, to whom – for them to choose from – I had presented a reading list on Victorian literature that amounted to an 'alternative canon' containing predominantly female authors, I found that they (a) had not even noticed the gender bias on the reading list, (b) had relatively little knowledge of what to expect in terms of canonised authors on a Victorian course, and (c) were less concerned with gender and 'the canon' than with, for example, the novelty value of any particular author. Which made me realise how much I as a teacher of English take 'the canon' for granted, accept its existence as 'real', construct my courses in response to it, and how little relevance it has to the students.

And I am not the only one caught in this trap. English as it is taught in Higher Education today is still very much governed by the notion of 'the canon' as became clear at the 1987 Higher education teachers of English (HETE) conference, held at the University of Kent. Although the title of the conference, 'Firing the canon', could be read as suggesting 'getting rid of', most of the sessions I attended were, in fact, about expansionist policies, and the conference might well have been about 'Extending the canon'. In much the same vein, in both a *Critical inquiry* issue devoted to 'the canon' (10, i, 1983), and an MLA publication entitled *Teaching women's literature from a regional perspective* (Hoffmann and Rosenfelt, 1982), the battle rages on the inclusion/exclusion field while the whole idea of 'the canon' remains essentially unexamined. Thus Charles Altieri pleads for 'an idea and an ideal of a literary canon' (Altieri, pp. 37–60), and Elizabeth Meese demands 'the whole truth', suggesting that 'the literary canon ought to be whole' (in Hoffmann and Rosenfelt, p. 15) while ignoring the implications of Louise Bernikow's statement (cited by Meese) that, 'What is commonly called literary history is actually a record of choices'.

If 'the canon' represents a record of choices then so do the courses we teach. Taking responsibility for these choices means making explicit the reasons for them, engaging with precisely those areas that have existed only in the negative, as silences and absences. And involving students in those choices. Letting neither them nor ourselves play the subservient role. 'Canon'-based English courses tend to proceed from a model of education that regards English as *the subject*, and the students as *objects*, the passive imbibers of a knowledge whose value is taken for granted. But on women's writing courses the students' knowledge and experience becomes an active ingredient in the learning process; not only that, material from other disciplines such as history, sociology, law, psychology constitutes an essential part of the inquiry, at which point the whole notion of English (*Studies*) as a discipline is opened for interrogation. The boundaries of the *subject* English are exploded by the inevitable inter-disciplinariness of women's writing courses, and by a student-centred approach to learning. What we are now talking about – moving towards – is the teaching and learning of intellectual strategies, methods of inquiry, the acquisition of transferable skills whose objects are the cultural dominants under which we labour. It is a policy for change and as such, of course, threatening to the territory and the authority of the subject English.

Notes

1 From F. R. Leavis's *The great tradition* (1948) to Dorothy van Ghent's *The English novel* (1952), Wayne C. Booth's *The rhetoric of fiction* (1961), and Raymond Williams's *The English novel* (1970) the story is uniformly the same; predictable (because always the same) 'great' authors beacon-like dominate the otherwise 'barren' literary landscape.

2 Malcolm S. Knowles (1978) discusses the research on and problematic of subject-oriented

learning.

3 Ann Cathey Carver offers some useful comments on this in 'From concept to classroom', in Hoffmann and Rosenfelt, p. 112 onwards.

4 See Martineau, *Autobiography* (London, 1983, 2 vols.), vol. 2, p. 115.

5 See Sanders (*Notes and Queries*, 228, iv (1983), pp. 293–4) for a discussion of 'the doctor as hero'.

6 'An abominable submission: Harriet Martineau's views on the role and place of woman', *Women's Studies*, 5 (1977), p. 29.

7 The choice of words 'from which it is impossible to shut women out' indicates the gate-keeping and exclusion that women writers were faced with in the literary world although it is impossible to say whether here this is considered a desirable or an undesirable thing.

8 This is described in painful detail in Vicinus (1972).

9 Valerie Sanders, *Reason over passion: Harriet Martineau and the Victorian novel* (Sussex and New York, 1986), p. 168.

15

Occupying the empty space: feminism and drama

Susanne Greenhalgh

I can take any empty space and call it a bare stage. A man walks across this empty space whilst someone is watching him, and this is all that is needed for an act of theatre to be engaged.[1]

> I am an instrument in the shape
> of a woman trying to translate pulsations
> into images   for the relief of the body
> and the reconstruction of the mind.   (Rich, 1979, p. 48)

Spatial metaphors come readily to the feminist writer and teacher. Whether we locate ourselves at the centre or the margins, occupy rooms of our own or the strongholds of patriarchy, speak of voids or of worlds, we view space as both significant and signifying. In her introduction to a collection of essays on women and space, Shirley Ardener argues that physical space and its social perception are 'mutually affecting spheres of reality' (p. 32), and Adrienne Rich has illustrated the relevance of such insights to the feminist teacher.

The undermining of self, of a woman's sense of her own right to occupy space and walk freely in the world, is deeply relevant to education. The capacity to think independently, to take intellectual risks, to assert ourselves mentally, is inseparable from our physical way of being in the world, our feelings of personal integrity. ... Look at a classroom: look at the many kinds of women's faces, postures, expressions. ... Listen to the voices of the women and the voices of the men; observe the space men allow themselves, physically and verbally, the male assumption that people will listen even when the majority of the group is female. Look at the faces of the silent, and of those who speak. Listen to a woman groping for language in which to express her mind . . . (*for it is not fitting that a woman speak in public*); or . . . throwing her words away, deprecating her own work by a reflex prejudgment: (*I do not deserve to take up time and space*.) (pp. 242, 243–4)

For Simone de Beauvoir this spatial inferiority is the inevitable physical and mental result of the process by which one becomes a 'woman', which takes place in a sphere 'everywhere enclosed, limited, dominated, by the male universe' (1953, p. 35). Within this 'allotted and confined space',[2] women are defined – and historically have defined themselves – not as agents, as speaking subjects, but as objects of the male gaze, dumb signs in the codes of masculine cultural representation, forever unable to build up 'a solid counter-universe from whence to challenge the males' (Beauvoir, p. 35).[3] As Julia Kristeva has argued, however, the patriarchal symbolic order, Beauvoir's 'male universe', does not simply *contain* all that it designates as feminine. Rather, it *marginalises* it, and the very act of positioning this 'other' at and as the boundaries of patriarchy serves both to distinguish and to determine what will be perceived as 'masculine' or 'feminine' at a given historical moment.[4] Indeed, symbolisation itself, and all signifying practices, may arise out of this 'problematic of space', as it is experienced in human infancy, in the alternation of the female carer's proximity and distance, absence and presence, through which pain, pleasure, and the sense of a separate self are generated.[5]

I am a teacher of drama, a subject which makes boundaries, margins, limits, its own special territory. Theatre *is* space, one can say: empty space demarcated physically and temporally from the flow of everyday life in order that certain human beings may be watched by other human beings, for their mutual pleasure.[6] In recent years much critical attention has been paid to the distinctive *liminality* of theatrical activity, its role in creating an area of experience that is both within and beyond the norms of structured social life, where possibilities of change and transformation – both private and public – can be rehearsed and enacted.[7] Drawing on theories of play and infant development, Richard Schechner has attempted to define this experience more precisely by employing the concept of 'restored behaviour'.

Preparing to do theater includes either memorising a score of gestures, sounds, and movements and/or achieving a mood where apparently 'external' gestures, sounds, and movements 'take over' the performer as in a trance . . . behaviour that is other is transformed into the performer's own; alienated or objectified parts of the performer's self – either his private self or his social self – are reintegrated and shown publicly in a total display.[8]

The educationalist Malcolm Ross sees the study of drama as leading to awareness both of 'the world of human protagonism . . . as it can be studied sociologically, psychologically and historically, and as dramatists and actors have made it look'; and of the ways in which 'one is a mimetic system, capable of causing others to suspend disbelief, and projecting and entering simulations of actuality, of organising oneself in different time-sequences and spatial figurations as a human being enacting for others'.[9] The performer employs her or his body to create a fictitious or artificial body which 'draws out/deforms/amplifies the normal tensions of the human body' and generates unpredictable patterns of surprise and recognition in the audience, so that 'theatrical pleasure arises and is maintained by an unbroken dialectic between the frustration and satisfaction of expectations'.[10] The student of drama must undergo such transformations continually whilst retaining the power to analyse as well as participate.

For the teacher of drama who is also a feminist there are special considerations, however. If a chief object of drama study is 'the world of human protagonism . . . as dramatists and actors have made it look', it is only too evident that this world and its portrayers have most often been male. Even when, in certain cultures, women have been admitted as performers, their bodies have generally been viewed as less capable of transformation than those of men, and sexual attractiveness, rather than the skills and techniques of effective disguise, has been regarded as their most essential talent. Although it is possible to recover the works of a handful of women dramatists from the past, these are individual exceptions to the rules that have excluded women from this most public of arts and professions rather than evidence of a female tradition surviving within the male sphere. The rise of the director as the central authority in western theatre has further institutionalised existing tendencies towards hierarchy and elitism, and the valuation of male action above all else. It is hardly surprising, therefore, that some feminist critics[11] have judged drama and theatre to be intrinsically male forms, privileging linear forms of crisis and conflict, and representing only these as the 'normal tensions of the human body'.

It might seem that feminist intervention in drama teaching will be restricted to what Elaine Showalter has termed feminist critique, 'the analysis of woman-as-sign in semiotic systems' (1985(a), p. 128), and certainly theatre, that richest of semiotic fields, offers rewarding opportunities for such approaches. Nevertheless, there is scope for *gynocritics* too, the examination of 'woman as writer . . . as the producer of textual meaning' (pp. 128–9). Although 'a specifically women's theatre may still be a theatre in search of a form',[12] and plays by women cannot always be assumed to be either feminist or feminine (Bassnett, p. 452; Wandor, 1986, pp. 130–2), the second half of the twentieth century has seen a notable increase in the activities of women as 'producers of textual meaning' in the theatre, as writers, directors, performers, and audiences. There are many kinds of 'texts' in drama, both written scripts and the performances developed either from an existing scenario or the interactions of a specific group of people working in defined conditions. 'Classic' male plays can be subverted in performances which reveal the ideological positions they dramatise (McLuskie, 1985, p. 106), and 'the presence of the female body and the female voice' can create 'new meanings and subversive tensions' in roles devised for men to play (Showalter, 1985(b), p. 80). Finally, to take account of the transformative, transgressive, and liminal energies of theatre, its deployment of the full resources of the human body, its physical engagement with otherness as a necessary condition of its very existence, is both to value the powers of drama literally to embody 'a world of human protagonism' that is other than male, and to be empowered to bring that 'counter-universe' into being.

Like all the women contributing to this collection, I teach within specific institutional contexts and constraints. I am a lecturer in a Department of Drama and Theatre Studies within a large Institute of Higher Education, formed by the federation of four voluntary denominational colleges with long histories as institutions for the training of women teachers. Now co-educational, the Institute offers a wide range of joint subject BA and BSc degrees, in addition to its BEd, PGCE, In-Service and postgraduate courses, all validated by a nearby university best known for its technological and scientific interests. Much stress is placed in recruitment literature on the Institute's 'collegiate identity' and the quality of 'pastoral care' this makes possible. In general it is marketed as 'safe space', caring rather than dauntingly challenging, offering opportunities for personal development via broadly-based study rather than impersonal specialist training. The majority of students continues to be female, and the student body as a whole is predominantly white and middle-class, a cause of growing concern to the administration. The words of John Ruskin, proposing educational objectives for one of the constituent colleges in 1881, still seem not inappropriate as a description of the model of achievement held out to the student.

> I have a deep and increasing sense of the wrong of all prizes and of every stimulus of a competitive kind. There should be a strict and high pass standard in all knowledge and skills required, but one which it should be dishonourable to fall short of, not a matter of exultation or ground of praise to reach. In all competitions, success is more or less unjust . . . while I intensely dislike all forms of competition, I believe the recognition of an uncontending and natural worth to be one of the most solemn duties alike of young and old.[13]

Within this setting Drama is a popular and well-resourced subject. Many students see it as offering a more directly vocational training than other subjects, providing an initial grounding in the skills and knowledge required for a career in professional or community theatre or as a teacher of drama. To some extent this status as a 'practical' subject gives it an image of unconventionality, even disreputability, compared with other disciplines. Drama is still a very young degree subject in Britain, emerging out of a combination of teachers' dissatisfaction with teaching it as a purely literary subject, growing awareness of the value of dramatic activity within the school curriculum, and demand for degree-level training for entry into the theatrical profession. Much energy has gone into establishing the specificity of Drama as an academic subject and convincing educational authorities and potential employers that performance and production are both valid modes of study and viable activities for assessment. A similar process has gone on in schools, leading to the introduction of Theatre Studies as an O and A level subject. Nevertheless, academics, students and parents often continue to view Drama as a less than wholly serious subject, perhaps because it is generally such a pleasurable activity. Located on the boundaries of many different subject areas, drawing its theories and procedures from a variety of disciplines, often appearing more play than work, Drama both studies and epitomises marginality within the institutional boundaries of education.

When I took up my post six years ago I joined a department in which over eighty per cent of the students were women but where not one woman playwright or director featured on the syllabus. Many of these women had ambitions to work in the theatre or media but there was no formalised discussion of either the history of women's lack of participation or analysis of the reasons for the current situation in Britain in which only a tiny minority finds lifetime employment in theatre, film, or television. Our students were playing male roles all the time, but this was viewed as a regrettable necessity rather than as an opportunity for using cross-gender casting to explore the sexual politics of a play, as Brecht proposed:

If a man had been playing that man he'd hardly have brought out his masculinity so forcibly; but because a woman played him (played the episode to be more precise) we realized that a lot of details we usually think of as general human characteristics are typically masculine. When it's a matter of sex, therefore, actors must show something of what an actress would bring to the interpretation of a man, and actresses something of what an actor would bring to that of a woman.[14]

Whilst I knew that I could employ and encourage feminist critique in all my classes, exploring the ways in which both on stage and in the audience, women have been kept 'to the sides, in recesses . . . or placed on display for the viewer' (Nancy Rheinhardt, in Langland and Gove, p. 29) in Greek, medieval, or Renaissance theatre, I also wanted to create a space where women and their work would be centre stage. This project had special urgency because of the proportion of our students who went on to become teachers. A feminist perspective in our classrooms would perhaps eventually lead to changes in all those classrooms around the country where drama was used both as a tool in the teaching of other subjects and as an activity in its own right. My colleagues, both male and female, were in general support of the idea of a 'feminist' course, and the third-year concentration on contemporary British theatre provided an opening in the form of a slot for new options under the general heading of 'Alternative and experimental theatre' (there was some discussion as to whether it should go under 'Political theatre' instead). Majoring students would also be required to devise a piece of practical performance arising out of the material and issues studied in the course, as writers, directors, or performers, in a 'Special study in theatre practice'; and workshop rehearsal, theatre visits, and film and video screenings would be integral, as in all our courses. Nevertheless, it was with a certain tentativeness that I put a syllabus together, and not only because I wanted to leave as much room as possible for student contributions to the shape the course might take. As Nancy Rheinhardt has pointed out, feminist criticism has been comparatively slow to address itself to the ancient arts of theatre compared with the attention given to the newer audio-visual media of film and television (Langland and Gove, pp. 25–8). I was still in search of my own theoretical guidelines, trying to sort out which of the feminist studies of literature, popular culture, and the media might be of real use to my students, and only vaguely confident of what might constitute distinctively feminist ways of working in the theatre. The title I gave the course that first year reflected my own uncertainty: 'Women and theatre: towards a feminist perspective'.

Three years later the course is called 'Representing women: feminist perspectives on the presence and presentation of women in theatre, film, and television', an unwieldy attempt to encapsulate those concerns that now seem central. Whereas in the first year I began by offering four classic male 'master pieces' for 'revisioning', now all the set plays are by women, as are the theoretical texts which are pre-required reading for the course, serving as an introductory basis for discussion and returned to throughout the course in relation to specific plays or theatre forms. Thus Woolf's A room of one's own is related not only to the dilemma of the woman artist but also to the dominance of domestic settings in naturalistic drama in theatre and television; psychoanalytic theory is approached via Hélène Cixous's play Portrait of Dora; materialist analysis informs discussion and observation of gay and feminist theatre collectives. Plays such as Churchill's Cloud nine or A mouthful of birds, which employ the circular rhythms of myth and ritual, rather than linear patterns of conflict and self-discovery, fragmenting time and space, and emphasising transformation and collective interdependency of characters rather than the spotlighting of a 'star', can be valuably set beside Kristeva's exploration of 'women's time' or her suggestions concerning Artaud.[15] Plays which centre on mother–daughter relationships such as Sharmian Mac-Donald's When I was a girl . . . provide a focus for discussion of Dinnerstein's theories of mothering,[16] as can improvisations from students' own experience. The issues of male violence and pornography discussed by Kappeler are explored through often gruelling workshops on scenes from Sara Daniel's Masterpieces, or Franca Rame's I don't move, I don't scream, my voice is gone, based on her own rape by Italian fascists. The taboos and prejudices relating to the presentation of sexuality on the stage became apparent both in study of the historical image of the actress (Juliet Blair, in Ardener, pp. 210–12) and in work on the inhibitions that students may feel working on scenes of masturbation and oral sex between women in plays like Churchill's Top girls or Timberlake Wertenbaker's The grace of Mary Traverse.[17] Of course there are far too many plays on the reading list to be discussed and rehearsed adequately in one term but students, surprised and excited to be exposed to so much women's work after two years without any, resist suggestions of a more selective approach. Coursework requirements – the only form of assessment of the option itself – allow the student every freedom is selecting both the plays to be discussed and the conceptual framework to be employed, so that a personal definition of feminism can be arrived at and argued for.

Such work remains safely within conventional academic bounds, however. Neatly presented and fully footnoted, it can be graded and re-graded by colleagues or external examiners uncommitted to active feminism. The perception that a student's whole outlook on the world has been altered is less important than her ability to command the skills of traditional academic discourse, spiced with some theoretical jargon regarded as 'appropriate' to the subject (i.e. on the booklist). However much our work together succeeds in being truly collective and non-hierarchical (and after all, I have put the course together, however many spaces I leave for the students to fill themselves) the course remains part of a system of credits which will add up to a class of degree upon which a job or study grant may depend. Although I may be attracted by ideas of student self-grading or pass–fail marks my course is one option among many, part of an overall degree programme in which feminist concerns play no real part other than as introduced by individual teachers. The assessment of the practical 'special studies' which emerge from the course presents even greater problems. These performances constitute a quite separate course, with its own conveners and criteria. Work from 'Representing women' is vaguely expected to focus on women in some way, but it is also supposed to 'work' as theatre. Performances evolved out of exploration of all the different ways in which women are working in the theatre, involving rehearsal processes which have engaged and deepened the student's political commitment to feminism, and called out powers of authority and responsibility she had not known she had, may thus be judged against implicit and unrecognised prejudices that continue to construct an effective theatrical event in terms of boldness, attack, and climactic action. It has been noted by a number of commentators that certain types of feminist theatre are, quite appropriately, 'closed' performances, aimed at specific kinds of audience who can 'read' them correctly,[18] designed to be 'consciousness raising' or 'discussion' theatre.[19] It is exactly this kind of theatre that students in the first stage of feminist commitment may wish to stage, and precisely these performances that may be judged as crude, limited, or biased by other observers. Examiners may be able to maintain an appearance of academic impartiality when reading an essay; it's much harder to do so when part of a responding audience, sharing a distinct discomfort as one of the targets of criticism, as 'part of the problem'.

But in the end it is exactly this kind of challenge that makes teaching drama as a feminist so exciting – the impossibility of separating feminist teaching from teaching feminism. In an institution which tends to view its large female membership as a weakness, despite – perhaps because of – its early links with women's education, feminist-influenced courses remain on the margins, but it is 'at the boundaries that the possibilities for change are found: at the boundaries in engagement with the center'.[20] There are many ways in which the characteristics of 'feminist pedagogy' described and analysed by writers such as Renate Klein can be considered part of most drama teaching – the fusion of theory and praxis; interactive and collaborative learning and teaching; the breaking down of barriers among participants to create an atmosphere of trust and community; the integration of cognitive and affective learning; and the development of systems of shared leadership. And many of the problems are the same, too. The drama teacher does not simply have to contend with her authority role as a teacher, but must often adopt the equally dominant persona of director whilst also acting as a receptive and responsive audience for her students' work. The conflicts, anger, and reversion to mother–daughter dynamics which may characterise the relationships between women students and teachers can have freer and more powerful scope within a classroom which is also – literally – an emotional and physical workshop, where feelings must be translated into performance images.[21] Within that performance and within the classroom both students and teacher play many roles, and in the process may come to understand better how such roles are constructed. As Gillian Skirrow has recently noted, there are subtle and as yet unanalysed relationships between sex/gender, acting and power (Baehr and Dyer, p. 165). It is only when the empty space of theatre is occupied by women that the full meaning and intensity of women's 'faces, postures, expressions . . . voices' can be registered and explored, only there that the body's shaping of itself can create new images of human protagonism, in pain and in pleasure.

Acknowledgements

My warm thanks are due to Val Taylor, Kate Briffa and Stacy Jenkinson, participants as teacher and students in the course in 1986–7, for support and advice during the writing of this essay.

Notes

1 Peter Brook, *The empty space* (London and New York, 1968), p. 9.
2 John Berger, *Ways of seeing* (London, 1972), p. 46.
3 See also Susanne Kappeler, *The pornography of representation* (London, 1986), pp. 68, 90; Laura Mulvey, 'Visual pleasure and narrative cinema', *Screen*, 16, No. 3 (1975), pp. 6–18.
4 Julia Kristeva, *Desire in language: a semiotic approach to literature and art*, ed. Leon S. Roudiez (Oxford, 1981), pp. 164–5. See Moi, 1985, pp. 150–67 for useful discussion of Kristeva's concept of marginality.
5 Julia Kristeva, 'Women's time', in Keohane, Rosaldo and Gelpi, pp. 33–4.
6 Brook, *The empty space*, pp. 9, 123–7; Anne Ubersfeld, *L'école du spectateur* (Paris, 1981), pp. 51–2.
7 See Victor Turner, *From ritual to theatre: the human seriousness of play* (New York, 1982).
8 Richard Schechner, 'Collective reflexivity: restoration of behaviour', in J. Ruby, ed., *A crack in the mirror* (Philadelphia, 1982), p. 73.
9 Malcolm Ross, *The creative arts* (London, 1978), p. 75.
10 Marco De Marinis, 'Dramaturgy of the spectator', *The drama review*, 31, No. 2 (1987), pp. 110, 112.
11 Gilbert and Gubar, p. 67; Rheinhardt, in Langland and Gove, pp. 29–39; Susan Bassnett-McGuire, 'Towards a theory of women's theatre', in Herta Schmid and Aloyisius van Kesteren, eds., *Semiotics of drama and theatre: new perspectives on the theory of drama and theatre* (Amsterdam, 1984), pp. 461–6.
12 Bassnett, p. 463.
13 Malcolm Cole, *Whiteland College May queen festival* (London, 1981), p. 13.
14 Bertolt Brecht, *The Messingkauf dialogues*, trans. John Willett (London, 1965), pp. 76–7.
15 See Bassnett (as above, n. 11), pp. 461–5.
16 Dorothy Dinnerstein, *The mermaid and the minotaur* (New York, 1976).
17 See Wandor, 1987, for a survey of post-war British drama in terms of gender.
18 De Marinis (see above, n. 10), p. 103.
19 Bassnett (see above, n. 11), pp. 456–61.
20 Helene Morgan, 'Power and empowerment', *WSIF*, 6, No. 2 (1983), pp. 131–4.
21 Juliet Blair, in Ardener, 1981; Gillian Skirrow, in Baehr and Dyer, p. 165.

Influence of a teacher
Margaret Beetham

This is the story of a seminar.

It was a wild February afternoon. The ill-fitting panes on the nine-teenth-century windows kept out the worst of the wind but not the cold, as a group of students gathered around their teacher to read a story written a hundred and fifty years earlier by an unknown author. 'Let us begin,' the teacher said . . .

Here I stop and wonder if this mode, which is that of melodrama and of the set-text of my seminar, is indeed the best for my story. Given the situation in Higher Education in Britain at the moment, farce might be more appropriate – or tragedy. By the time you read this, small group teaching of the kind I want to discuss may no longer be possible in my institution. This piece may itself be a historical document of some curio-sity. I decide, after all, to try old-fashioned realism.

What follows, therefore, is a realist fiction. It is my account of a particular seminar in the spring term of 1987 at Manchester Polytechnic. However, it also represents a set of processes in which I and my collea-gues and our students have been, and are still, engaged. It explores some of the questions which concern me as a feminist teacher in Higher Education. I teach a Women's Writing option for third-year students, which is now well-established. Most of my teaching, however, goes on in the context of large compulsory courses and with groups of students like the one which gathered on that cold afternoon last winter. So I begin . . .

It is grey Monday afternoon. I am about to take a seminar with a group of thirteen students, ten women and three men. I note that there should be sixteen of them but, seated as we are at a long table, the group is already almost too large for easy discussion. The curiously elongated room is one of several made by partitioning a space in a nineteenth-century building originally designed for dispensing Victorian values and 'relief' to the poor of Manchester. Now I prepare to dispense education to this group of students from the BA Humanities Social Studies Degree. It's a large degree in which students choose two discipline areas out of a possible nine in which to be examined. But today, finals is a long way off – or so it seems to this group in the middle of their second year. They know each other, but only from this seminar; the other hour of this two-hour course takes the form of a lecture to over a hundred of them in raked rows. This is a seminar in the Culture, Society and Text course. For the students, as for me, the sweeping claims of this title have become part of the routine, a set of intials, 'CST', the nineteenth-century cultural studies course, which is a compulsory part of the English half of this degree.

Each of us has a copy of the course booklet of texts for seminar discussion, including those the students have been asked to prepare for today. (Inevitably, one student has left his (sic) behind.) Today these relate to the lecture I gave this morning on 'the construction of the feminine in middle-class discourse of the 1830s and 1840s'. There is a range of material; popular poems, articles, extracts from magazines and books addressed to women on their domestic role, including Sarah Ellis's *Women of England*.

These are clearly not the canonical texts of the great tradition. However, they are unlikely to appear in any alternative feminist account of women's writing, even though they are addressed to women, may have been written by women and seek to define that which is distinctive about women. Precisely because they celebrate and reinforce the difference of women from men only in terms of the domestic ideal, for me – as for most feminists – these texts present a problem. Are they simply repressive, simply expressions of dominant male power? The students turn the pages of their reprographed copies.

I suggest we look first at a short story called 'Influence of a wife' which appeared in 1840 in an American periodical called *The mother's magazine*, which circulated in England. For me the appearance of this text on this table is evidence of a particular history, one in which the personal, the public and the academic are intertwined. I review it briefly as I wait for the group to find the place.

Uppermost in my mind, is the history of the development of this particular course and my involvement in it since I came into the department ten years ago. At this stage there were two implicit structures at work in the nineteenth-century cultural studies course. One was that of class; dominant middle-class culture was posed against working-class culture, which was seen as subordinate or, sometimes, oppositional or alternative. The other structure was that of the more traditional History of Ideas course. Mill, Arnold and Ruskin were read as major theorists whose work provided a critique of the dominant ideology – though a critique which was always contained. I think it would be fair to say that these two elements fitted together rather badly.

Awkward and inconsistent as it was, the cultural studies course has been and is still for me an interesting place in which to develop a feminist teaching practice. In it my colleagues and I have been engaged in situating cultural traditions in terms of power; political power, social power, rhetorical and linguistic power. This has meant that we are always concerned with how literature is shaped by exclusion and silence as well as inclusion and voice. In practice, too, the staff has been committed to team-teaching; the group plans the course together, divides up the lectures, finds seminar texts we can agree on – either in the familiar works of the major novelists, poets and theorists or in obscure and popular forms, like women's magazines. The course is always under review, theoretical debates are thrashed out again and again and lecture patterns change – as do the texts.

The magazine story which we are about to read in my fictional seminar group is there because of precisely such a process of discussion. When I began to teach in the department, the cultural silencing of women had not been recognised in the course. Yet then – as now – most of the students on the English strand of our degrees were women. Then – as now – the staffing of the department provided a cultural text which was not difficult to read; the manual workers divided into two groups, visible male porters and invisible female cleaners; the clerical staff, all women; the senior academic staff, all men. Until I was appointed all the academic staff were men; now the English section is three and a half women (yes, 3.5) to nine men – a proportion roughly the inverse of the ratio of women to men among the students.

Now, as these texts in front of my group indicate, there is a whole section of the course which is specifically addressed to the nature of patriarchy and to the way the feminine came to be defined in opposition to the masculine in the early nineteenth century. But questions of gender recur throughout the course and appear in relation to other texts. When I began raising the question of giving space on the course to the role of women, it seemed as if it might be added to the cultural studies mixture like another ingredient; add a pinch of discussion of the role of women here, stir in a dose of feminist theory there. Now, I realise that it has radically transformed the whole cake. The binary opposition of dominant/subordinant cultures, which was already creaking to accommodate the culture theorists like Arnold and Ruskin, was not able to sustain the introduction of a 'third term', that of the woman. It is not just that subsequent revisions of the course have all included the question of the role of women in culture and the construction of gender as a central part. More significantly perhaps, the course has increasingly moved away from any attempt to set up simple oppositions like literary/popular or middle-class/working-class or even masculine/feminine in favour of a more complex set of questions and problems.

In describing gender as the question which disrupted the course pattern of two cultures, dominant and oppositional, I am making it tidier in retrospect than it was and I may be thought to be claiming some kind of credit for making things happen which is certainly not mine. It is true that I think of the history of the course in autobiographical terms – as a woman, I wanted to address the issue of gender. But these developments in our courses have come out of collective staff discussion and – even more important – have developed under pressure from student demand and enthusiasm. Beyond that, they cannot be separated from wider developments in women's studies and in cultural studies courses. Nor would any of this have been possible without the Women's Liberation Movement and its challenge to the traditional divisions including those which separate personal life and academic work.

So, I come back to a familiar problem. Central to the way we study culture on this course is the argument that the texts we read are constructed historically in various ways (by ideology, by literary tradition, by the institutions of publishing, by race, class and gender). But readers, too, have their histories. Not only the texts we read but the selves we are must be understood as 'made' in various ways by the social and cultural.

As I sit here, then, I think of myself and the history from which I read the texts. And once again I feel the familiar contradictions; the tension between the self I feel I am and those explanations of the self which I can give. And that other set of tensions around the text, which is on the table in all its particularity but which is also the product of social and narrative conventions. In an abstract way I know what I want to do in reading the text in the seminar. It is in part to set the idea of the self-explanatory text and the self-sufficient reader against the argument that the reader and the text are constructed. These ideas, however, are potentially threatening to me, as well as – I suspect – to the students.

And where are the students in this history? What are they thinking as they turn the pages of The mother's magazine? They have had no access to the discussion which shaped the course. For me its shape is contingent and fluid. For them it is fixed; the texts are given. They appear in the course booklet and must be read. Unlike the texts set on their other courses, however, these do not conform to the model of the literary work as satisfyingly complex or important in its own right. The students have just come, on this occasion, let us say, from the poetry course in which they study Milton, Dryden, Pope, Wordsworth . . . Reading the great fathers of the literary tradition can present difficulties for our students, many of whom come into Higher Education with very little sense of the canon. However, this does not make it any easier for them to accept a text which is apparently just as repressive, just as distant from them, as Milton, but which rests its claims only on the authority of the teacher or the course or even on some theoretical concept like 'patriarchy'.

The seminar discussion of The mother's magazine, therefore, begins against a resistance from some students. One of them says to me, only half-jokingly, that she has come to do English because she wants to read Jane Austen, not some obscure woman whose writing was so dreadful that no one has bothered to reprint it since 1843 or whenever. Her particular enthusiasm is not shared by the others in the group, but they understand what she means. They want access to the culture, self-improvement or even pleasure, which is vested in recognised works of genius like Emma or Hamlet. These non-canonical texts threaten their sense of literature and of what studying literature is for. This is compounded here because 'CST' is a compulsory course. They can't escape it.

The question of the definition of Literature is one to which we keep returning and I am ready to argue once again that if they choose to do a course in Literature they should be prepared to examine their assumptions about what constitutes the literary. But today I refuse to get involved in such discussion because I am aware of another and deeper current of resistance, which is particular to this subject and this seminar.

In setting these texts and putting the question of gender at the centre of this part of the course we are using institutional structures and power to question the norms of that power. All our students will leave this course at least aware that gender definitions are open to discussion. The nature of culture as gendered culture is put into question, even for those who would never opt for a special study in Women's Writing or Feminist Criticism. But that creates its own problems.

I sense a resistance, not just to the definition of literature which the course offers, but also to this subject and the mode of its presentation. I have given a lecture on the domestic ideology of the nineteenth century in the morning. These students know that I am a feminist. They think they know what I think. Some of them, especially the men in the group, find this threatening. Some have simply stayed away from this seminar and so avoided the problem. One has forgotten his text. Those who have come, feel uncomfortable. I am an authority but I am also a woman, the only woman staff member on the course. In my position of authority I have just given them a lecture, that most authoritative of modes of address. Within the student culture of the group the men feel part of an embattled minority.

Most of the women, too, feel awkward, about discussing gender in this way and in this context. They resist the label 'feminist' with its inevitable association. They are not 'nutty', like me, but neither do they have my authority. On one hand – here the current flows the other way – they welcome this recognition in the course that they exist and that they are not men. They want to talk about how they perceive the role of 'Woman' which they play. On the other hand, this is a seminar: there is an essay question set on these texts. The definition of the feminine, which is so close to them, is here being held at the distance demanded by the academic setting. They sit in a rather confused silence and I, hoping for a space in which the theoretical and the personal can be safely dealt with, hesitate before it.

I glance at the first page of

'Influence of a wife'

'Why do you keep me so long at the door?' said Edward F. passionately to his wife. The night had passed but its cold wind had entered the house, as Mrs. F. with a sorrowful heart undid the lock.

'It is late, Edward, and I could not keep from slumbering.' He said nothing in reply to this but flung himself into a chair, and gazed intently at the fire. . . .

'Tell me, Edward for heaven's sake tell me! we are ruined! is it not so?'

Edward had not a word to say to his wife; but a man's tears are more awful than his words . . .

'Well, be it so, Edward; our children may suffer from our fall but it will redouble my exertions for them. And as for myself, . . . a woman's love is like a plant which shows its strength the more it is trodden on . . . (*The mother's magazine* (1840), p. 138).

The task for the seminar is to answer the question, 'How can we read this text?' But related to that are other questions, especially, 'What kind of reader does this text imply?' and 'Who do you think might have read it?' Since the latter is a historical question, I also ask (and try to answer) the question, 'What do you need to know to answer these questions?'

First reactions to the mother's magazine piece are of distance and of rejection. To the students, 1840 seems a long time ago and the stylised expression is uncongenial. They argue that we can only read this as addressed to other, historically distant readers, those repressed women of the nineteenth century who were so much less strong and aware than we are. One of the women fastens on the image, 'A woman's love is like a plant which shows its strength the more it is trodden on', and argues that no woman would say that and if indeed, as seemed the case, this story was addressed to women readers, if not written by a woman, then they were very different from any women she knew today.

This takes us into a discussion of whether the piece is realist or not. I point to the stylised dialogue and the imagistic opening in which the cold wind of male anger and the competitive world of commerce blow into the domestic haven. The students are familiar with the melodramatic mode from elsewhere in the course. They look rather more closely at the passage. One student suddenly says that the simile is an example of the powerful association of femininity with powerlessness and the link between sexuality and hurting rather than a realistic bit of characteristion.

In the silence which follows this, one of the mature women students half-humorously, half-angrily, says, 'My ex-husband's mother used to say things just like that and he believed her. That is why he is my ex-'. Setting aside as uninteresting questions of 'realism', she claims the passage for her experience, an experience she wants now to distance herself from and examine, but which she recognises as 'real'. Reminiscences break out all over the room. 'The nuns at school . . .' and 'Yes, then he said . . .'

This is one of those moments which you may recognise as you read; the eruption into the seminar of experience, which is posed *against* the academic. It is a familiar dilemma; shall I let the discussion go on and, if so, will it lapse into 'mere' anecdote? Is it not precisely this connection of what they know with what the course offers which I should nurture?

I ask how we can reconcile the sense of distance felt at first with that familiarity they are now claiming. We agree that there is discontinuity.

This passage was written a hundred and fifty years ago and speaks to its historical moment but – the walls of the oddly-shaped room press in on us – do we still inhabit patterns of thought which were laid down in that distant period from which these documents and this building come? We are talking about the emergence of the first industrial urban society. Perhaps it is not surprising that here in the decaying industrial centre of Lancashire we inherit their ideas along with their street plans. Some of the women agree; 'nothing has changed', they say. The rest differ: 'there may still be these ideas around among some old-fashioned people, like your mother-in-law, but we don't accept the description of Woman this passage offers us; we have moved on.'

From the argument which this provokes we go back to our earlier discussion of literary mode. I ask if we should understand the story not as description but as polemic. I suggest that it is a symbolic representation which is an intervention into a debate or struggle over what it means to be a woman. It asserts the dominant view but that view has to be asserted because it was contested then, just as the definitions of gender are contested now. We can make subversive readings now because we read out of a history of challenge to the definitions of Woman offered in the story but should we rule out the possibility of subversive readings in the 1840s? What about *Jane Eyre*, after all, a novel they had all read in the first year?

So we come back to the historical readers of this text and how they relate to the reader positioned by the text. *The mother's magazine* story seems to assume a female middle-class readership but the copy from which I took the extract was in the Mechanics' Institute Library in Manchester and, judging from the ticket pasted in the front, was extensively borrowed. 'Could it have been read by working-class women?', they ask, 'or even by men?' 'How would a man read it?' Women are so used to reading texts which position them as men that the question of how a man might read a text which positioned him as a woman intrigues the group.

The men had contributed almost nothing to this discussion so far. Now, one of them, rather hesitantly, talks about the way the man in the story is presented. In particular, he is interested in the way the man can only be redeemed by the love of the woman and by that recognition of his own weakness which leads him to cry, a moment marked by the authorial comment, 'a man's tears are more awful than his words'. Now it is the men's turn for anecdotes – about such memories as that of the rugby injury which had to be borne without complaint, because 'boys don't cry'. Was the story an attempt to feminise the man or a more radical attempt to glorify the 'feminine' qualities of sensitivity and self-sacrifice as against 'masculine' self-reliance and refusal of emotion?

This reading produces first an outcry, 'typical'; 'men want it both ways'. Then a pause, as we think about the way the narrative deals with masculine/feminine difference. But one woman wants to pursue the question of class. She points out the middle-class fantasy involved in the resolution, in which a woman's devotion solves even financial problems, and she deplores the absence from the story of any grasp of finance or the world of work outside the home. For working-class women, devotion wasn't going to produce a rich father-in-law conveniently out of the night, was it? There were other differences here – including those of class – which we ought to address, she argues.

I try to pull together the strands of the discussion: the idea of gender definition as contested, the historical dimensions of distance and continuity, the question of reading as a trying-out of social roles, but it all slips away from me as the students realise that it is time to rush off to another class. The cold wind of institutional constraint enters the room as the door is flung open by the next group. I gather my books together and go to teach . . . Pope's 'The rape of the lock'.

This is the stuff of my teaching and what makes me stay in the job. But, as I look back over the seminar, I feel, as I do so often, a sense of dissatisfaction – not least with what seems like a failure to bring it all to a proper conclusion.

Here, too, I confront a similar problem. How can I draw together into a tidy bundle all the loose ends, all the tangle of questions which even one seminar produces? I feel a cold draught from the world of publishers' deadlines, as I struggle to order complexity into some neat conclusions about power and knowledge, knowledge and power.

As a teacher I have power; constrained it may be, delimited, shot through with powerlessness, but nevertheless, I must acknowledge my power. I must also understand its limits. Perhaps this provides a clue to the problem of making an ending. It is beyond the limits of my power to hand my students a tidy package of ideas labelled 'feminist'. They, too, have power. I can leave it to them. I cannot give my readers a neat solution to the problems of being a feminist and a teacher. I can leave it to you.

Meanwhile, there is next week's seminar.

Acknowledgements

I am grateful to my colleagues and students on the Culture, Society and Text Course at Manchester Polytechnic and to my friends in the Polytechnic Feminist Research Group and the All Saints Women's Group, without whom this would not have been possible. Special thanks here to Liz Yorke for all her support, to Peta Turvey for reminding me of the power of the teacher and to Elspeth Graham, from whom I am always learning. Her chapter in this volume is complementary to mine.

Afterword
Penny Florence

'There was a wall. It did not look important . . . where it crossed the roadway, instead of having a gate it degenerated into mere geometry, a line, an idea of boundary. But the idea was real. It was important. For seven generations there had been nothing in the world more important than that wall'.[1]

As I begin to write I find myself shifting between the roles of teacher and taught. I shall not try to eradicate those movements from what I leave as written.

I also realise that in writing an afterword I have taken up a position in relation to the book analogous to the position I always choose/ choose? in relation to institutions. Even when I am physically within, I place myself outside the boundary-idea, where I feel the strongest. The risk of marginalisation is calculated.

The point of this afterword is to reflect on some of the kind/s of change implied by the other contributions to this book, and by the underlying idea of it. The editors chose to concentrate on practice rather than theory, and on feminist teaching within formal Further or Higher education, rather than in the women's movement or other spaces.[2]

Nevertheless, they agreed that a more theoretical moment from a less precise perspective might be useful. Like the individual essays, the book itself strains against the categories within which it is working. This is a kind of disjunction many feminists will recognise. My intention is to re-state it in terms of form and meaning, with the aim of floating some general feminist thoughts about cultural and educational relationships, the dynamic between thinkers, thought and their context/s.

Literature is a good starting point for reasons other than the local one, that teaching literature is the subject of this book. Literature occupies a position in feminism different from that which it occupies within overall culture. This is because imaginative writing has often been the only site where women and feminists could generate meaning. Literature therefore creates and inhabits a less definable, more volatile space in relation to reality than it does for the men who have created present-day institutions. For many of us that space is politicised and its power is literal. We know at first hand that it changes lives, whether we are involved with it as readers or as writers. We also know that the power is not exclusive to what we are supposed to believe is high art.

Some men know some of these things.[3] But theirs is not an identical experience; that is why 'Women's culture/writing' is not an essentialist category. In fact, our experience of the conditions of cultural production – and examples abound in the essays in this book – makes an essentialist conception of literature untenable. For me 'women's culture' is a necessary and useful category in the specific sense that it fulfils a need many of us experience. Still more important is the general sense that it opens on to greater understanding of the relationship between mental and social constructs and how cultural concepts are generated.[4] This is true as regards both women and other groupings, including the overall.

The asymmetry between men's and women's experience is the reason why we cannot dispense with working on gender as cultural determinant. It is also why men have very different work to do on it than women. 'Masculinist' and 'Feminist' could never in this culture be opposite terms, because all other determinants than gender would have to be the same. And oppositions only clarify within the same system.

As soon as she speaks/writes 'women's' cultural history a person splits neutral, ungendered classification into three: women's, men's and the overall. By attending to the specific in this way she and he affect the general.

Women's cultural history is further made up of an uneasy and contradictory combination of the patriarchal[5] – white, western men's – tradition which has hitherto masqueraded as complete and ungendered, and our own separate history, insofar as it can be reconstructed. Our position within both strands has been in some sense (de)formed by the men's tradition and it imposes on us certain tasks and subject matter.

As feminists, therefore, we are the inheritors of a displaced tradition that sits uneasily in contemporary institutions. By now, most of us know that our tradition draws on an incompletely recorded past, even more full of gaps, riddles and coded messages than history inevitably is,

because that past has been both systematically and unconsciously erased
– 'systematically' meaning deliberately and thoroughly, and according to
a patriarchal system. We also know that matters have twice erupted, with
the Suffragists[6] and the Sixties/Seventies movements, both of them white
and middle-class-led, and both strained with the contradictory and enor-
mous tasks that faced them.

We now need to know what our historical development[7] means for
the detail of the projects that face us in the present. It certainly sets us a
different agenda from men's cult/ural history. We need to know, for
example, how it was that the Suffragists were contained and what are the
differences between them and contemporary feminists that are crucial to
avoiding the same fate – perhaps, for example, that we benefit from the
understandings gained by the Black Power movement.

What the Suffragists achieved, however, did not disappear, just as it did
not emerge from nowhere. It went underground, to resurface within the
Women's Movement/s, part of a less public, but those who experienced
it know how powerful, 'other' knowledge, discovered through con-
sciousness-raising, internal debate, reading groups, collective work. It
began to be possible to make sense of much that the received tradition
denied.

As feminist cultural workers we benefit from these ways of thinking
and learning at the same time as experiencing the conflict they cause as
we use them to develop categories of thought of a more patriarchal
pedigree, such as critical methods and textual strategies. It is an example
of the ever-present problem within our supposed liberal democracy of
how the internal and anarchic organisation of the suppressed both
relates to and can communicate with the mainstream without loss of
integrity. Or exhaustion or being ripped off. We have power; but our
power speaks a different language. How do we bring the unconscious to
consciousness?

Understanding historical difference of this kind clarifies how and why
thinking women have been kept outside the boundaries of academe. The
predominance of women arts undergraduates/students, and their substantial presence overall, is not reflected in permanent staff posts,
research fellowships or professorships. All the teachers writing these
essays courageously allow the marks of marginalisation, exclusion, isolation, insidious pressure to show.

Our history also shows how the reasons for our exclusion/invisibility
are almost inextricable from the development of these institutions which
women find unsuitable/inimical/a strain. We have worked in forms that

had no literary or philosophical recognition – a reflection of the conditions of production as much as of gender.

We have also undergone the simultaneous ridicule and suppression of women's organisations, including feminist gatherings and the informal form/s of the Movement; the mass media's puerile attitudinising is nothing new. It's part of a pattern of suppression that has gone on since the Beguines,[8] and doubtless before. This is not paranoia. It is political realism.

'If you are an Anarchist why do you work with the power system betraying your World and the Odonial Hope or are you here to bring us that hope?' (p. 163)

Being outside systems has its advantages. Women's shorter history in relation to institutions of education, and our lack of vested interest in their wholesale preservation, gives us the opportunity to elaborate a more dispassionate view of them. I know the one thing the ranting feminist is supposed to be incapable of is disinterestedness. But everyone has an ideology, especially those paid to think. And I see very little evidence of the negative potential inherent in any passionate commitment to an idea in these pages. Having a considered and declared ideology is more conducive to disinterest than sham objectivity.

In its separated existence, furthermore, elements of women's culture can be seen more clearly, less masked by structures which are built on its assumed absence. Women's culture can appear as more incoherent and ephemeral than either men's or the overall when viewed from a pan-societal perspective, and this conceals our contribution, which can be involuntary, to both. But the tracks of that contribution are there. The new directions, both past and future, in which they lead are necessary both to white, western women, and to others.

Separatism, in whatever form, is not an institution. It is a strategy and a state of mind. Its usefulness dissolves if it is misrecognised as a solution. We are interdependent. We have no alternative but to grapple with patriarchy. We have to fight for our share of money and resources. Ultimately we are fighting for our lives.

It is both cause for optimism and for serious concern that no society can afford to ignore the consequences of injustice and untruth. This is why neither feminism nor its allies can leave the dominant to destroy itself. (This is a tone that used to make my tutors smile. I am not smiling.)

What feminist demands for justice have to do with the classrooms of institutions of education must surely be clear from the contributions to this book. Teaching, furthermore, is not the only activity that goes on in institutions of further education. Many outsiders would be shocked to know how little status it often has.

Rather than teaching, what is rewarded is contributing to a self-defined body of intellectual knowledge. I know some of it is excellent. That is not the point. If there were nothing to be gained from injustice, the world would be run by the just. The point is to connect the experiences recounted by the teachers in this book with some of the supposedly neutral considerations that problematised their work. In this way it becomes clear that the right to define what is intellectual/aesthetically fine and the power to disseminate/elaborate that belief is not merely an 'academic' idea.

One problem common to all the essays in this book is that feminist courses and essays do not fit into the institutions that host them. As well as asking 'why don't they fit? I want to ask 'what does the misfit signify?' On what level is it appropriate to answer the question?

One desceptively simple signified is that they are doing work which in some sense runs counter to the rest of the work being done.

It is work that has to be done and the tools to do it have to be developed, together with the necessary will to understand the costs and consequences of supp/oppression.

Feminism understands experience in structural terms. For example, in this collection of essays many of the teachers and students have identified a broad pattern: (this is much simplified) students and teachers feel euphoria when they take for themselves the space to articulate their ideas in a form which they feel to be appropriate; they then feel a complex of responses to these ideas for which there is no ready explanation, no clear basis for analysis, and which can quickly lead to negative feelings such as threat, alienation or failure. This is due neither to our inferiority nor to the incoherence of our ideas. It is due to the fact that the value we have assigned finds no external confirmation in its contextual, institutional logic and is therefore vulnerable. It is a structural problem.

What is more, it is one which reflects a weakness/lack in the patriarchal structure, even though it appears to reflect a weakness/lack of feminism. Our weakness in this respect is purely strategic, and it is an inevitable moment in a conflict of values where the dominant colonial/patriarchal[9] structure projects its weaknesses on to those whose strengths it exploits.[10] The underrepresented do not. Feminists, Black thinkers from the Third World, and in the West from Black Power onwards, some Socialists and some Marxists know that to do so is ultimately debilitating.[11]

Feminist thinking is often lamentably reduced or rendered invisible by patriarchal readings. The nature of the questions and issues is misrecognised – not because the issues themselves lack coherence, not always because of ill-will, but because of the inadequacy of patriarchal tools in relation to the task in hand. They are as damaging to our soil as the European plough proved to be to Africa.

The nature of the issue here is the enactment of historical conflict. (The weakness of my thinking, I have always been told, is a certain wildness; some interesting insights, but flawed judgement.)

The successes and difficulties outlined in this book are all part of a pattern which should not be trivialised. It is not coincidental that it should be a feminist book that brings together teaching practice, course content, institutional relationships, students' experience and aesthetics. It is all part of re-articulating the relationship between abstraction and experience. It is an interrogation of received notions of how ideas emerge and what determines the logic of their development: to what extent that logic is carried within the ideas, the language/s, the people or the institutional context.

In terms of aesthetics, the problems of form raised within these pages are similarly crucial. Earlier in this century, the Russian Formalists had already located how important it is to understand that aesthetic form is inseparable from a society's meanings, producing and being produced by them. It is also vital to understand in detail how form expresses the dynamic of which it is part.

If we do understand this, then it is no surprise that women find themselves working in undervalued areas or in forms which do not fit. Since form is as linked to how we experience external structures as it is to innate structure, we would expect a misfit. The problem is again compounded by how value either accrues or is attributed to certain forms over others in the guise of making objective judgements according to absolute standards. The particular forms referred to in this book are autobiography,[12] collective work, popular literature and what might be called multiple forms, in which there are several shifts of voice and convention.

There are others, including fantasy and science fiction; in fact the list is surprisingly long. What matters is that we should analyse what the invalidation of any form of cultural expression signifies – a huge example must be the colonial plunder of African and other 'primitive' art by nineteenth- and twentieth-century painters. (I am, I understand, prone to knee-jerk reductionism. I think I am trying to see what those painters

saw, rather than their expert commentators, and therefore to understand my colonial debt.)

Furthermore it is sometimes true that there is nowhere to go but
men's texts for some highly developed areas of form. This is to do with
injustice, not biology. The oppressor grows where the oppressed does
not. This is why it is far more important to prioritise understanding
cultural dynamics in an atmosphere of mutual respect than it is either to
establish whether this form or this text is 'as good' as that, or to protect
what is selected to stand for 'our cultural heritage'.

Why patriarchy's obsessional and competitive quest for some echo of
'the idea'? It's still there, even in the more fashionable -isms and
discourses. It's a red herring as monstrous as the idea of a personal god.
What greater proof of man's (sic) internalised boundaries? Or of the
power of ideas?

I want to open up these effete intelligences that hide from difference.
My schooldays are scarred with the separations that resulted from their
thinking – Nancy who wore a leather jacket and was in the D stream,
Eddie who did art and Barbara whose Dad was Polish and unemployed,
disabled in the war (the? war), so her English wasn't too good. What
have I lost of their intelligences? What do I do with the pain of that
loss?

Why do the patriarchal academics hide? All the empty rhetoric
about academic freedom! They are not actually outside the economy.
Nor are they above history. For all their learning, don't they recognise
the symptoms of decadence?

Men are accustomed to naming what they think as 'objective'. Since
their thought patterns elide the connections between abstraction and
experience, they do not know that they know what it feels like to
encounter a dislocation between them. (Some of their poets do. That's
why they are poets.) Even when they agree, for example, with a non-ess-
entialist view of literature, they can neither connect it with feeling nor
accept the consequences both personal and theoretical. They might
know what they can make their ideas mean; they refuse, in the end, to
know what this signifies.

The Odonian Society was conceived as a permanent revolution, and revolution
begins in the thinking mind. (p. 276)

One of the basic differences between patriarchy and feminism is that
patriarchy is built on control while feminism seeks to empower. A
system of ideas that aims to protect a series of established interests and

values has an entirely different dynamic from one which aims to open up new areas. The former will tend to preserve, the latter to seek change. Thus it is built into patriarchal logic that it should mistake conformity for clarity, whereas feminism does not automatically value it over the contradictions of process-oriented thinking.[13] Feminism can more readily accommodate occasions when the texture in which logical thought is embedded should not be pared away or the resultant clarity will be false.

Imagine education without the need for money. It may be impossible, but a hypothesis does not have to be realisable to be useful. It can delineate a boundary.

I was talking to an economist. I was in the first flush of having read Freud on mental economy and was trying to draw analogies, even just to play with idea of a relationship, literal or metaphorical, between the academic discipline of economics, the distribution of wealth and thought structures and operations. We both perceived stupidity in the exchange, but located it in each other. What I was trying to propose was the idea of an economist as 'one who studies economies' rather than 'one who studies money'.[14] The economist felt I had not grasped the essence of his (sic) profession. Ah! the essence.

The essays in this book afford a glimpse of a different economy of knowledge. It derives from experiences as dramatic as a revelation and as undramatic as the fact that many women teach in their role as mothers and our career patterns and expectations so far differ from men's. Given that variance in mental and financial economy we are clearly going to want change. Access isn't simply a matter of opening the same narrow door. You do not honour the differently abled by placing a red carpet on a grand staircase. You develop your architecture – and therefore the idea of which it is an expression. Change of this nature is an opportunity, even a necessity.

A society defines for itself what knowledge is useful to it. The implicit myth of a neutral and definable entity which needs protection is a sign of a moribund system,[15] one which has lost the sense of education as a social dynamic, concerned with empowerment, not control or conformity.

Education is still a patronage system which excludes women, or forces us to exclude ourselves, and which is yet perceived as benevolent by (some of) those involved. It is in fact built on the fear that there is a contradiction between democracy and excellence. Only when you resist it does the violence of this exclusion and fear become apparent. And then, in the patriarchal way, the meaning of the negativity is distorted by being projected on to the women who released it. The oppressed are characterised as violent. So it is arranged, Blacks cause riots, feminists are aggressive.

This book did not set out to foreground the task of re-thinking the nature of institutionalised education as we know it. Apart from being a different book, re-thinking education would also be a very long book, and hardly the subject of an afterword. (I have, like a good girl, learnt to prize modesty over ambitiousness in my thinking.) What I have tried to do with the freedom I have been given in this chapter is just to hold your attention on the implicit fact that the process of which the women teaching in this book are part constitutes just that: a re-thinking of education. I want you to pause before leaving these pages to allow through into consciousness at least the possibility of a new educational reality.

Acknowledgement

Thanks to Harvester Press for kind permission to draw on my forthcoming book, *Reading as a woman*.

Notes

1 Ursula LeGuin, *The dispossessed* (London, Collins/Grafton, 1986, 9, 163, 276.
2 This book, for example, itself draws on an informal organisation of women teaching in higher education. Many of the contributors are members of Network, and the book was to some extent realised through it.
3 For the sake of brevity I have said 'men' when I know, or hope, there will be a few exceptions.
4 Lack of space makes some unqualified assertions unavoidable. Sorry.
5 As in notes 3 and 4 above, I am aware of cutting across some matters for the sake of others.
6 'Suffragists' is an American term, which I prefer to 'Suffragettes'.
7 Clearly a very selective summary.
8 The Beguines were medieval lay sisterhoods, associated with nunneries, but engaged in secular work. They became powerful and were outlawed. 'Beguine' has been corrupted to mean 'a flirtation'.
9 See note 5.
10 See the process outlined in the penultimate paragraph.
11 Slippage between value-judgments and fact are all too common. It is a disadvantage in the values-game that feminism is fundamentally revolutionary and relativist, and so does not seek to institutionalise itself. This gives our arguments less status than those of the 'neutral universalists', especially in institutions. (I suspect that very little is truly universal, not even birth and death when you consider the capacity of some creatures to transform.)
12 There is some very interesting work being done on autobiography, for example, by Linda Anderson, *At the threshold of the self: Women and Autobiography*, 'Women Writing: A Challenge

to theory', ed. Moira Monteith, Brighton/N.Y., 1986.
13 A good example is the experience recounted by Maggie Humm in this collection of essays, where women's autobiographies, submitted as an entrance qualification to the polytechnic, were perceived as inferior to the 'clearer' men's.
14 'Economist': one who manages a household. This is the first definition in the OED.
15 It may well be the case that universities and polytechnics need certain forms of political and economic protection. The danger is in how this need is interpreted.

Contributors

ISOBEL ARMSTRONG is Professor of English at the University of Southampton. She has taught courses in feminist criticism for some years and is currently involved in setting up an interdisciplinary MA in Women's Studies. She has published widely on Victorian poetry and is now editing a collection of Victorian women's poetry.

MARGARET BEETHAM is Senior Lecturer in the Department of English and History at Manchester Polytechnic. She teaches nineteenth-century literature and cultural studies as well as a course on twentieth-century women's writing. She is also involved in developing policy on women in the Polytechnic and is Chair of the Polytechnic Advisory Group on Women in Education.

DEBORAH CAMERON is Lecturer in English Language at Roehampton Institute of Higher Education. She is the author of *Feminism and linguistic theory* (1985), but she has also taken a feminist approach to a broad range of topics, from reproductive technology to sexual murder. She is committed to extending the educational process beyond the confines of traditional institutions.

ALISON EASTON is Lecturer in English at the University of Lancaster. She teaches mainly American literature and courses on women writers and feminist criticism. She is a founder member of the Women's Studies Research Centre at Lancaster. Current projects include a study of Hawthorne and a study of the image of the mirror and notions of female selfhood in British and American fiction and poetry.

PENNY FLORENCE is a freelance writer and maker of films and videos. She has worked in universities and colleges but says: 'I was assailed by endless self-doubt and waves of "inexplicable" anger . . . Though institutions have affected me, they have rarely nourished me. I survive through women and our networks.' She is the author of *Mallarmé, Manet and Redon* (1986) and is currently working on a book about women's culture in relation to patriarchal institutions of thought.

ELSPETH GRAHAM is Lecturer in the Department of English and History at

Manchester Polytechnic. She teaches seventeenth-century literature and cultural studies and is currently co-editing a collection of seventeenth-century women's autobiographical writing. She is a founder member of the Manchester Feminist Research Group.

SUSANNE GREENHALGH is Lecturer in Drama at Roehampton Institute of Higher Education. Her research is on patriarchy, politics and drama in the seventeenth century, the sexual politics of Shakespeare in modern performances, and women directors. She has directed several plays with all-women casts and a feminist interpretation.

GABRIELE GRIFFIN is Lecturer II in English at Nene College, Northampton. She teaches nineteenth- and twentieth-century literature as well as women's writing courses, and is interested in psychoanalytic criticism and women's studies. Her current research is on moral philosophy and feminism, focussing on Simone Weil and Iris Murdoch, and on problems of lesbian identity in twentieth- century women's writing.

ANN HANCOCK is Lecturer in English at Bedford College of Higher Education. She has taught English and Communications at all levels though in recent years has been involved mainly with A level English and with the English literature component of a BA degree in Combined Studies.

ELAINE HOBBY has taught at the Cambridgeshire College of Arts and Technology and now lectures in Women's Studies in the Department of English and Drama at Loughborough University. She is a socialist and lesbian who has been an active feminist for twelve years. Her research is in seventeenth-century women's writing and she is the author of *Virtue of necessity* (1988), a study of women's writing published between 1649 and 1688.

MAGGIE HUMM is Co-ordinator of Women's Studies in the School for Independent Study at North East London Polytechnic. She has published widely on education and feminism, including *Feminist criticism* (1986) and *An annotated biography of feminist criticism* (1987). She is currently writing two books: *A dictionary of feminist theory* and *Strategies of contemporary women writers*.

LYNETTE HUNTER is Lecturer in Bibliography and Textual Studies in the School of English, University of Leeds. She has published on twentieth-century writing and post-Renaissance rhetoric, including work on the alternative worlds in women's writing. Other research interests include Canadian literature and the history of science. She is currently editing a three-volume bibliography of nineteenth-century household and cookery books.

LESLEY JEFFRIES is Lecturer in English Language at the University of Leeds. Her research interests include grammatical style and the language of literature. She is currently writing a book on the language of twentieth-century poetry.

LESLEY JOHNSON is Lecturer in English at the University of Leeds. She has published on the Old French fabliaux and on Robert Henryson and is now working on a study of the historiography of Medieval Romance.

VIVIEN JONES is Lecturer in English at the University of Leeds. She has published on Henry James and Jane Austen and is now working on women and writing in the eighteenth century.

MOIRA MONTEITH is Senior Lecturer in English at Sheffield City Polytechnic. She has published on Doris Lessing, Marge Piercy and Ursula Le Guin and is editor of *Women's writing: a challenge to theory* (1986). She teaches a creative writing course and is interested in the ways women write to create or explore other dimensions for themselves beyond the roles prescribed by society.

SU REID is Senior Lecturer and Head of Literature at Teesside Polytechnic. She teaches nineteenth- and twentieth-century English and American literature, including two feminist courses which she has initiated. She is the founder and co-ordinator of the Teesside Polytechnic Women's Forum. Current research includes feminist readings of modernist texts and a project for a book of essays about the experiences of women as mature students. She is also writing a book on *To the lighthouse*.

MARGARET REYNOLDS was Lecturer in English at the University of Leeds 1986–7 and is now Lecturer in English at King's College, London. She has edited Elizabeth Barrett Browning's *Aurora Leigh* and is currently editing *Bleak House* and working on Christina Rossetti. She is the editor of *The Dickensian*.

SUSAN SELLERS is a member of the Centre d'Etudes Féminines in Paris. She has also worked in Southern Africa and South America. She has published mainly on French feminism and the work of Hélène Cixous, including *Writing differences: readings from the seminar of Hélène Cixous* (1989) and *Language and sexual difference: feminist writing in France* (1988). She is currently involved in a research project with the University of Amsterdam (Department of Andragology) on women's learning.

LOUISE STEWART developed an interest in feminism and literature as an undergraduate at Liverpool and went on to take the MA in Women and Literature at Hull. With Leigh Chambers, she produced *Aurora*, a magazine of women's creative writing. She is currently working in publishing in Oxford.

PATSY STONEMAN is Lecturer in English at the University of Hull. Her teaching and research is in nineteenth and twentieth century literature. She has published on George Eliot, the Brontës and Elizabeth Gaskell.

ANN THOMPSON is Senior Lecturer in English at the University of Liverpool. She teaches Renaissance literature, American literature and film studies as well as women writers and feminist criticism. She has published widely on Shakespeare, including books on source study and on metaphor, and she has edited *The taming of the shrew*. Current research is on Shakespeare editing, feminist readings, and metonymy.

HELEN WILCOX is Lecturer in English at the University of Liverpool. She teaches a wide range of literature from the Renaissance to the twentieth century as well as women writers and feminist criticism. She is currently co-editing a collection of seventeenth-century women's autobiographical writing and is editing the works of George Herbert.

Bibliography

Abel, Elizabeth, ed., *Writing and sexual difference* (Brighton, 1982).

Acker, Sandra and David Warren Piper, eds., *Is higher education fair to women?* (Guildford, Surrey, 1984).

Altieri, Charles, 'An idea and ideal of a literary canon', *Critical inquiry* 10, i (September 1983), pp. 37–60.

Anderson, Linda, 'At the threshold of the self: women and autobiography', in Monteith, 1986, pp. 54–71.

Ardener, Shirley, ed., *Women and space: ground rules and social maps* (London, 1981).

Auerbach, Nina, *Communities of women* (Cambridge, Mass., 1978).

Baehr, Helen and Gillian Dyer, *Boxed in: women and television* (London, 1987).

Beauvoir, Simone de, *The second sex*, trans. H. M. Parshley (London, 1953).

Belsey, Catherine, 'A space in the syllabus?', *Literature, teaching, politics*, 1 (1982), pp. 58–65.

Bernheimer, Charles and Claire Keohane, eds., *In Dora's case: Freud hysteria feminism* (London, 1985).

Bowles, Gloria and Renate Duelli Klein, eds., *Theories of women's studies* (London and New York, 1983).

Bunch, Charlotte and Sandra Pollack, eds., *Learning our way: essays in feminist education* (New York, 1983).

Cameron, Deborah, *Feminism and linguistic theory* (London, 1985).

Chodorow, Nancy, *The reproduction of mothering* (Berkeley, 1978).

Cixous, Hélène, 'The laugh of the Medusa', in Marks and de Courtivron, 1981, pp. 245–64.

Culler, Jonathan, *On deconstruction: theories and criticism after structuralism* (Ithaca, New York, 1982 and London, 1983).

Culley, Margo and Catherine Portuges, eds., *Gendered subjects: the dynamics of feminist teaching* (Boston and London, 1985).

Daly, Mary, *Beyond God the father: towards a philosophy of women's liberation* (Boston, Mass., 1973, 1985, and London, 1986).

Daly, Mary, *Gyn/ecology* (London, 1979).

Davis, Barbara Hillyer, 'Teaching the feminist minority', *Women's studies quarterly*, 9, no. 4 (1981), pp. 7–9.

Eagleton, Terry, *Literary theory: an introduction* (Oxford, 1983).

Evans, Mary, 'The teacher's tale: on teaching women's studies', *Women's studies international forum*, 6, No. 3 (1983), pp. 325–30.

Fish, Stanley, *Is there a text in this class? the authority of interpretive communities* (Cambridge, Mass., 1980).

French, Marilyn, *Shakespeare's division of experience* (London, 1982).

French, Marilyn, *Beyond power: on women, men, and morals* (London, 1985).

Gilbert, Sandra M. and Susan Gubar, *The madwoman in the attic: the woman writer and the nineteenth-century literary imagination* (New Haven and London, 1979).

Greene, Gayle and Coppelia Kahn, eds., *Making a difference: feminist literary criticism* (London and New York, 1985).

Hey, Valerie, 'The woman in the moon: women's studies and the academy', *WSIF*, 6, No. 3 (1983), pp. 299–304.

Hoffmann, Leonore and Deborah Rosenfelt, eds., *Teaching women's literature from a regional perspective* (New York, 1982).

Jacobus, Mary, ed., *Women writing and writing about women* (London and New York, 1979).

Jelinek, Estelle, *Women's autobiography* (Bloomington, Indiana, 1980).

Kaplan, Cora, *Sea changes: culture and feminism* (London, 1986).

Kelly, Joan, *Women history and theory: the essays of Joan Kelly* (London and Chicago, 1984).

Keohane, Nannerl O., Michelle Z. Rosaldo and Barbara C. Gelpi, eds., *Feminist theory: a critique of ideology* (Brighton, 1982).

Klein, Renate D., 'The dynamics of the women's studies classroom: a review essay of the teaching practice of women's studies in higher education', *WSIF*, 10, No. 2 (1987), pp. 187–206.

Knowles, Malcolm S., *The adult learner: a neglected species* (London, 1978).

Kristeva, Julia, *About Chinese women* (New York and London, 1986). 1986 (a).

Kristeva, Julia, 'Women's time', in Moi, 1986, pp. 187–213. 1986 (b).

Langland, Elizabeth and Walter Gove, eds., *A feminist perspective in the academy: the difference it makes* (Chicago and London, 1981).

Marks, Elaine and Isabelle de Courtivron, eds., *New French feminisms* (Brighton, 1981).

McLuskie, Kathleen, 'The patriarchal bard: feminist criticism and Shakespeare', in Dollimore, Jonathan and Alan Sinfield, eds., *Political Shakespeare: new essays in cultural materialism* (Manchester and Ithaca, N.Y., 1985).

Miller, Nancy K., ed., *The poetics of gender* (New York and Guildford, 1986).

Mitchell, Juliet and Jacqueline Rose, eds., and translators, *Feminine sexuality: Jacques Lacan and the Ecole Freudienne* (London and Basingstoke, 1982).

Moi, Toril, *Sexual/textual politics: feminist literary theory* (London and New York, 1985).

Moi, Toril, ed., *The Kristeva reader* (Oxford, 1986).

Monteith, Moira, ed., *Women's writing: a challenge to theory* (Brighton, 1986).

Olsen, Tillie, *Silences*, (New York, 1979 and London, 1980).

Perry, William G., 'Students' use and misuse of reading skills: a report to a faculty', *Harvard Educational Review*, 29 (1959), pp. 193–200. Reprinted in Melnik, Amelia and John Merritt, eds., *Reading today and tomorrow* (London, 1972), pp. 370–7.

Rich, Adrienne, *On lies, secrets and silence: selected prose 1966–1978* (New York, 1979 and London, 1980).

Rowntree, Derek, *Educational technology in curriculum development* (London, New York, San Francisco, 1982).

Ruether, Rosemary Radford, *Sexism and god-talk: toward a feminist theology* (London, 1983).

Russ, Joanna, *How to suppress women's writing* (London, 1983).

Ruthven, K. K., *Feminist literary studies: an introduction* (Cambridge, Melbourne, New York, 1984).

Sedgwick, Eve Kosovsky, *Between men: English literature and male homosocial desire* (New York, 1985).

Sellers, Susan, ed., *Writing differences: readings from the seminar of Hélène Cixous* (Milton Keynes and New York, 1988).

Showalter, Elaine, *A literature of their own* (London, 1978).

Showalter, Elaine, 'Towards a feminist poetics', in Jacobus, 1979, pp. 22–41; also reprinted in Showalter, 1985 (a), pp. 125–43.

Showalter, Elaine, ed., *The new feminist criticism* (New York, 1985 and London, 1986). 1985 (a).

Showalter, Elaine, 'Representing Ophelia: women, madness, and the responsibilities of feminist criticism', in Parker, Patricia and Geoffrey Hartman, eds., *Shakespeare and the question of theory* (London and New York, 1985). 1985(b).

Spender, Dale, ed., *Men's studies modified: the impact of feminism on the academic disciplines* (New York and Oxford, 1981).

Spender, Dale, *Man made language* (2nd ed., London, Melbourne, Boston, Mass., 1985).

Spender, Dale and Elizabeth Sarah, eds., *Learning to lose: sexism and education* (London, 1980).

Thorne, Barrie and Nancy Henley, eds., *Language and sex: difference and dominance* (Rowley, Mass., 1975).

Vicinus, Martha, ed., *Suffer and be still: women in the Victorian age* (Indiana and London, 1972).

Wandor, Michelene, *Carry on, understudies: theatre and sexual politics* (London, 1986).

Wandor, Michelene, *Look back in gender: sexuality and the family in post-war British drama* (London, 1987).

Woolf, Virginia, *A room of one's own* (London, 1929).

Index